THE BEAVERBROOK GIRL

THE
BEAVERBROOK
GIRL

An Autobiography

JANET AITKEN KIDD

COLLINS
8 Grafton Street, London W1
1987

William Collins Sons & Co Ltd
London · Glasgow · Sydney · Auckland
Toronto · Johannesburg

BRITISH LIBRARY CATALOGUING IN PUBLICATION DATA

Kidd, Janet
The Beaverbrook girl.
1. Kidd, Janet   2. England—Biography
I. Title
942.082′092′4   CT788.K4/

ISBN 0—00—217602—5

First published 1987

Photoset in Monophoto Imprint
by Ace Filmsetting Ltd, Frome, Somerset
Made and printed in Great Britain by
William Collins Sons & Co Ltd, Glasgow

To my daughter Jane
with thanks for all her help and encouragement

and to my son Johnny
who has given me so much love and care

Acknowledgements

For the help I was given in writing this book, I am most grateful to the following: Michael Syson, Jane Kidd, A. J. P. Taylor, Captain John Coote, Phyllis Smith, Lawrence Johnson and the House of Lords Library.

Illustrations

Foreword

I have always been fascinated by the thought of so much history passing within the span of a single lifetime. I was born into a leisurely age of country pursuits, close-knit families, and horse-drawn carriages, yet my grandchildren may well fly to Australia in three hours and never feel the need to read a book to pass their leisure hours.

This book is for them, however, in the hope that they will gain the same satisfaction as I have gained from living life to the full, always with optimism and enthusiasm; the same qualities which I cherished most in my father.

Janet Aitken Kidd,
1986

Preface

At nine o'clock on the calm, misty morning of 6 December 1917, the French munitions ship *Mont Blanc* nosed her way into the harbour of Halifax, Nova Scotia, and collided with the Norwegian tramp steamer *Imo*, which was feeling her way out. The resultant explosion killed sixteen hundred people and injured thousands more. Less importantly, it destroyed waterfront installations, warehouses, office blocks, government buildings, and my birth certificate. An anchor shank was found three miles away.

So I was not officially recognized as a person for many years, until R. B. Bennett, ex-Prime Minister of Canada and a lifelong friend of my father's, went to Canada House in London and sorted it all out.

R.B. was a fabulous person and I'm sure he would have been invited to the bonfire party. It was held on the evening of 9 July 1908 in the garden of our home on the Arm of Halifax, to celebrate my arrival. If my mother had been watching from the open window of her bedroom, where I had been born earlier that day, she would have seen them gathered there in the firelight; friends and relations, many of whom I would come to know and love in the ensuing years.

Of her own family, the Drurys, her brothers Victor and Chipman were bound to have been there, such was their fondness for her. Of her three beautiful sisters, only Arabella would have been with them. Ethel, the eldest, was far away at the time, and Helen still at college.

On the Aitken side, her in-laws, she would have seen my three aunts, Rahno, Jean, who was known as 'Gyp', and Laura; also their brother Allan. I don't think uncles Traven, Magnus and Arthur were there. Nor was Aunt Nan, or poor little Kathy who had died of diptheria, aged seven. There had been ten of them in all. So there was one more still to come – my father.

I can imagine my mother staring into the darkness to pick him out in the flickering light of the fire. William Maxwell Aitken, small and compact, with a big head, a wide grin and neat feet. She probably saw him talking to R.B. or perhaps Sir Robert Borden, a more recent friend who would also one day be Canada's prime minister. Or maybe he was handing a glass to his old school friend James Dunn, who was to make and lose one fortune, then make another. And she would have heard them laughing.

They laughed a lot in those days, my father and his friends. For the first ten years of the century they helped themselves and each other to the power and the wealth that dangled before them like so much ripe fruit on a tree.

'I didn't make the boom,' Father once said, 'I just saw it coming and rode in on the tide.' And he wasn't the only one. Fortunes were made overnight. When James Dunn died, leaving sixty-five million dollars, he had the last laugh of all. But that comes later.

When I was born, Father was not yet thirty. He was already a dollar millionaire and fast becoming a dollar multimillionaire, a fact noted with some surprise and no small gratification by my grandparents. The Reverend William Aitken's love and indulgence for his restless and often wayward son was to some extent at odds with the harsh discipline of his Presbyterian faith. Having trumpeted his way from his native Scotland into an Ontario pulpit, he continued to lambast the faithful with threats of hell and damnation in the awesome tradition of John Knox. His wife, Jane, was made of even sterner stuff. She ruled the manse and bore him their ten children without complaint, disciplining herself and her family into a happy and well-organized unit. Unfortunately, she suffered from chronic asthma, a condition passed on to her children, killing two of them, and afflicting most others – myself included.

Father declined the ecclesiastical life expected of a son of the manse and embarked on the road to fame and fortune with the encouragement, if not the active support, of both his parents. It would not be at all surprising if my grandparents were dubious of their gifted but feckless son's ultimate success, for his start was un-promising. Having been rejected by Dalhousie University (an insult he never forgot), he worked in a drug store, then became a journalist and a lawyer's clerk. Between times he bought and sold a bowling alley. With the profit, he purchased a consignment of frozen meat and lost the lot in an unexpected thaw. He was eighteen years old.

Nothing seemed to go right for him during the last years of the old century. He sold insurance and lost his own money and more trying to beat the odds at cards and dice. This financial downturn was offset by his first success as a political campaign manager in Calgary, where his friend R.B. was running for the Northwest Legislature. Father ran the campaign, uninvited, yet with boundless enthusiasm. R.B. won, but found himself faced with pre-election promises that would be hard, if not impossible, to keep. His anger was short-lived, however; he was on his way to the top.

Father returned east in an agony of frustration and tried to join the army. The Boer War had already prompted brother Magnus to enlist, but Father was rejected. Although physically strong, he was tense with nervous energy after a time of strain and activity. And then, as so often happened in later life, he would be struck down by the pervading threat of asthma.

With the new century came his twenty-first birthday and the start of his success. It was sudden and dramatic, as if he had been asleep, and had then woken to find it happening all around him. The boom was on. Canada at last was growing up. Railways, industry, agriculture, shipping, mining and finance. All were expanding and the working man had money to spend.

Father saw this as much as anyone else, and earlier than most. Expansion required money. And who better to invest in the nation's future wealth than the men and women who made it? So he sold bonds. And such was his own confidence in the future that he guaranteed to replace any money lost. This was no idle boast made in the euphoria of enthusiasm, but the result of careful analysis, sound judgement, integrity, dynamic salesmanship and tremendous energy. People trusted him. He was ruthless but he kept his promises. And he never looked back.

Much has already been written about the few years it took Father to become a millionaire. From bond salesman he moved to company promotion and from there into the mysterious snake-pit of investment banking. He came through it all unscathed to merge companies into conglomerates: cement, steel, paper, electricity. He made many friends along the way, and some enemies too, the most powerful of which were the giant Canadian Pacific Railway and the Bank of Montreal.

He could now offer his help to each member of the family according to his or her needs. And this he did, not out of bravado, but simple generosity and affection. He financed his younger sisters, Gyp and Laura, through school and university, paid for his mother's medical care and offered money open-handedly to his father. If there were strings attached, they were insignificant. He wrote to his brother Arthur:

> . . . You are at liberty to call on me at any time for financial assistance during your educational period. Of course you understand that I do not wish to assist you to extravagances, but for such expenditures that you may feel necessary, I will be glad to help you along.

He was twenty-three when he wrote that letter.

Then, two years later in 1905, while staying with R.B. in a cottage on the St Lawrence river, he met Gladys Drury. It happened at a ball given by her father, General Charles Drury, commanding the Royal Military College at Kingston, and head of an old and aristocratic Canadian family that could be traced back to the storming of the Heights of Abraham. He and his wife were launching their three beautiful daughters into society.

The outcome of this ball was that my mother was the first to be launched; not so much into society but into a love affair which was to lead her, six months later, to the altar of the garrison church. It was a whirlwind romance for those days, leaving all concerned breathless by the speed and ardour of my father's courtship. The general, at first cool and reserved, had finally capitulated in the face of an onslaught which included an abundance of charm, consideration and genuine affection, punctuated by a series of carefully selected gifts. Another merger had been successfully completed.

It was to be two and a half years before I was born, and another two before the family left for England. During that time Father visited London twice. The first occasion was in 1908, and the second was soon after his already neglected wife in Canada had given birth to my brother Max in February 1910. On his first trip to London he met a fellow Canadian, Bonar Law, already a powerful figure in the Unionist Party. At first, they were mutually unimpressed. 'The shape of his head's all wrong,' Father reported. On the second trip he stayed long enough to borrow five million dollars and return to confound the Bank of Montreal and bring off the biggest deal of his life. When he had finished, on the morning of 17 July, the Steel Company of Canada was an accomplished fact, and my father was a multimillionaire.

That same evening, we left for England.

I

Everyone has a first memory, I suppose, although childhood memories tend to be erratic; amazingly detailed and perceptive on some occasions, fanciful and vague on others. My first memory is of being wet, very wet. I was hanging on to Father's hand, to prevent myself from being blown away, when a solid curtain of salt spray came in over the guard rail and turned me from a cuddly, chortling little girl, in a fluffy white fur coat and bonnet, into something resembling a screaming, half-drowned gerbil. We were half way across the Atlantic.

I was still howling with fear and shock when I reached my mother in the warmth and safety of her cabin. She must have fixed Father with an accusing look, because, either from guilt, or in an effort to stop the terrible noise I was making, he promised to buy me a pony. I stopped.

'No, not *now*. When we get to England.'

England? Where was that? I wanted to go home. My mother calmed me. Her gentleness and understanding were irresistible and would remain so as long as she lived. Throughout my childhood and youth, she would not only be my champion but also a refuge. To me she was as beautiful as she was kind; someone to whom I could take my troubles, and for whom I reserved a very special love. She could be firm when required, but I never saw her angry or bitter, even though towards the end of her life she was driven to the brink of despair. And above all she was constant, always providing some kind of rational calm in times of trouble which gave us – my brothers and I – a counterpoint to the heights and depths of Father's passions, his apparent injustices, and his unpredictability.

So it was to Mother whom I turned when, after several months, the pony had failed to appear at our new home – a long, white, rambling house, called Worplesdon Court, in Surrey. She smiled rather wistfully and asked me to be patient . . . Father had been away much of the time. But there seemed to be great things brewing somewhere because, when he did arrive home, he would usually be accompanied by friends whose excited talk, and on one occasion shouts of celebration, seemed to fill every room and passage.

One of his friends was a tall man who smoked a pipe and would emerge from Father's study like a train coming out of a tunnel. He didn't come often but he was always treated with a lot of respect. I called him Mr Smoke and hid behind things when he passed. Then there was Mr Sad. He had a drooping moustache and never seemed to smile. He was always hanging about, not really going where the others were going, and seemed rather alone. I felt a bit sorry for him but never said so because he never seemed to notice I was there.

I remember when I heard my Canadian nanny call Father an MP. Not to his face of course, but it sounded rude enough for me to go scuttling off to Mother to ask her what it meant. Mother, no doubt surprised that the missing pony appeared momentarily to be forgotten, took me somewhere quiet and gently explained that Father was now a Member of Parliament. She did it in such a way that it all seemed quite natural after only a few months in England. And she had to do it again a few months later when Father was knighted. Someone had called him 'Sir Max'.

One day at breakfast, maybe a year or so later, I noticed everyone looking at me, and trying not to smile. It was enough. I bolted for the stables and saw two long ears protruding over the half-open door of a loosebox. A moment later, and it was love at first sight. The donkey stared back. It had a garland of flowers round its neck and a label which I have kept to this day. 'To my only daughter, with much affection from her daddy.' I hugged the donkey and then rushed back to hug Father. He told me that there was still some harness to come and a small governess cart, but his grin faded a bit as he added, 'Make the most of it, child. We may be going back to Canada soon.'

But we didn't go back to Canada. Canada came to us in the shape of my two aunts, Laura and Helen. Laura was a remarkably intelligent girl with whom I would share much happiness and sorrow. Helen, my mother's younger sister, was a beauty. She was to break many hearts, including Philip Sassoon's and Cole Porter's, on her way to Westminster Cathedral where she married Evelyn Fitzgerald in the twenties.

It didn't take me long to learn to ride my donkey and drive him in the governess cart. Max was still too young for these adventures, but our poor, long-suffering nanny in her white starched dress and apron down to her ankles spent hours stumbling along behind us, trying to hoist herself on to the step to save worrying her bunion.

Father seemed a bit distracted during all this, and I didn't see much of Mr Smoke either. But Mr Sad would appear from time to time. He would stand staring at us soulfully as we clattered past, me in my heaven, Nanny no doubt pondering on how best and how quickly she could hand in her notice and go back to Canada. And go she did, at about the same time Father bought our second and last home, Cherkley Court.

I grew to know and love this house over the years to come. Architecturally it had little to recommend it, but the view from each of its thirty-one rooms was breathtaking. Over a period of months, Mother, assisted by Laura and Helen, turned it into a warm and hospitable home. They started by taking advantage of the fact that much of the interior had been burned in a recent fire. Central heating was installed in every room – an unknown luxury in 1912. Then came the carpets and the furniture; deep armchairs and sofas in brocades of flaming colours. To these were added antiques of every kind, chosen by Mother from scores of different shops and sales, filling the well-proportioned rooms with the soft glow of light on polished wood.

Father added a tennis court, a squash court and, in later years, a swimming pool and a cinema. He reserved one room for himself. It was to be his study, and it was soon filled with books given to him as a gift by his friend Mr Smoke – who I now knew to be Bonar Law. How many men and women of power, talent, wealth and influence were to tread that corridor leading to his study? For me, at the age of five, it was all a bit spooky until I got used to it.

Our rooms were upstairs, light and airy, each with a wonderful view over the Surrey hills. On the roof a great bell was fixed to the top of one of the twin towers, and from up there no other building could be seen. The drive itself was over a mile long, and beyond the spacious lawns was one of the most famous yew forests in England. As a child I was irresistibly drawn to it; a wonderland of fantastic shapes, with the trees dense in places, then giving way to grassy paths and revealing hidden glades. Cherkley was a child's paradise. I couldn't wait for my donkey and cart to arrive so that I could drive over all three hundred acres of it.

Time went by and although the donkey still failed to appear, another far more important newcomer arrived. My brother Peter was born in March. I remember gazing with some curiosity at this tiny, red-headed person, not knowing how much we would mean to each other in later years.

But for now, Max was my constant companion. Although he was only three, we were quickly to establish a childhood bond, a sort of mutual protection society. It started with the departure of our Canadian nanny. Max and I waited with some trepidation for the arrival of her replacement. Enter 'the Brute'. I have conveniently forgotten her name. This dreadful creature would pinch our noses to force the slimy tapioca down our throats then beat us when it made us sick. She gouged out our ears and noses with cotton wool on sticks to ensure that we were thoroughly clean before bed. She was cunning too, setting little traps for us knowing we would transgress, then bearing down on us like an enraged griffin, all starch, medical smell and hard hands.

She perpetrated most of her crimes when Mother and Father were away. They were away a lot, returning every third week to give us what were known as 'spoiling weekends'. We were happy then, leaping at them with such joy they never noticed the tears of relief, or indeed the tears of dread when Monday came and it was time for them to go. There were 'wish times' too, when Father or Mother were tucking us into bed. For some reason we never wished ill of the Brute. Max would want a new toy car or plane and my wish, always, was for my donkey. Or if that was not possible, a pony. *Please*, a pony.

20

Things were better when Aunt Laura came to live with us.
None of our large staff, from the butler down, dared stand up to
Nanny. But when Laura was there, the Brute watched her step.
Then our parents started coming home more often. Mr Sad was
there again and even if he still didn't notice me, I was always
pleased to see him. He only seemed to take an interest in Peter
although he was still just a baby. I asked Mother why. 'That's
Rudyard Kipling, darling. He's Peter's godfather.'

Father went away again in 1913. People said he was ill but
Mother told us he was just feeling 'under the weather' because
things hadn't been going right for him. When he had seen enough
doctors, he got bored and came home. Soon afterwards a lot of
marvellous people came to Cherkley. Among the first to arrive was
a man who brought his horse with him and left it in the stables. One
day, to my indescribable joy, he lifted me on to its back and walked
it round the yard. The world seemed a wonderful place from up
there. I could see the great arched neck and mane stretching out
before me and hear the clack of hooves on the cobbles beating time
to the man's whistling. Unfortunately he left before I could enlist
his support in getting a pony of my own. I didn't see him again for
a while. When I did, I learned that his real name was Frederick
Edwin Smith (later Lord Birkenhead). Everyone called him F.E.

I had almost given up hope of ever seeing my donkey again.
Every time I caught up with Father, I would rush up to him and
start pleading all over again. It was always the same. He would
pick me up, hug me, show me to whoever it was he was with, make
another promise which usually included the word 'soon', put me
down and walk away. I felt betrayed. Then that night he would
come to my room and read to me. He would be so kind and loving
I'd forgive him. He had a tree house built for me in the yew forest
and I would sit there for hours, alone, positively willing him to
keep his promises and buy me a pony, or at least bring back the
donkey.

But nothing happened, until one day a small Irishman with
twinkling eyes, white hair and a beard walked in the front door
and into my life. His name was Tim Healy. He was always immaculately dressed and smelled of sweet lavender. I called him Tim and

he became my best friend. There was a lot of talk about Ireland at the time. Bonar Law, when he visited, was very preoccupied and Rudyard Kipling always seemed very sad. But Tim would come looking for me, all smiles, and together we would head for the forest. He helped me make my tree house bigger and more secure, 'borrowing' a ladder from the stables and nailing extra planks to the existing structure. He told me about leprechauns and the 'little people' who lived in his country, and listened carefully to my hopes and fears; mainly about the pony that wasn't, and the Brute that was. Knowing I went there every day and spent so much time alone, he filled my small world with surprises, leaving chocolate horses, dogs or birds waiting for me on the platform.

'The little people like you,' he would say, laughing, when I breathlessly reported these finds. Somebody must have done, because one day the Brute just wasn't there anymore. And a few weeks later, I found this message pinned to the bark of the tree:

> A secret message we relay
> to little Janet as you play.
> A pony of your own we say
> will come to you on Christmas Day.

It was coal black with a long mane and tail, and a coat that glistened in the bright, cold morning. The trouble was that no one could ride it. I was the first to climb on its back and was promptly thrown into a flower bed. Bonar Law's son, Richard, was the next to try and he met the same fate. After a great deal of sound, practical advice, and an offer of £5 from Father to anyone who could stay on, Richard tried again, as did the stable lad and the gardener's son. Father kept his money. I doubt if all the buck-jumpers in America or pig-rooters in Australia could have matched this one. It repeatedly shot skywards from a standing start, its back humped and its nose between its feet. I burst into tears and could do no more than watch my pony, a bit wild-eyed by now but still beautiful, being led away, never to be seen again. Tim told me that the 'little people' had sent the wrong pony. They were fond of playing tricks on people, he said, and agreed without too much conviction that maybe they'd send another one. But it was some time before they did.

Father was constantly taking my ponies and horses away from me throughout my childhood and early teens. As far as I was concerned, it was the ultimate punishment and he knew it. Just as suddenly as one pony was taken away, another, or maybe two, would appear in the stables. Sometimes the slightest misdeed on my part would be enough; at other times, he would be indulgent and forgiving. I never knew where I was with him, from one pony to the next.

With the departure of the Brute, Cherkley became a far happier home for Max and me. The front of the house always seemed to be full of guests coming and going, with secretaries and valets following in their wake. Our own staff consisted of Mr Rennie, the tall and handsome butler, his two footmen in green livery and white gloves, a chef, three kitchenmaids and four housemaids, one of whom always dressed as if for a ball and made eyes at the visiting valets.

Then, one day, Miss Evans arrived. She was engaged as housekeeper and this exalted position she held in our family for fifty-seven years. She was devoted to Mother and we all loved her in return. Her room became a refuge more than once. Our German governess, Ada Krelle, was also much liked by us all. She combined a deep understanding of children with the ability to make them want to learn. She would sometimes have to come and fetch me from my tree house, but she never complained, and her proprietary attitude towards us was remarkable. She once wrote to Father:

Dear Sir,
Janet Aitken thanks you for the twenty sixpences you sent her. Would you be so kind in future as not to send her any such amount again without my authority.

Yours sincerely,
Ada Krelle

Thanks to Ada Krelle and the *Daily Express*, which had begun to make a fairly regular appearance at that time, I knew what the Prime Minister looked like. Mr Asquith came to Cherkley in 1913. Remembering what happened three years later, I'm not surprised that I never saw Mr Asquith again. I remember, too, the furious argument that went on between Rudyard Kipling and Tim Healy.

This can only have been about Ireland, and when Father, who believed very simply in self-determination (by majority vote of course), became embroiled, things got really bad. But that came later, after I met 'the Loved One'. His name was David Lloyd George and he was my first love. Whenever he came to Cherkley, I would find out about it and follow him around like a devoted dog. He used to walk up and down the terrace outside, deep in thought, while I trotted along beside him. I loved the way his long white hair became ruffled in the wind. Far from being irritated or embarrassed by this unsolicited attention, he would welcome me with a happy smile and include me in his mental deliberations. I had no idea what he was talking about, but I was totally fascinated by his voice and the way he would turn to look down at me as if seeking my approval.

'We should grant Home Rule don't you think, Janet?' he might have said. 'But leave out Ulster.' Another few strides, then, 'Your father agrees, you know. So does Churchill.' Who? I would nod happily and trot on until he abruptly turned into Father's study and left me behind.

He would often come to our playroom, as did his secretary, Frances Stevenson. She became a great favourite with Max and me, but whenever the Loved One was there, I had to stop whatever I was doing. I would then become speechless, gazing at him in wonder. He told us about his beloved Wales and, listening to him, I swore he would be the only love of my life. I was even jealous of his wife.

Before and during the first Great War, tuberculosis from milk was rampant, infecting many children in the glands or lungs. I contracted it in the glands. It was probably the most painful experience of my life. They bundled me up to London, to the Hyde Park Hotel where Father had a permanent suite. Having sterilized one of the rooms and turned it into an operating theatre, the nurses poured ether on some lint, clamped it on my protesting face and called in Sir John Bland, known to his contemporaries as 'the butcher'. I woke up feeling horribly sick with a wound in my neck and a gland missing. The next day the stitches burst and I was returned to the horror room to be resewn.

24

Sir John was, in fact, a brilliant surgeon, but his bedside manner was such that he scared me witless. So when, after two months of pain and boiled milk at Cherkley, another gland erupted, the thought of a repeat performance was too much. They got me as far as the Hyde Park Hotel, but the smell of ether was more than I could take. I bolted, tearing along a passage and down the stairs into the main entrance-lobby. Once there, I hid behind the hall porter's desk. I was betrayed. Sir John arrived and I was dragged out, screaming and kicking, to have a needle stuck into my backside.

They operated on me a third time, and I was desperately ill. Superb nursing saved me, I think; and my mother's love. Father gave me a spaniel puppy and a huge grin of encouragement as I fought against the pain. It wasn't easy.

Then one day *he* arrived, my first and only love. He sat on the bed, held my hand, and spoke to me in that wonderful, luminous voice. I have never forgotten what he said:

'Wisdom comes with pain, little Janet. And life is full of pain. So wisdom comes with age, you see. You're so young, but wiser now.'

The Loved One had worked his magic once again.

*   *   *

I was in my seventh year when the Great War came. I knew *who* we were fighting because one morning in the early summer of 1914 Ada Krelle came to kiss us goodbye. Mother explained. She didn't want to leave us but thought it best for everyone if she returned to the fatherland. Max and I felt deserted. The English were going to fight the Germans? No one could tell us why.

For four years the obscenity of Mons, Ypres, the Somme, Verdun, Passendale, Gallipoli, Loos, Arras, Vimy Ridge and countless other places of organized slaughter passed serenely over my head. We heard about the heroes. But were they not *all* heroes? Was the airman whirling about in a dangerous sky more valorous than the unknown private from a little known regiment, who gritted his teeth when the whistle blew, rose up to go 'over the top' and fell back dead with a bullet through his face?

25

Father had gone to Canada with Tim Healy to get help. They told me half a million men responded, over sixty thousand never to return. He was appointed Canadian Eye Witness, which involved reporting the war for Canada on paper, wireless and film. He was so successful, they said, that the Americans began to think the Canadians were the only people fighting. 'The British should try publicity too,' Father retorted.

Mother took me to London to see him off to France. He wore khaki breeches and high, polished boots. It was a tearful scene in the lobby of the Hyde Park Hotel; a tableau which became all too familiar in the years to come. It was a bit scary, too, for a six-year-old, made more so by talk on every side of German 'frightfulness'.

At Cherkley, the routine went on much as before although the number of men on the staff, and horses in the stables, had been drastically reduced. With Father gone, the only person to walk the deserted corridors was Rudyard Kipling, who came to visit Mother from his home in Sussex. I think it was because there was nobody else around to talk to on that blustery autumn day that I remember seeing Rudyard Kipling standing by a window. He looked so lonely. I went and stood beside him, hoping he would notice me and perhaps say something. I knew he couldn't see very well because he always wore those thick lenses. I was just about to give up when he fumbled in his pocket, brought out a handkerchief and started to wipe, first his eyes, then his glasses. When he turned away, he still hadn't noticed me. But I knew he had been crying.

I kept it a secret, as children do sometimes about these things. I was to learn the truth later: John Kipling, his only son, was killed in action with the Irish Guards at the battle of Loos on 2 October 1915. He was just eighteen but had gone off to the war in spite of his own weak eyes.

Then Uncle Allan arrived from France. He bore with him a wound from a German bullet, a Military Cross and an enormous Canadian flag which I flew from the roof on a specially constructed pole. He wouldn't talk about the war but I could see how thin and tense he was. When he got better he used to smile more. He followed Mother everywhere and I think he fell in love with her a bit. Suddenly, he was gone again, but I wouldn't let anyone take the flag down. It went on flying up there for months. Uncle Allan survived the war. He was one of my favourite uncles and I think Father's favourite brother. Afterwards, with Father's help, he became rich, then married and had three children. I hope he was happy, for he deserved to be.

When Father came home, the war had only been going for two years and Cherkley was to embark on one of the most vital periods in its history, starting with the arrival of three more Canadians. R. B. Bennett, I loved. Sir Robert Borden, I liked but never really knew. The third man I didn't like at all. His name was Sam Hughes and he was a general. He clanked about Cherkley patronizing people in a loud voice, behaving as if trying to maintain some popular image of himself which wasn't him at all. I found out later that he fought with everybody, including the Germans, and was finally sent back home so that others could get on with the war in peace. Sir Robert was Prime Minister. He had wavy, white hair (reminding me of the Loved One), a droopy moustache and warm brown eyes. He liked to go for long walks before breakfast and would sometimes take me, protesting, and Elsie Kipling, less protesting, with him.

R. B. Bennett had a rather portly, immaculately dressed figure. He used to come into our playroom preceded by a Bible, which he always carried with him, and a box of chocolates. He neither smoked nor drank, but chocolates were his passion. He was humorous, friendly and kind, dispensing his 'goodies' to Max, Peter and me whenever we saw him. He did this before meals too, which would upset Mother, although she always found it hard to be cross with him. He was one of Father's oldest friends and would one day retire from politics and come to live close by.

Then the greatest of all 'goody'-dispensers arrived. His name was Winston Churchill, and his pockets were always full of delicious, sticky fruitdrops. Watched by his somewhat aloof wife, Clemmie, he would tumble out of the car, grinning broadly, and hug every child in sight, some of them total strangers to him. His own children, Diana and Randolph, would invariably arrive with him and, having shared out the fruitdrops, he would involve us all in some childish game whith entailed chasing each other all over the lawn. He did this within moments of arrival as if he had been looking forward to it throughout the drive from London. To save time, he would get his chauffeur to start honking the horn of their big, black car when they were only half way down the drive. Then Max and I would be waiting for them.

Clemmie disapproved of these games, as she evidently disapproved of almost everything to do with the Aitken family. She distrusted Father and thought him a bad influence on her husband. No doubt she had read Disraeli's remark about the country liking 'grave statesmen', and the sight of Winston, whose political career was at that time approaching the doldrums, capering about the lawn with a bunch of kids, simply did not fit the image she required for him. Someone important might be watching, as indeed there often was. But it didn't matter. Winston just loved children, and we loved him in return, treating him, whenever possible, as one of us. So we would play until he had had enough, then out would come the big cigar. He would light up and disappear into Father's study.

It was always a dining-room lunch when the Churchills were at Cherkley. Father never succeeded in treating children as grown-ups and must have watched with some admiration as Winston brought us all under control yet made us feel at ease. When the pudding came, he would sometimes stand up and conduct us while we sang 'Roses round the door . . .', followed by 'The Jones Boys', a song from New Brunswick which was Father's favourite. I can hear them still; Father and Winston bellowing away with little thought for timing, key or rhythm. And we loved it, Max and I. No wonder we looked forward to Churchill days and to the sound of that familiar car horn coming down the drive.

The year 1916 was a great one for Father. But although four memorable events occurred in his life, I know that beneath the high points of achievement, and the celebration they incurred, there ran a constant awareness of the horrors and carnage of a war which seemed so remote yet so unending. When he allowed his grief to show, it was to me he showed it, often unwittingly. We had established a routine between us at this time, a routine which was to last five or six years. Each morning I would arrive, and climb into his bed for breakfast. Sometimes we would fight about some broken promise of his (a pony no doubt) and I would rush out and slam the door. But far more often, we would laugh together or listen to each other's hopes, fears or worries. He was thirty-seven and I was only eight, but from these moments of closeness, a love and understanding grew between us which was erratic, volatile and deep; a relationship of father and daughter, but above all of two very similar people. 'The boys are like you,' he once wrote to Mother, 'Janet, I'm afraid, is like me.'

So I witnessed his sadness and his joy, as I munched my way through cereal and eggs. I knew how pleased he was when his first book, *Canada in Flanders*, was published, and something of his inner satisfaction at gaining control of the *Daily Express* in November of that year. 'It'll mean a lot of work for somebody,' I remember him saying. And he said the same thing two years later when he started the *Sunday Express*. It meant work and another two million pounds of his own money before it made a profit.

Father was not a good member of the House of Commons, although he did take care of his constituency at Ashton-under-Lyne. He seldom went to the House, and when he did, he didn't vote and he didn't speak. I don't think the other Members appreciated his barnstorming type of delivery. So he stayed silent. In fact I've heard it said that the only person to say less than Father in the House was his son, my brother Max, in the parliament of 1945–50.

So perhaps the news that he had been elevated to the Upper House didn't really upset him that much, although his usual ebullient enthusiasm for his own personal progress was, on this occasion, sadly missing. I remember that winter breakfast when, in an angry voice muffled by blankets, he declared, 'I'm a Lord.' That evening the family was summoned to discuss what he should call himself. He asked for suggestions. 'Beaverbrook' was one of the more jocular offerings, but it stuck. I think Father treasured his memories of the little creatures since, as a boy, he had watched them swimming about in a local river near his home.

So Beaverbrook it was, and Rudyard Kipling undertook to design a coat of arms. Whether or not Father thought he deserved this title, I'll never know. But I think few would deny that by the time he died, he had earned it. And earning it was what mattered to him. Max understood this. 'There'll only be one Lord Beaver-brook as long as I'm alive,' he said, and refused to take the title when Father died. Perhaps the title should have died with him.

In earlier years I had discussed this peculiarly British phenome-non with Father. 'The Exchequer likes titles,' he would say. 'Avoids payouts for services rendered, as in the United States.' But on the strange business of inherited titles, he would become more effusive. He didn't think anyone much approved of them, except in the case of working members of the Royal Family. That in itself was justification enough. But would a duke or an earl or a baron be a lesser person without a title? If so, then it is no more than a prop to boost a sagging ego or some inbred feeling of inadequacy. Or would they perhaps, by their own endeavours, still warrant the power and prestige accorded them?

The political machinations that led to Father's peerage and the fourth great happening of 1916 were mostly carried out in London, at Father's suite in the Hyde Park Hotel, and in the homes of Lloyd George and Bonar Law. When it was all over, Asquith was out. Lloyd George and Bonar Law were in. As a political fixer, Father appears to have had few equals. But apart from his own ambitions and his genuine love and admiration for Bonar Law, I think he correctly gauged the mood of the time and believed Lloyd George to be the best prime minister to hasten the end of the awful, wasting war. 'George'll do it,' he would say.

One morning, as I climbed into his bed for breakfast, Father said, 'Stop biting your nails.' I extracted a promise from him that if I managed to, he would buy me a pony and trap. He wasn't the only one who could drive a bargain. This time he kept his promise. Six weeks later, when I presented my long, polished nails, I demanded my reward. It came in the form of a cheque for £400 and a warning not to exceed it. So off I went with the head groom to Mr Nigel Coleman's Hackney Stud and bought a prize pony, complete with small, black show waggon. The harness and carriage were extra, so I had overrun the budget. How to tell Father? He was quite capable of being cross. With a scowl and a few harsh words, he could reduce me to tears then watch in silence as I ran from the room, banging the door behind me. A reconciliation would usually follow – sometimes with a present of money or too much praise for something I didn't deserve, and a hug and a kiss.

Max learned just to do what he was told. Peter got the worst of it. In time, he developed a habit of retiring into himself and saying nothing. This was his form of self-defence, to be carried to extremes later on when he virtually cut Father out of his life and went his own way. I reacted to Father, and in some ways managed to give as good as I got.

I know now that Father detested self-pity, in himself as much as in others. I soon developed a child cunning, an ability to turn on, or off, rage and tears at will. Being an emotional child anyway, I found I could psyche myself up beforehand by thinking hard about the injustices and the misery he had caused us, particularly Peter. Then I would burst in on him with an act worthy of Lillian Gish in her prime.

For the harness and carriage I chose tears. It was a masterly performance producing a flood of them as I blurted out my misdeed, peering at him speculatively over my sodden hanky. He waited until I had quite finished, then grinned, sat down and wrote a cheque for the extra. Did he *know*? A few weeks later, having driven my new pony and waggon all over the Cherkley estate for practice, I considered myself ready for the Small Hackney Class at the Royal Richmond Show. We started well enough, trotting proudly round the main ring in front of an enthusiastic crowd, who voiced their appreciation with soft murmurings of 'Oh, how sweet!' and 'Well done!' But something was wrong. We were going a bit too fast. Yes, definitely too fast. The charmed murmurings changed to terrified screams as my pony broke into a gallop before hurling itself through the ropes and into the crowd, dragging me and the show waggon with it.

Luckily no one was hurt. But the next morning they were gone; pony, waggon, harness – the lot. That afternoon I passed Father in the front hall. For a second or two we stared at each other in silence. When he turned away, I ran upstairs and started to bite my nails to stop myself crying. It was to be sixty years before I drove in a ring again.

The tree house became important after that. I would spend

hours up there, pondering on my bad luck and deciding which of the many children who lived in, and visited, Cherkley should be allowed to climb up and share my tree house with me. Max was almost a founder member and could come up whenever he liked, although he seemed to take little interest in it. Peter could come too, with help. I always welcomed him. He seemed to have more dreams and secrets than I did. Then there was Jean Rogers, a very pretty girl who often stayed with us for long periods of time, being taught by our governess. We all loved her, Father particularly, who wrote wrote her this letter when finally she left us:

Dear Jean,
For my part I would like to turn back the clock and keep you always in the school room where your beauty and charm first captured my heart.

Yours with love,
Beaverbrook

Mary and George Holmden were neighbours. She was definitely my best friend at the time and shared my love of horses, having one of her own. They were both allowed in the tree house; Diana and Randolph Churchill too. Randolph was always the first to plot some crime against the 'establishment' of adults. Of the Law children, Richard was my favourite. I hardly knew Isobel, but Catherine, who was my age, was partly brought up by my mother, as her own mother had died when she was very young. Although there was a certain amount of antagonism between us, there were also moments of genuinely warm respect and affection, and she became a friend of mine. Elsie Kipling and Megan Lloyd George would both have been welcome because they were such good storytellers. But somehow I think they had risen above such childish pranks. Then there were the two Freddies. One was called Furneaux, the son of F.E., and the other March. He would one day be the Duke of Richmond and Gordon. Both were marvellous companions and definitely members of my tree-house club.

It was a place for fantasy and dreams. We plotted and we planned, and later on we appointed each other members of the tree 'Cabinet'. I was to be Prime Minister ('But you're a *girl*'), and I think Freddy

March was Chancellor of the Exchequer. It all happened in the tree house. One day, George Holmden proposed marriage, and Freddy Furneaux, who didn't bother with that sort of stuff, gave me my first kiss.

I must have been a terrible child at times. Apart from hitting poor Catherine Law, I fought a lot with Max, whom I considered a 'yes man' to Father, and who seemed to be aping him in his desire to tease and goad me. One day he was clomping round on a new little flower bed I had planted with flowers of my own.

> 'Giddy, giddy gout,
> y' petticoat's hanging out!'

So I clobbered him, too, with a trowel. He had twelve stitches put in his head. I lost another pony and spent twenty-four hours in bed.

Although memories of events so long ago are still vivid, it is sometimes hard to place them accurately in time. But one such memory lingers on, and I am sure now that it happened in the winter of 1916–17. It was one of those calm, cold afternoons with a touch of mist that would turn to fog before the day was over. I was preparing to leave my hunched position in the tree house, when I saw Winston Churchill standing alone on the path below me. He stood quite still, gazing away into the forest, hands clenched behind his back, cigar gripped in his teeth. I was about to call out a welcome when something stopped me; something in his attitude. Or was it his face? He looked so angry and alone, so different from the smiling man who gave us all so much happiness. Then a voice, Clemmie's, called him away. I don't remember exactly what she said, but I do remember being hurt and aggrieved by it. It was as if we were not good people, or even trustworthy any more. When Winston left, I climbed down. The sun had dipped behind the trees and soon it would be dark.

2

'Write a poem,' said Father, 'every week.' So this unwelcome chore was added to the routine. Every Saturday night I had to lean another finished offering against the clock over the fireplace in his bathroom. And at every Sunday breakfast session, he would comment on it. Most of them were awful. He was a member of the Government now; the Minister of Information, and often the house would be full of American and Canadian journalists, and others from countries I had never even heard of. He told me Winston was in the Government too and seemed surprised at my pleasure and relief.

'Winston and I,' he said to me many years later, 'are the only two people to have served in *both* wartime cabinets.' Their relationship was deep and lasting, often stormy but born of a mutual respect for each other's prodigious energy and abilities. And they made each other laugh. But there wasn't much laughter in the last few months of 1918. A million Britons had died, Father told me. The flower of a generation, lost. 'The old politicians will linger on,' he said. 'Who will come to take their place?'

I knew he was ill. This was no ordinary depression leading to asthma and restlessness. This time he was in real pain. In October he resigned from the Government. His fights with Balfour and the Foreign Office were no more than a secondary reason. He was ill and tired, and he'd had enough. 'It will be over soon anyway,' he said. And it was. When the news reached us, I ran up on to the roof and rang the great bell as hard as I could. I kept on ringing it until my happy, laughing mother came and took me away. But first she helped me ring the bell, then she hugged and kissed me as the tears poured down both our faces. I think she was surprised how much the end of the war meant to her ten-year-old daughter.

Uncle Allan was safe now. No more dying. The foreigners would go away, the men and the horses would return. And Father would be well again. They told him it was actinomycosis, a rare disease which invariably proved fatal. It had started as toothache the previous August and was to linger on well into the new year. He consulted two dentists, a throat surgeon and a cancer specialist in Harley Street. But it was a little-known Portuguese man who finally cured him, pouring a daily dose of four hundred drops of iodine down his throat until the offending fungus was arrested and could be completely removed.

During these months of severe pain and mental anguish, Father not only continued to run the Government's publicity, but also launched the *Sunday Express*. He did some, but not all, of this from his bed, where I visited him continually. One afternoon he smelt tobacco in my hair when I leaned over to kiss him. 'You've been smoking a cigarette!' he croaked. In a furious rage, he sent for the nice Irish nurse who had let me smoke part of hers, and promptly fired her. Nothing I could say would make him change his mind. He looked ferocious, having grown a beard to hide the fresh scars on his neck. Later, he wrote about his illness. 'It had not been my intention to die,' he said.

Father celebrated his complete recovery by disappearing up to London. Earlier he had moved from his suite in the Hyde Park Hotel to a delapidated property in Fulham called The Vineyard. By the time I got there, he had turned this small Tudor house into a charming and restful home. Here he could invite his friends and political associates to intimate gatherings, secluded from the outside world. The things Father bought would often go wrong; cars wouldn't work, suits didn't fit. But The Vineyard was a success for him in every way. He installed a cinema projector in the small dining room and resurrected the tennis court.

Tennis was a fashionable game in the twenties. At Cherkley, where everything was done on a much grander scale, tennis was the focal point of summer weekends, when Father and a host of his friends would arrive from London. Partly in an effort to wean me away from my main passion, riding, Father encouraged us to play tennis. When this didn't work, he insisted, hiring some of the best coaches in the country. Max and I showed no lasting interest for the game, but Peter improved over the years until he finally became good enough to win a South of England Championship. I think this was one of the very few occasions when he did anything of which Father approved.

So it was tennis, five days a week, slogging the balls back and forth over the net, or more often into it, then walking miles to pick them up so we could start all over again. And the weekends were worse. I was the ball boy. Father's main opponent was always F.E., now Lord Birkenhead. I don't remember ever seeing him in formal clothes but when he and Father approached the court at Cherkley, their sartorial splendour was a sight to see. They wore whites, blazers, scarves and carried two rackets each. I would follow with the new box of balls.

They might have been on the Centre Court at Wimbledon for all the formalities they observed: bouncing balls, testing racket strings and the height of the net before tossing for service, then slowly disrobing for the knock-up. 'Balls, please.' Father would imperiously hold out his racket. We were off. They would start sedately enough, graciously acknowledging each other's winning shots and the subdued murmurings of applause from the spectators. Among these would be Mother, who was no mean player herself and a popular doubles partner, James Dunn, Father's boyhood friend, now a knight and a millionaire, his attractive daughter, Mona, whom F.E. clearly fancied, and sometimes A. J. Balfour and Bonar Law.

Philip Sassoon was often there too, standing as near as he could to the devastatingly pretty Aunt Helen, while behind them two new voices commented freely on the play. One voice sounded like pure cockney, while the other was high-pitched and squeaky. H. G. Wells and Arnold Bennett had arrived. They stood like Tweedle Dee and Tweedle Dum, each to the other a friend, an enemy, a critic and a champion; writers of immense talent and integrity, who, unlike their contemporary, John Buchan, refused honours and titles with as much vehemence as the latter pursued them.

After a while the pace would begin to hot up, and good court manners gave way to spontaneous invective. When this in turn

36

degenerated into physical expressions of their frustration, things got interesting. 'Get it!' Father would shout, as a ball sailed high out of the court into the trees. I spent hours retrieving them, sometimes longer than strictly necessary, nudging balls further into the undergrowth so I could slope about in the shade a bit longer pretending to look for them. Meanwhile, on the court the titanic battle would rage on. More shouts as other balls would arc up over the great elms. 'Another coming!' Laughter from the delighted spectators would hang on the still, summer air as I stumbled about from tree to tree.

Father was quite mean about his tennis balls. When it was all over, I had to retrieve a full box of them before I could leave the court. Sometimes F.E. would hand me a racket before I could get away. 'Come on, Janet. Hit some back.' To please him I would. But he was never inspired sufficiently to include me in the Olympic team he took to Paris three years later – in any capacity. He was such a nice person. They all were, really. It's just that when they played tennis, they took it so seriously; bashing those beastly balls about, losing their tempers and looking ridiculous. Lloyd George preferred golf.

Father was a good host but a bad guest. He seldom went anywhere socially, unless it was abroad, or to the house of one of his political friends, for a political reason. He liked to be in control of things; to steer the conversation this way or that, to test people, even to embarrass them a bit. He hated cant, hypocrisy and people who tried to bluff him. He could be withering in his disapproval and lavish with his praise. He was particular about food and drink, and, whatever else it was, being entertained at Cherkley was never dull. So because of his power, or perhaps his magnetic personality, the world came to him.

He had already decided to quit Canada for good, returning there only for visits. 'You can't live in two continents at once,' Kipling told him, and Father agreed. He got his brother Allan to wind up his Canadian affairs and decided to stay in England. But I think he felt he owed a debt to Canada. Perhaps it was because he had taken so much out that he now wanted to put something back. In 1921, he ran a successful campaign in the *Daily Express* to lift an embargo on cattle imports from Canada, and already the romantic theories of Empire Free Trade were forming in his mind. In keeping his Canadian passport and citizenship, his motives were not only patriotic. He also knew what he was doing from a financial point of view.

One criticism aimed at Father was that he was never wholly serious, to the point of being irreverent. Unlike the other press barons, Northcliffe and Rothermere, Father was rich before he started. They ran their newspapers for profit, while Father ran his for power. So I think people were a bit afraid of him, not because of his power alone but because of his disconcerting attitude to gaining it and using it. To many he was an *enfant terrible*; a child with a loaded gun running through the corridors of power. A frightening thought. But he *was* serious, and having committed himself to something or someone he believed in, such as Empire Free Trade or, in the case of a person, Bonar Law, he remained committed and wholly serious to the bitter end.

He was a staunch friend, and vindictive to only a few enemies. He liked people but hated and feared the thought of boring them or being bored by them. Boredom was his worst enemy. Perhaps that was one of the reasons why he would come to get me in the middle of the night. He would wake me up, help me into my favourite maribou dressing gown and drag me down to meet his dinner guests. I think he was quite proud of me but I hated it. 'Oh, Daddy, no. Not again!' Through eyes half-closed with sleep, I would peer at the elegance and splendour around me; the immaculate boiled shirts and cuffs, the strings of pearls and the glittering bracelets, and hear the enthusiastic chorus of welcome as I slurped at a glass of wine or chewed on a nut.

'Recitation!' demanded a guest. Oh, God! Someone's been here before, I thought. There was no escape. Father would stand me beside him (he always sat in the middle, never at the end of the table) and I would have to recite, looking nervously at their faces to see who was smiling and who was not. They always smiled; all except one. Arnold Bennett was already a social tyro. Looking at him, one's eyes were somehow drawn away from the strange face with the ragged moustache and undershot jaw, downwards past the flower in his button-hole and the immaculately frilled shirt front to rest on his gold fobs and watch chain, or, as H. G. Wells called them, his 'gastric jewellery'. He never smiled or applauded as the others did. Why should he? But always those heavy insomniac's eyes would stare at me as if contemplating something rather unpleasant. In later years I would think of him every time I heard W. C. Fields's wonderful remark, that anyone not liking children or dogs couldn't be all bad. Nevertheless, Arnold Bennett helped people, particularly young and unknown writers.

H. G. Wells was a bit of a problem. He seemed to argue with everyone, except Arnold Bennett, and it got worse as he grew older. 'Go and talk to Mr Wells,' Mother would say. And for a few moments at least, Mr Wells would forget the world's impending doom and disaster to give me images of stars and planets where people walked in peace, men and women were equal, and children could rule the universe. His smile, when it came, was warm, and his voice was gentle. The images have remained in my mind ever since. But he was always in trouble with adults; his wife, girl-friends – everyone sooner or later. Like his old friend Arnold Bennett, I think his humble background made him feel insecure. He wanted to ·change the world and make people wake up before it was too late. He wanted them to *listen*. If only he'd had Bernard Shaw's sense of humour.

Two new personalities arrived on the scene at this point. I think I first saw them on one of those nocturnal occasions in my maribou dressing gown. Both Canadians, they were often referred to by Father as 'the bellhop and the piano tuner', simply because E. J. Robertson had worked his way through college in a local hotel, and Beverley Baxter had wanted to be a concert pianist. But as Manager and Editor respectively of his power-base, the *Daily Express* and *Sunday Express*, they wouldn't have lasted long if they hadn't both been brilliant. 'Amateurs,' scoffed Northcliffe from his lofty pinnacle, then died before he could eat his words.

Father chose the right people for the job with unerring instinct. Another inspired choice was Valentine, Lord Castlerosse. He was the court jester – a diligent gossip whose se!f-elected role was to know everything that was happening on the political and social scene. He seemed to know everybody, and everybody in time would know him as a result of his 'Londonder's Log' in the *Sunday Express*. It was compulsive reading in those days, featuring a line of the most celebrated and beautiful faces every week. At dinner he was superb, only interrupting his prodigious intake to raise his glass and gaze lugubriously over the proceedings in such a way that people would lean closer as if trying to hear what he was thinking. He used to view me with an expression of quizzical interest, pondering perhaps on the amusement he might derive by taking such an innocent to a brothel. He succeeded in doing this twice in later years, no doubt gaining immense pleasure from my outrage and incredulity. Like Father, he could be easily bored.

Of the ladies present, one would have stood out head and shoulders above the rest – Lady Diana, *née* Manners, daughter of the Duke of Rutland, newly married to Duff Cooper. Her brilliance, beauty and grace seemed so effortless, so perfect in every way. I can add nothing new to what has already been written about Diana Cooper, except perhaps to say that she was one of Father's few very special people. He gave her a motorcar for a wedding present, and she responded by making him godfather to her son, John Julius Cooper.

Dinner parties at Cherkley could get pretty wild on occasions. Father would hire a jazz band and, if I wasn't sent back to bed quickly enough, I would see some strange happenings as guests lurched and swooped about the dance floor or draped themselves exhausted on chairs, sofas and window seats. It was all 'ripping' fun. Champagne flowed, the music blared, and the drone of conversation would increase, punctuated by hoots of laughter from the dining room where the hard core would be reacting, no doubt, to some particularly racy story, or the spontaneous if barbed wit of Valentine Castlerosse. Slightly drunk myself from one glass of wine, I would stumble upstairs, once climbing over the supine figure of the tennis coach, asleep with his head on a drum.

One morning a fresh face appeared on the staff. Her name was Miss Dexter. Dex, like Miss Evans, the housekeeper, was special. She was tall, lively and good looking. Utterly loyal to us children, she would show remarkable courage in standing up to Father, a quality much admired by us all. Four years later, she married the handsome butler, Mr Rennie. Their son is my godchild. In due time she became my mother's and my lady's maid also and we kept in touch constantly until she died suddenly in 1984 at the age of ninety-two.

I always tried to sit beside Dex at the film shows, hoping she could do something to stop me being thrown out. The whole household would be present on these occasions: kitchenmaids and chambermaids in the front; footmen, grooms, gardeners and chauffeurs behind them; then the chef, the butler and Miss Evans. Next would come the governess, Dex, myself and Jean Rogers. Father, Mother and their guests would sit in splendid isolation on a platform at the back. Max and Peter were usually away at their prep school in Leatherhead.

The cinema was one of Father's passions. He was not interested in making films but the finished product always fascinated him. Had it not been for his newspapers, I think he might have joined the ranks of the mighty in the dog-eat-dog world of film distribution and exhibition. He had already dabbled in it, and was to do so again. But until the coming of the 'talkies' in 1927, the cinema was no more than an infant relation to the theatre and posed no threat of competition.

We loved it, sitting rigid in our seats, enthralled by the brilliance of Chaplin, the adventures of the swashbuckling Fairbanks and the unbelievable sweetness of Mary Pickford. But when Theda Bara, 'the vamp', or Gloria Swanson took the screen, I held my breath. And if Rudolf Valentino appeared I knew my moments were numbered. At the first sign of an approaching kiss, Father's voice would ring out: 'Janet. Leave the cinema!' The projector would be stopped and I would be led protesting from the room, followed by Jean Rogers who didn't protest hard enough. Why! What on earth were they going to do? The maids would giggle and nudge each other, impatient for us to be gone, while the footmen tried to keep straight faces. They never turned round.

'It's a kissing scene,' Dex would explain. 'Your father thinks you're both too young.'

'But . . .' Visions of Freddy Furneaux in the tree house came flooding back. Was that all? At fourteen, I wanted to know. It became important to me that I *should* know. The answers were near at hand.

*　　　*　　　*

I think I may have inherited my deep love of horses from my great-grandfather. As the elected head of the Orange Movement in Canada, he liked to ride through the streets of Toronto every twelfth of July at the head of the procession, expounding his beliefs and, by tradition, pointing his long orange stick at those who disagreed with him.

This in itself was unremarkable, but the fact that he chose to do it on a pure-bred Arab stallion was not. When out of the pulpit, I'm told he was a very nice man and had the ability to know a good horse when he saw one. I knew Baby was something special the moment I first clapped eyes on him. A dun, with black mane and tail, he arrived as a replacement for his predecessor, lost after another furious row with Father. I first saw him when he was being walked round the yard under the critical gaze of our head groom, John Thorn.

'This one's better, Miss Janet.' He had got used to the rapid turnover in the stables and was reluctant to approve of anything too much in case it had to go the next morning. 'We must try to 'ang on to 'im if we can.' This time the soft West Country voice failed to disguise a note of entreaty.

John Thorn was about thirty, and had been with us for two years. He had a wiry build and a hard, brown face, slightly discoloured by powder burns. I remember he brought with him one of those army saddles with padded, wooden strakes and a high cantle. I asked him once if he had been a lancer, or maybe even a hussar.

'Yeomanry, miss,' he said. Being ignorant of army matters, I left it at that. I think I saw more of John Thorn than anybody else during this time. No one else at Cherkley seemed in the least bit interested in horses, except perhaps Max, who would climb on one occasionally. But his heart wasn't in it. 'Doesn't go fast enough,' he would say, and return to his model cars.

So my life hinged around John Thorn and the world he represented – a world of cold winter mornings, the smell of saddle soap, horse sweat, manure and fresh hay. And in the summer mornings, the sweet aroma of crushed grass in the show ring and the long hours spent watching them graze in the paddocks. I never got tired of seeing him ride. Too often we have heard about someone being so good, he or she looked 'part of the horse'. But that's exactly how he did look. And he seemed to understand me when no one else even tried. Girls are inclined to be a bit sentimental about their horses. All part of the growing-up process, I suppose. But John Thorn would smile and stand patiently waiting while I kissed a 'thank you' on Baby's velvet muzzle after a long and wonderful day's hunting. Then he would lead him away.

I had been 'blooded' – smeared on the face with the blood of a fox as a reward for being in at the kill – at the age of nine. I am glad to say that this habit has now more or less disappeared, but at the time it was, for all of us, the ultimate accolade. I didn't wash for a week. But now, at fourteen, the kill, although perhaps a boon to some farmers, was of no importance to me whatsoever. In fact, I always hoped the fox would get away – after, that is, he'd given us a wonderful chase over most of the county.

It was the day that mattered most, the short winter day. We would start in total darkness and sometimes hack fifteen miles to the meet. My tin of sandwiches and thermos of tea would be waiting for me on the kitchen table. John Thorn would be waiting too, his own sandwiches and a khaki-covered canteen, containing something stronger than tea, already packed in his saddle bag.

'Mornin', Miss. Just the two of us again then, is it?'

'Yes, John.' I had long since stopped calling him 'Mr Thorn'. He was at the very centre of my life. So off we'd go, the darkness slowly giving way to a moist, grey morning with a touch of warm wind from the west. Soon we would be discussing the blackness of the hedges (a sure sign of strong scent), and then, at some pre-arranged rendezvous in the middle of nowhere, Mary Holmden would be waiting, and we would ride on together.

Our days with the Surrey Union hounds were always memorable. There were few roads in 1921 and the countryside was unspoilt.

Mary and I had developed a strong friendship. Rain or shine, these were the happiest days in our young lives. And sometimes it rained so hard we couldn't see our horses' ears. Baby was the best horse I'd ever had. There are moments out hunting when, in the excitement and euphoria of the chase, one has to throw caution to the wind and simply take a chance. Laid fences on banks, hidden ditches, sunken fields, wire and other unforeseen entanglements are all challenges to skill and experience. But once the decision is taken and you are committed, it is the horse that pulls you through, or over, coping with the hidden menace in the few seconds remaining to him, before the danger is past and you are thundering on again, easing the weight from his back, calculating the distance before the next obstacle.

I learnt very early on that a horse is receptive, capable of retaining knowledge from teaching and experience, and that he has a noble heart. 'A good horse is what you make him,' John Thorn once said. 'He'll scare like anyone else when the shrapnel's flying. But he'll trust you if you're worth it. If you're on his back and you show him courage, he'll show you his in return.' It was the second longest speech I ever heard him make.

When we checked, Mary and I would turn to each other, faces flushed, glorying in it, oblivious to everything except the moment. When I looked round for John, he would be right behind us, standing his horse with the reins looped over one arm. He would smile back at me before pulling the cork from his flask and raising it to his lips. I'd know then that he was pleased.

We covered amazing distances. Horse-boxes were still things of the future, so we piled ourselves and our animals into trains whenever possible for the trip back to Leatherhead. Most trains pulled horse-waggons at the rear in those days. John Thorn would remain with them while Mary and I joined our friends in one of the carriages for what we called our 'rag-time'.

We knew them all; children from other big houses in our part of the county. In the winter we hunted together, and in the summer months we competed fiercely at every gymkhana and horse show, particularly the Royal Richmond Show. This was where we went for most of our serious competitions. I was something of a 'star',

44

having won Best Child Rider for three years in a row. But we were all pretty good, and brushes, masks, pads, rosettes, pots and pans made many of our tack rooms resemble a cross between a silversmith, haberdashery and taxidermist. The competition was fierce, but Baby was my trump card.

By the time we reached Leatherhead, we were all exhausted from the pulling and pushing, the shouting and the laughter. We must have been awful. But somehow it never occurred to us to leave so much as a toffee paper in the compartment, let alone to vandalize it.

It was completely dark by the time we did the four and a half mile hack back to Cherkley. We never carried lamps. Half way there, Mary would branch off to her home and John Thorn and I would ride on together, finishing the day as we had started it, just the two of us.

The darkness was the basic cause of the rumpus. I arrived home one evening and walked up the steps to the front door, unaware that I had oil on my boot. I then left a trail of it across the hall and up the stairs to my room. The storm broke next morning.

'He'll go today,' raged Father. 'Teach you to be more careful where you put your feet!' Oh, no! He was going to take my whole world away. I sobbed and screamed, pleaded, shouted and nearly passed out with the shock, the horror and injustice of it all. He means it. He'll do it, as he had done it so many times before. But this was Baby. Oh *why* . . . ?

Then a voice spoke behind him: 'That's not fair, Lord Beaverbrook! The oil came from the forecourt, left there by one of *your* friends. I've checked. If people have cars that leak oil all over the place, what can you expect?'

Father swung round. 'She should have looked where she was going.'

'It was *dark*.'

They stared at each other. I held my breath. Then Father pushed past her down the stairs and Dex, my champion, smiled up at me and winked. Baby was safe. My world was intact once more.

*   *   *

Two people left Cherkley shortly afterwards, never to return. One evening in the cinema, when Gloria Swanson started to go all misty, I knew a kissing scene was coming up. Sure enough it did and I was promptly ejected, along with sweet Jean Rogers. Angry and confused, I made my way to the stables and confronted John Thorn, alone in his tack room.

'What comes after kissing, John?'

He looked up from polishing a buckle and smiled. 'Throw you out again, did they, Miss Janet?'

I could see nothing to smile about. 'What comes afterwards? What do people *do*? Tell me.'

He stood up and hung the gleaming bridle on its peg. 'Ain't my place to do that, Miss Janet. Why not ask your mother?'

'No. You're the best friend I've got. *You* tell me.'

'There's more to life than kissing. You'll find out soon enough. You got plenty of time.' He was about to leave when I grabbed his arm.

'No. Tell me now. It's about love, isn't it? About making babies? I know that much. But what? *How*? I *order* you to tell me, John.'

So he did; John Thorn, ex-cavalryman, companion, mentor, and the best friend I had. He took one long look at my face and his eyes became serious. I think he knew what would happen. He told me the facts of life the only way he knew how – in language that D. H. Lawrence would no doubt have approved of, but which left me in a state of shock and outrage. In near panic, I fled back to the house, disgusted, disillusioned, to sit on my bed in silence, chewing a sodden handkerchief, eyes staring at the wall.

It was never the same after that. Gone was the wonderful friendship. I was formal with him, and remote: I simply couldn't look him in the face anymore. Two weeks later he left. He just went away, taking with him his old army saddle with the high cantle, and later, much later, my undying gratitude.

The second person to leave Cherkley, never to return, was Rudyard Kipling, who had come to seem as much a part of the house as we were. It was all about Ireland, I knew that, and his fundamental disagreements with Father and Tim, who wanted the Irish to rule themselves. For Kipling, sad, dear Rudyard

Kipling, the British Empire was life itself. He could not watch any part of it die. He wrote a poem in the Cherkley visitors' book, and on the day John Thorn left, I read part of it again:

> The four best gifts beneath the sun,
> Love, peace and health and honest friends.

3

When the Greeks occupied Smyrna (now Izmir) as a reward for being on the winning side in the war, they reckoned without Kemal Atatürk. This remarkable man had rejuvenated his defeated country, so often referred to as 'the sick man of Europe', and by August 1922 was busy throwing the intruders into the sea.

Father, having been urged by the Aga Khan and government officials to meet Kemal Atatürk and see for himself what a Muslim Turkish Nationalist could do when he tried, set off for Constantinople in the same month, taking with him his valet and a clutch of secretaries. He also took Max and me, as part of our education.

After a long and tedious train journey, we sailed from the Italian port of Brindisi and headed east into the Levant. I never found out exactly how Father persuaded the captain to alter course, but this he did, and instead of the domes and spires of Constantinople, the first thing Max and I saw from our position on the guard rail was the burning port of Smyrna, in Asia Minor.

When Greek fights Turk, the resultant brutality, born of centuries of religious and territorial enmity, can add new dimensions of obscenity to the already blood-soaked annals of war. It was an experience that was to live with me, and haunt me, all my life.

We arrived in the evening to see flames rising a hundred feet above the town. Great dust and smoke clouds mushroomed upwards to mix with the rays of the setting sun and turn the horizon blood red, flecked with yellow, green and black. The ship moved close enough inshore to anchor for all of us on board to hear the roar of the flames, the crackle of gunfire, the shouting and the screams. The last Greek defenders were overrun before our eyes, then men, women and children were bayoneted and thrown into the sea. We had arrived in time to witness the last few dreadful moments.

No one swam out to us. No boats appeared with cargoes of refugees, and if they had, I doubt if they would have been picked up. Such an act, no matter how humanitarian, could evidently have been interpreted as favouring one side against the other. So we sailed away, not wanting to be involved; leaving behind us the agonized screams, the diminishing rattle of gunfire and the pathetic bundles of lifeless humanity floating on the placid waters of the bay. It was not our affair.

At twelve and thirteen years old respectively, Max and I heard, saw and smelt these terrible things from a distance of no more than a quarter of a mile. We might have been standing on another planet. It was not until later that the full shock and horror of it penetrated our young minds. It never occurred to us to ask why; why we had not stayed to help. Nor did we wonder how *they* had felt; they who had waited to die, and had seen a gilded world of peace and luxury come to watch them in their agony, then glide silently away above its own reflection of a thousand twinkling lights.

No one was allowed ashore in Constantinople, except Father. With his special letters of introduction, he was whisked away to meet the great Atatürk. When he returned, we were promptly transferred to another ship which weighed anchor within the hour for Piraeus and Brindisi. There was an air of urgency about things now. In Piraeus we saw the battered remnants of another Greek army disembarking amid the litter of their discarded material and equipment. The expressions on the soldiers' faces were of shock and disillusionment, almost of resignation. We stayed long enough for Father to cable a lurid description of this scene to the *Express*, then left for Brindisi. From there, a series of clattering trains and a ferry returned us to England, to Cherkley, and to Mother. That same evening, Father left for London.

The events that followed have been carefully recorded by both historians and biographers. To his consternation, Father was told that Lloyd George, F. E. Smith and Churchill had already decided on war with Turkey, and to that end had cabled the Dominions for their support. Each day for the next three weeks, Father used every weapon at his disposal to prevent the war. He repeatedly called on each of his old friends in turn, entertaining them at The

Vineyard, together or separately, whenever he could. He coun-
selled peace, patience, negotiation in the face of the outrage expressed by Lloyd George, always pro-Greek, and the sabre-
rattling of Churchill who, with F. E. Smith, had supported Turkey
but now abruptly switched camps and fell in behind their leader.
Father used the full weight of his newspapers to enlist public
support. And in the end, he persuaded his old friend Bonar Law
to return from France and add his weight to the cause of peace and
sanity.

He nearly failed. On 29 September the Government authorised
an ultimatum to Turkey which, had it been delivered, might well
have plunged us into war. But it was not delivered, thanks to the
good sense of General Harrington, commanding the beleaguered
British forces at Chanak, who either didn't believe it, tore it up, or
conveniently lost it. On 10 October an armistice was signed at
Mudros.

The failure of the British Government's pro-Greek policy precipitated a political crisis which resulted in Bonar Law becoming
Leader of the Conservative party, and then Prime Minister. Lloyd
George, the Loved One, was out. But Law had needed to be
pushed, and Father pushed him. 'I did not create the opportunity,'
he said, 'I took advantage of it.' He had said it before; in 1910,
referring to the Canadian economic boom, and again in 1916 with
the fall of Asquith. Now, in 1922, he might have reaped his greatest
reward. But there were strings attached – two of them.

One morning, through the open door of his bathroom at Cherkley, I saw Father in his dressing gown, striding up and down with
an expression of furious preoccupation on his face. He noticed me
and stopped.

'They've offered me Chancellor of the Exchequer,' he said, and
resumed his pacing. I waited, not knowing the profound importance of this statement. 'Want to live at number eleven Downing
Street?'

'Not if it means giving up Cherkley,' I answered.

He stopped his pacing again and turned towards me. 'It means,'
he growled, 'giving up my newspapers, and I won't do it.'
Stanley Baldwin got the job in the end, and Father took me to

London to wish good luck to Bonar Law on his way to Buckingham Palace to kiss the king. We lumbered down the Mall in a black barouche of a car and swept in through the massive wrought-iron gates with their gold spikes, past policemen and guards who saluted and waved us on. Then across the great forecourt, under the archway and into a courtyard where a small army of uniformed footmen and courtiers took him away. Apart· from the inevitable chauffeur, there were not many people about when I crept rather nervously out of the back of the car and looked around me.

'Their horses are rather fine,' Bonar Law had broken silence to observe on our way round Queen Victoria's statue. I had noticed he was no longer smoking his pipe. He was right. They were. Or the one I saw was. It emerged from the direction of the mews with a man on its back. How on earth had he got up there? The animal was the size of a small elephant; coal black and glistening from tossing mane to shining hooves. It came sedately towards me and stopped, chewing its gleaming, foam-flecked bit.

I looked up. The officer in a tunic bedecked with black frills looked down. His eyes were bright blue, set in a smooth, hard face which was perfectly symmetrical and bisected by an immaculate moustache above a firm mouth and chin. He was like a god, staring down at me from a great height, while I, a mere mortal intruding upon the slopes of his Olympus, stared back with increasing nervousness.

'Good morning,' he said in a high-pitched, metallic voice.

'What's his name?' I asked. 'He's perfect.'

'God' touched the mane with a gloved hand and looked thoughtful for a second. Then he smiled, showing a row of straight, white teeth. 'Max,' he said, 'I think.'

*   *   *

Father's attitude to foreign affairs was global, hingeing on an expansionist-inflationist policy for the UK and the Empire, primarily the Dominions. His mental map of the world no doubt envisaged a potentially dangerous gap between Gibraltar and the Indian subcontinent, safeguarded by Suez and Aden in defence of our principal trade route. On the Near East he was consistent: 'Out!' he would say, stabbing the air with his cheese knife to emphasize the point. 'Pull out. Involvement in Mespot and Palestine can only lead to trouble. We'll always be the "bad guy" whatever we do. Out!'

History was to prove him right, I'm afraid. Years later, with the problem still unsolved and many British lives lost, he focused his resentment on the unfortunate A. J. Balfour, his one-time tennis partner and the chief architect of the famous declaration that promised a national home for the Jews in Palestine. 'The man was a hermaphrodite,' Father said, as if that explained everything. 'No one ever saw him naked.' Sadly I was not present to hear A. J. P. Taylor's choice rejoinder: he asked if it was usual for Father to see cabinet ministers naked.

Father's sentiments appeared to be pro-Jewish and anti-Zionist. I well remember how strong they were. The occasion was a dinner party at Cherkley and I was sitting beside him. The topic of conversation was once again Palestine.

'How can we support thirty thousand Jews against three hundred thousand Arabs?' he asked. 'How can we ask our army to do that?' No one answered. '*Out* then!' He swung the cheese knife sideways and stabbed me in the arm. I still bear the scar.

So I was a bit surprised when Father told us we were going to Palestine for a holiday. The whole family went with him: Mother, Max, Peter and me, together with Aunt Helen, Dex, James Douglas, the editor of the *Sunday Express*, and Father's secretary. It was February 1923.

We joined the *Mauretania* at Southampton and headed for Gibraltar in unseasonal calms. The swimming pool is the thing I remember best about that great liner. It was deep down between decks, surrounded by marble pillars and exotic plants growing in huge Greek urns. It was built entirely of blue and green mosaic tiles in which the tepid water glittered like some vast jewel. My brothers and I were dragged from our aquatic paradise to see, first Naples and Vesuvius, then the ruins of Pompeii where the adults spent hours peering at the 2000-year-old pornography, having directed us children elsewhere.

At Piraeus I was glad that nothing remained of the military shambles I had seen six months previously, and Athens provided me with my first view of the Parthenon, which perhaps more than any other single experience inspired me later to want to draw and paint. From Greece we sailed, thankfully, past Smyrna and into the Sea of Marmara, past the Golden Horn to the harbour of Constantinople. Once more, Father left us the moment we docked. He had another appointment with Kemal Atatürk, who this time was deeply grateful, not surprisingly, for Father's successful efforts to avoid a war between the two countries.

In the days that followed, I was shown the Topkapi Palace, the Blue Mosque and the Byzantine masterpiece of St Sophia. I also saw the whirling dervishes, who danced about on spikes and hot coals while the smell of their burning feet revolted all but the hardiest of enthusiasts. I couldn't get out of the place fast enough. Then it was Palestine; Haifa and the beautiful train ride to Jerusalem, where an officer from General Allenby's staff met us and took us to the King David Hotel, a remarkably luxurious place until the day twenty-three years later, when Menachem Begin and his friends of the Haganah blew it up together with its British residents. Allenby, whom I had met before at Cherkley, also longed for the day we could get out of Palestine.

Father was now courted by prominent Jews and Arabs alike, each seeking to influence him and thus advance their cause through his newspapers. Wherever he went he took me with him. We dined with the Jewish gentlemen in the city, then climbed into a British army vehicle for the ride into the desert, to the beautiful rainbow-coloured tent of Amin Al Husseini, the President of the Supreme Muslim Council, where we sat on velvet cushions and ate with our fingers. 'You have an excellent case gentlemen,' Father told each in turn. 'As soon as I return to London, I will discuss your problems with members of the Foreign Office.'

The Church of the Holy Sepulchre and the Wailing Wall came next. But both seemed equally strange to me, the former having no visible link with our Presbyterian faith, nor, except for the crucifix itself, our little church at Mickleham near Cherkley. At the Wailing Wall, my two young brothers had to be restrained by

53

the police from playing some boistrous game which involved running round the worshippers. When the reason was explained to them, they were both genuinely contrite. After that, we left by train for Cairo.

All I could see of the Sinai Desert, when I worked up the energy to look out of the carriage window, was a sea of pulsing yellow sand under a milk-white sky. We had run out of water and I was hotter than I'd ever been in my life. I said so. 'You don't sweat, dear,' Mother said, 'it's rude. Max sweats. You perspire.' So I perspired, as did the sandwiches, all the way to Cairo where I wallowed in water at Shepherds Hotel, then slept for twenty-four hours.

After visits by Viscount Allenby and Ahmad Fuad, head of the Egyptian State (none of whose retinue looked *quite* like Rudolph Valentino), we moved to the Mena House, a superb hotel close to the awe-inspiring pyramids of Gizeh. Here we rode camels, rushing about the desert on these ungainly, endearing beasts, followed by shouts from Father, who was mainly confined to posing for the camera. 'Don't let it spit in your eye, Janet!'

We were well on the way to Luxor when our time in Egypt was abruptly terminated. From our deckchairs under a blue and white awning, we were admiring the breathtaking beauty of the Nile at sunset, when a fast launch overhauled us in mid-stream and a voice called Father's name. A few seconds later, he held an urgent cable in his hands. It told him that his dearest friend, Bonar Law, was dying, and I had never seen a look of greater sadness or despair on his face. Within minutes he had gone, taking Max with him, leaving us to follow in our own time.

We finally reached Cherkley in May, and were told that Father had taken his old friend to Le Touquet and was doing everything he could to make the last months of his life more bearable. For instance, to make him feel he was dying a rich man, Father bought hundreds and hundreds more of his named shares on the Stock Exchange to make the price rise – then advised him to sell at treble the price which Bonar had bought them at. Five months later he was dead, from cancer of the throat.

Bonar Law had held office for such a very short time. Perhaps he would never have made a great prime minister even if he had lived, because he was just too straight, too honest. I know Father admired him for these virtues alone, but I also suspect he saw in Bonar Law a greatness of spirit and depth of integrity which he himself could not aspire to. This could cause conflict between them, as indeed it did over Palestine. The policy of isolation, the negation of responsibility, was not for Bonar Law. He would *try* to do the right thing because he was an honourable man and promises were made to be kept. I never really knew Bonar Law. But I believe Father truly loved him.

*   *   *

When Sir Edward Hulton retired to the south of France, he sold his entire newspaper empire to Father, who in turn sold most of it to Lord Rothermere, who then sold the rest to the Berry brothers. When everyone had sorted themselves out, Father had acquired the *Evening Standard* for the price of a phone call, and Lord Rothermere was richer by almost £2,000,000. Perhaps it was this remarkable deal that precipitated an expansive mood in Father, or perhaps it was just because he was now in his mid-forties. Anyway, he quickly bought a yacht, *Miramichi*, and rented a fine London home – Stornoway House in St James's Park.

He also bought for his children three shining new bicycles. They were red, white and blue, and I got the white one. Very soon afterwards, the red bicycle was a twisted mass of metal lying underneath the family Daimler on top of my nine-year-old brother, Peter. He was unconscious and horribly cut about the head and face as a result of a head-on collision in the driveway. With the help of blood transfusions, Mother's amazing calmness and self-control, and the fire brigade, who lifted the heavy car from his body, Peter's life was saved. In the ensuing weeks, I spent hours sitting at his bedside, talking to him, hoping he could hear me through the bandages which covered his entire head. It had been a very close thing. Father never left Cherkley until Peter was fully recovered. When he did go, he went to Canada. And he was still there when the next, near-fatal accident occurred.

We were in our open Cadillac this time, on our way through the

New Forest to Sidmouth, and the sea air which Mother thought would be good for Peter's continued recovery. Mother, Peter and a nurse were sitting in the back, behind a raised windshield. I was in the front beside Mac, the chauffeur and Father's ex-batman, who was still deeply upset after the last accident. I remember looking round excitedly for a sight of the wild ponies, when suddenly I knew no more. I came round, lying in the road, pouring blood from a horrendous gash down one side of my face and a severed artery above one eye. I had gone through the windscreen.

I owe my life to a dentist. I never knew his name. He ran from his house close by and, having tourniqueted the artery, he took me to the nearby home of Lord and Lady Harcourt, who were friends of Mother. A doctor came and stitched me up. The Harcourts were good, kind people, and their beautiful home near Lyndhurst was a perfect place for Peter, who had not been seriously hurt in this, his second car crash in a few weeks, and I to recover.

Plastic surgery for both of us came later, carried out by Mr Trotter of Harley Street, who inserted a silver plate above my eye and tidied me up enough so that people didn't actually shudder when they looked at me. Important for a girl. 'She'll be scarred for life!' cried Father when he got back from Canada. He didn't seem to mind about Peter's wounds so much.

The first person I wanted to see was Mac, the chauffeur. He had been waiting outside my door for days, I was told. When I did see him I was horrified. His hair seemed to have gone completely white. Poor Mac. Two head-on collisions and neither of them his fault. I tried to cheer him up but he just sat there, his eyes clouded with misery. When Max arrived from school, he looked me straight in the face without flinching then grinned a wide grin. 'Gosh, Janie. What a beautiful black eye!' I hugged him hard, as I always did when things were tough.

In the end I didn't look too bad, after the stitches had been removed and the cuts had had time to heal. I was fifteen and, like most girls of that age, had become interested in boys, music and dancing to the exclusion of almost all else – except riding, of course. I had filled out a bit too, and I suppose people found me attractive enough if they didn't get too close to the wrong side of my face.

When the navy arrived in the shape of Dick Pugh and Prince George of Kent, things definitely began to look up. On days when Father was in London, these two happy midshipmen would arrive at Cherkley in a sports car with the most enormous dog which filled the back seat, like a dowager duchess on her way to Ascot. It belonged to Prince George and I think it was called Gladstone (or Palmerston – definitely not Disraeli!). Apart from its size, it was friendly and inquisitive.

Mary Holmden was usually with me and the four of us, plus dog, would creep away to the schoolroom or my sitting room. Then out would come the gramophone and we'd roll back the carpet. It was Gladstone who caused our downfall. His master and I were so engrossed in our impersonation of Fred and Adele Astaire, dancing on the tables, that we failed to notice he'd got bored and left. On his way out of the front door, he had evidently encountered Father coming in, and had embraced him rather sloppily in the hall. This had not been a difficult feat for Gladstone, who stood all of six feet with his front paws on somebody's shoulders.

Father screamed for the butler, demanding to know who owned the Alsatian and how it had got into the house. Mr Rennie was saved from answering by the faint strains of 'Lady Be Good' and a good deal of thumping coming from upstairs. The result of all this was that my two marvellous midshipmen, who had done so much for my morale, were sent packing, as was Gladstone, 'never to darken our door again'. Mary was sent home, and I was sent to school.

*   *   *

I think Father must have bribed the headmistress of Leatherhead Court. Either that, or she was an amazingly tolerant and understanding woman, because I tried my hardest to get expelled. Apart from spilling bath water through the ceiling, faking illness and encouraging other girls to break every rule in the book, I once again enlisted the help of the navy to bring a little colour and excitement into what I considered to be a dreary world.

All to no avail. Sports cars turning up in the middle of the night, walks in the moonlight, music and laughter when all others were asleep. I tried everything. Nothing worked. I was committed to an open prison, because of Father's jealousy and injustice. When I did work, I found I was well up to the academic standard of the other girls. Governesses had done a good job on me, and now I wish I had calmed down enough to make better use, in particular, of the art classes. The teacher was good and I was interested, in spite of my deep sense of resentment at being there at all.

It lasted a year, during which time wonderful things were happening in the outside world. Aunt Laura, Father's sister, left Edinburgh University and married Douglas Ramsey, a Scottish landowner from Selkirk; the beautiful Aunt Helen, Mother's sister, had finally dismayed her many admirers by marrying Evelyn Fitzgerald; and Father had erected a large illuminated cross in the garden at Cherkley. He stuck it on a slight hill from where it could glow down an avenue, straight into the window of the dining room. No one seems to know exactly why he did this, or what it was meant to represent. Personally, I think it was a sort of tongue-in-cheek remembrance of John Knox and the Presbyterian trumpetings of his youth. And I missed seeing Lloyd George when he came again to Cherkley in November 1923, with Winston and F.E. I don't know what they talked about, maybe Free Trade, maybe the repayment of the colossal US war loan. Either way, it would have made good listening. 'Don't pay it,' Father would have insisted. 'Not yet. If you do, it will lead to deflation, which will mean a General Strike, which will, in turn, cause mass unemployment. Wait.' Sometimes I think Father was a bit psychic.

I was released from my open prison at Leatherhead in 1924, and in September of that year I was sent to Paris, to a well-known finishing school run by the Ozanne sisters. I was now sixteen. Here, far from being the precocious teenage rebel and the envy of my friends, I found myself in the company of rich, rare and beautiful people; girls my own age or older who had about them an aura of worldly sophistication which I wished I had too. Most of us were pre-debs, destined for the English marriage market, to which dubious end the three Ozanne sisters, determined, open-minded, intelligent women, endeavoured to instil in us a little French, a lot of poise, and a keen sense of where and when.

Here was an 'open prison' with a difference. Paris, that most seductive of cities, lay on our doorstep, and often one of the Ozannes, probably Lily, would take us walking in the Bois de Boulogne or escort us to the ballet, the opera or the Comédie Française. I made some good friends among the inmates: Peggy Walker, Tanis Guinness, whose family was in banking, and Leslie Campbell who was to become my closest friend for years. I also met the fabulously wealthy Nancy Cunard, busy cutting a furrow of her own, who lived with Henry Crowder, a black jazz pianist, and who one day insisted on undergoing an appendix operation without an anaesthetic. Nancy could love and hate with equal ferocity. Among the former was Aldous Huxley, and among the latter, her mother.

I was learning, and I wanted to learn more. For this reason apart from any other, I was lucky to meet Michael Arlen. His bestselling novel, *The Green Hat*, had just become the rage of London, profoundly shocking the older generation and exciting the younger. The outrageous activities and tragic demise of its heroine, Iris Storm, as she went about her one-girl battle against conventional society, was the talk of the town.

Michael, whose real name was long and unpronounceable, was Bulgarian by birth and had escaped from Armenia during one of the terrible Turkish massacres. Now, suddenly, he was rich and very famous, and, because he was also much admired by the Ozannes, I was allowed out to lunch with him. I found him utterly charming, his behaviour exemplary, going no further than repeated invitations accompanied by gifts of flowers. He told me about the things that were happening in 1924; about the Prince of Wales breaking bones steeplechasing, and Ramsey MacDonald forming the first Labour Government. He talked of Diana Cooper's success in *The Miracle* on Broadway, and a new play, *The Vortex*, by a new author, Noel Coward. He spoke of crime too, a hitherto unknown subject; how Chang, the dope king, had at last been caught, and Mrs Merrick fined forty shillings for selling liquor without a licence in one of her fashionable, though dubious, basement 'clubs', which included royalty among their patrons.

I listened and I was fascinated, for Michael Arlen was no ordinary man. When *The Green Hat* had run its course on both stage and screen, with Katherine Cornell and Greta Garbo respectively, he gracefully retired before either he or his work could be called 'dated'. In London, Iris Storm was played by Tallulah Bankhead, who was about to scythe her own outrageous swath through society in a real-life imitation of the part.

Father would often visit Paris while I was there, staying at the Ritz and dining at Maxim's. He took me to lunch with the British ambassador and his wife, Lord and Lady Crewe, at the British Embassy, and having dropped me back at the Ozannes', would retire to the Pigalle, or wherever else his fancy beckoned. Mother, when she came with him, would retire to bed. It was probably Valentine Castlerosse, on one of his *tours gastronomiques* to Paris and the home of his first love, Jacqueline Forzanne, who told Father about Michael Arlen. And it was no doubt Father who told Valentine to tell him if he found out anything. One day, Father told me on the phone, 'Michael has got a bad reputation with women. I forbid you *ever* to see him again.' Michael was standing beside me at the time, so Father repeated it all to him, loudly. The Ozannes looked on helplessly. When it was over, Michael smiled and kissed me decorously on the cheek. 'Good luck, Janet,' he said, 'I won't forget you, ever.'

*   *   *

I was almost seventeen when I returned to England in June 1925. The heavy atmosphere of Paris, and perhaps the influence of Michael Arlen, had given me a veneer of sophistication, an almost cynical awareness of what was going on, far beyond my years. But it was only a veneer, pasted thinly over my real interests, shared with Leslie Campbell, of music, fashion, make-up and young men. In politics, the Conservatives were back in power under Stanley Baldwin, for whom Father nurtured a secret and lasting dislike. Lloyd George was evidently discredited. Churchill walked in fear of his wife. F.E. was now madly in love with Mona Dunn and couldn't concentrate, and Father had developed a love of music and the theatre. This was his 'actress' period, and like everything else he did in life, he did it to the full for as long as the mood lasted.

I arrived home to find Mother contemplating an out-sized bath, installed for the use of Lord Castlerosse during his increasingly frequent visits to Cherkley. Valentine treated her with due deference as the wife of the man who was buttering his bread. As with Arnold Bennett, Father's other intimate crony, Valentine could come and go as he liked. But Mother was not happy. Max and Peter were away at school and her joy at having me home again betrayed an inner loneliness I could only guess at – until I went to London.

Stornoway House had been leased from the crown. It was a fine building in Cleveland Row, overlooking Green Park on one side and the courtyard of St James's Palace on the other. The ballroom was impressive. Father showed me round. 'Got it for you, darling, really. For your coming out.' I didn't quite believe that. The old friends were gone, replaced now by bright, young people he had known for only a few weeks or months. There were exceptions of course. Valentine Castlerosse was still very much in evidence and fast becoming a force to contend with. The ladies of society and stage waylaid him in the street, positively quivering with desire to be included in the next edition of the Londoner's Log. He knew them all, did Valentine.

But the following year he bit off more than he could chew when he met Doris Delavigne, an exclusive *poule de luxe*, who, I am told, later made him a most 'uncomfortable' wife. She gave his insane jealousy plenty to work on. He once received a reverse-charge telephone call from New York in the middle of the night. It was Randolph Churchill.

'You'll never guess where I am, Valentine.'

'Where are you?'

'In bed with your wife.'

Father met most of Valentine's friends. Arnold Bennett no doubt affected a few introductions too. He swam in a rather different pond, concentrating his energy, his money and his dwindling health trying to keep up with the furious pace of the twenties, while peering nostalgically over his shoulder at the old friends who knew him for his talent. Among these were Bernard Shaw, Somerset Maugham and, of course, H. G. Wells. His weekly articles in the *Evening Standard* kept him in funds, and with a yacht and a town house of his own, he moved among the rich and famous with the assurance of a bull elephant in a herd of water buffalo.

Another 'introducer' who had appeared on the scene was Freddy Lonsdale, already lionized by society for his book, *The Maid of the Mountains*, which was then dramatized for the London stage, starring Jose Collins. It made Freddy a fortune, as did *The Last of Mrs Cheyne* and others. Unfortunately, unlike Michael Arlen, he didn't know when to cut and run. Father had met Jose Collins, a plumpish girl with dark hair and a beautiful voice, who brought her own accompanist to Cherkley for weekend entertainment. He thought she was wonderful and he evidently wasn't the only one. She had recently become Lady Innes-Ker, thereby following in the best traditions of Rosie Boote and Gertie Millar, who had already become the Marchioness of Headfort and the Countess of Dudley.

Father was well armed for his foray into the world of entertainment. He had already equipped himself with a majority shareholding in the country's largest cinema chain, thus inviting producers, actresses and cabaret stars to swarm about him. Among the latter were the sparkingly talkative Dolly sisters, who had been around for some time at the Kit Cat Club. Before long, Gordon Selfridge, their original patron, and Father were batting them back and forth between them like a couple of ping pong balls. The prettiest was Jenny, who, alas, eventually ran up a gambling bill of £90,000 which no one felt inclined to pay. She committed suicide. There were serious talents too, among them Gertie Lawrence and Bea Lillie, both on 'darling' terms with Father, but both moving too fast for more than fleeting relationships.

One massive talent, however, stopped long enough to cause the worst, most bitter row I ever had with Father. Tallulah Bankhead was larger than life. With Noel Coward's *Fallen Angels* already to her credit, she took on Michael Arlen's heroine in *The Green Hat* as if it were her own living story. She did almost everything except crash a yellow Hispano-Suiza into a tree and kill herself. Father, at the peak of his 'Walter Mitty' phase, got caught up in Tallulah's web with predictable results. I remember her hair more than anything else about her. Not so much the colour of it, but the way it glowed and fell in gentle curves about her forehead and wide-set, slumberous eyes. Father seemed to be getting too fond of Tallulah and I couldn't bear the thought of him hurting my beloved mother. When I told him so, a very bad argument followed. Father was defiant, telling me to shut up and mind my own business. Looking back on it, it was as if he had *wanted* to do what he did, where and when he did it, in line with Tallulah's own creed; flying in the face of every conventional morality.

Ironically, it was a film producer who brought this lurid phase of Father's life to an end. His name was Richard Norton, the son of Lord Grantley, who himself had a roving eye for a pretty face and a poor sense of marital loyalty. He did it unwittingly, by introducing Father to his beautiful wife, Jean. Jean Norton was different. She was intelligent and kind, and well aware of what was happening as the summer months passed and she and Father fell genuinely in love. Gone were the actresses and the crazy times. Gone the Dolly sisters, Bankhead, Collins and their like. Jean saw to that. Father was himself again.

Mother's reaction was typical of her; relief on the one hand, for Father's own sake as much as hers, and on the other, sadness and a profound sense of loss as she recognized his relationship with Jean Norton for what it was; serious and perhaps lasting. She tried her best to explain her feelings to me, asking me again not to be angry on her behalf. Her unselfishness was amazing. But I could see how hurt she really was. And when Father brought Jean to Cherkley, although Mother was kind to her and obviously liked her, she had had enough. Late one night, she came to my room and sat on my bed. Impulsively she grabbed my hand, then smiled. 'Let's go to Canada,' she said. I loved her so deeply I would have gone anywhere with her, so Canada it was.

4

Montreal did not seem a very happy place in 1925. Even then the antagonism of the French-speaking inhabitants in some districts was manifested by rowdy marches, violence and shouts for independence. Mother, Dex and I arrived in the autumn. We stayed with her brother Chip Drury, and for a few weeks, at least, she was happier and more relaxed than I had ever seen her. Her sisters Ethel and Arabella came and went, as did Father's brother Allan, whom I was particularly pleased to see looking happy and prosperous.

Then, suddenly, as winter closed in, Mother fell ill, complaining of severe headaches and dizziness. She was admitted to the Victoria Hospital but insisted I go ahead with our plans to ski every weekend in the Laurentians. I went with Chip, and together we enjoyed to the full the glittering ski slopes and the warm evenings round the fire in our timber-built hotel. They were wonderful days, made more so by the arrival in my life of a blond, good-looking French-Canadian called Jacques Hubert, whose company we both delighted in, and with whom I had my first serious, though totally innocent, affair. I adored him.

When Mother was well enough, she went to Atlantic City with Dex to stay with her brother Victor, leaving me with Chip and the romantic attentions of Jacques. On Christmas Eve, I was staggering out of a store with my arms full of presents, surrounded by fairy lights and carol singers, when, without warning, a terrible pain hit me in the stomach and I collapsed in the snow. Appendicitis. I was rushed to hospital and woke with tubes sticking out of me in a room full of flowers, with Jacques peering anxiously from the foot of the bed. He was holding a letter for me, from London.

Janet Janet I adore you,
Come and live in London Town.
I will give you pearls and pendants,
And a nice new velvet gown.

Thus Father wrote, adding that he had seen Lady Mountbatten, also recovering from surgery, that Lady Eleanor Smith, F.E.'s daughter, had sadly joined the Band of Hope, and lastly that the Kit Cat Club had been raided by the police when he was *not* there. 'Look after your beautiful mother,' he finished. 'I long to see her again, before I die of old age.'

My beautiful mother had returned to Montreal. A few weeks later we were on our way to Vancouver. We travelled on the Canadian Pacific Railway, and it was memorable, all three thousand miles of it. Forests, lakes and endless plains were to be seen from our three adjoining drawing rooms with soft carpets, velvet sofas and silk blinds with golden tassels. At Toronto we stopped long enough to have soft drinks with various Aitken and Drury relations who came to meet us. They still had a form of prohibition there. Then on to Moose Jaw, where Indians and tall men in wide-awake hats on raw-boned cow ponies sat watching us as if waiting for something to happen or for someone to come.

After Maple Creek and Calgary we entered the Rocky Mountains, and were privileged to see a panorama of magnificence beyond description. From the observation car I watched the great shining peaks pass, the rushing rivers and steep ravines. I watched till my eyes ached, for each valley was different, each mountain alone and remote in its untouched grandeur. Vancouver left me with memories of more relations, a spectacular city with west-facing slopes of huge redwoods, and endless rain sweeping in from the Pacific.

Then we headed south into the United States, to California and Los Angeles. I've heard it said that Americans have no sense of humour but an enormous sense of fun. I don't believe this was ever true, but fun in the twenties was what everyone was seeking. Four years previously the Mountbattens had visited Hollywood, or 'Fun City' as it is sometimes called, and had clearly had a lot of 'fun'.

They stayed with the Fairbanks at Pickfair and made an amateur film with Charlie Chaplin. Just how much fun the Americans got out of this in return, I'm not sure, but the Mountbattens had obviously kept in touch, and it was probably because of Edwina's friendship with Father that we, in turn, were invited to stay at Pickfair.

We didn't stay long, but we did meet a lot of people. Douglas Fairbanks and Mary Pickford were famous, very famous. As the 'King' and 'Queen' of Hollywood, they were always being asked to entertain foreign royalty or dignitaries from just about any country that had a cinema. They were nice, friendly and informal, although Fairbanks always seemed to be acting. He was a small man who would suddenly appear out of a door or window, smiling his famous smile and posing as if for a hidden camera. We found this disconcerting at first, but soon got used to it because he was such a warm and friendly person. As 'King' of 'Fun City', he had a lot to live up to.

We didn't see much of Mary Pickford because she was working at the time and left for the studio long before we sat down for breakfast. When we did meet her, she was as sweet and friendly as her image on the screen; a slightly plump, shy little person who seemed so ordinary that one found it hard to realize she was already at the very top of her profession, had married the 'King' and was the sweetheart of the Western world.

We visited Sam Goldwyn, who showed us round his 'lot'. We gazed in wonder at the streets of wooden houses with no backs, the Western cow-towns and so on. He was charming, but I suspect it was Father's influence in the UK as a major distributor of his films that made him so. We met Charlie Chaplin, a quiet, rather dour little man; Valentino, who was so small it embarrassed me; Pearl White, unmarked by being forever bound to railway lines; Norma Shearer, a fellow Canadian; John Gilbert, Gloria Swanson, Lillian Gish and the Astaires – all nice people.

We were also introduced to Greta Garbo and Robert Taylor who impressed me – not so much for their devastating good looks, but because he seemed so genuine, and she so surprised, almost reluctant, to be there at all; a legend in the making. I also spoke to

Edward G. Robinson, who appeared from behind a studio 'flat' looking so much like Father it was uncanny. I told him so.

If I appear to have been a bit nonchalant about Hollywood, remember, I was seventeen years old and inwardly full of awe. It was 1926 and talkies were in. The 'vamp' had given way to the 'it' girl and the cinema embarking on a golden era which was to last for thirty years. But at that age, one's romantic notions tend to be rather personal and secret. Much of the time I was thinking about Jacques Hubert on the ski slopes and was neither willing nor able to equate my feelings for him with the phoniness of 'Fun City' and the silver screen. I suppose I probably was a bit 'blasé'; a popular attitude of the time, when some said the silliness of American films only went to enhance the English sense of inbred superiority. In other words, we took it too seriously. We had no sense of 'fun'.

When we left Pickfair, Mother and Dex returned to Montreal where she was to have further medical checkups. I went to visit Aunt Rahno, Father's eldest sister, at that time the administrator of the Good Samaritan Hospital in Los Angeles. I was alone when the earthquake hit. From total silence things started rattling and vibrating as if a heavy truck was passing outside in the street. But there was no truck and no street. By the time I realized what was happening, most of Aunt Rahno's possessions were clattering about on the floor and I was scrambling after them, trying to save the more precious objects from certain destruction. The noise scared me most; a sort of thundering, made more awful by the stillness that had preceded it. As the shockwaves grew more violent, I lurched towards the door with pictures and hanging lights swinging and dancing around me.

I was on my knees, clutching a vase, half-covered by a table-cloth, when the door burst open and I heard peals of laughter mingled with the unholy racket. Aunt Rahno was that sort of person. Grinning and wheezing, for she had been running and was a hopeless asthmatic, she dragged me under the stairs where we remained until the madness had passed. I have never forgotten that crazy half hour during which the earth outside went berserk, as if some giant hand was trying to prise it loose from its foundations.

Aunt Rahno was a big woman in every way: a large mouth, wide

67

smile, a great deal of intelligence and a huge sense of humour. I can't remember what we talked about as our world shook and heaved around us, but I remember that soon I was laughing too, a bit hysterically perhaps, but no longer so scared by the immensity of nature's furious energy. For me, Aunt Rahno turned things from being incomprehensible to acceptable in a matter of minutes. But the only things we laughed *at* were our own human selves, and our insignificance when confronted with such awesome power.

When it was all over, and it was time for me to leave, I made a promise to myself that one day I would go back to see Aunt Rahno again. She had taught me something very valuable; to accept those things over which we have no control; life, death, tidal waves, hurricanes, volcanoes and earthquakes. Our helplessness in the face of this sort of adversity was something I had hitherto considered profoundly unfair. Aunt Rahno disagreed, and I loved her for it. I had to learn the lesson all over again, because she died before I was able to see her again.

*   *   *

Government House, Ottawa, was our next stop. Here, Mother and I were the guests of the Canadian ambassador and his wife, Lord and Lady Willingdon, who ran their establishment with taste, affluence, and an old-world sense of decorum I found impressive, if a trifle overpowering. The Governor General himself was that type of distinguished, middle-aged English gentleman who contrives to make one feel at ease against a background of severely traditional behaviour requiring punctuality, formality and a keen dress sense. Butlers abounded, as did green-coated footmen, maids of all kinds, secretaries and a cohort of aides-de-camp who attended His Excellency with grave and courteous bearing.

The one-hour bell for dinner had just completed its mournful chime when I saw a particularly splendid uniform emerge from Lord Willingdon's study carrying a sheaf of papers. Instant memories of the courtyard of Buckingham Palace! Unhorsed he was just as magnificent, moving with an easy grace; tall, slim and heroic. The clean-cut profile passed me, unseeing. It was Apollo.

I fled to my room, determined to look my best at dinner, to catch his pale blue eye at least, and fervently hoping he remembered me.

So I bathed while the maid laid out my best dress. Then I started excitedly on my hair. Curlers were tricky things in those days. If you got it wrong, you crimped away to no effect. In my case, before I knew it, smoke was rising and a small fire had started in my hair. Not surprisingly, I panicked. Screaming for help, I ran out of my bedroom into the passage, trailing smoke behind me. I saw him before I heard him: 'Oh, I say. Rotten luck.' I remember a blur of movement, then a red fire bucket descending over my head, soaking me from top to toe.

I was confined to bed for two days after that. I lay there asking myself why it had to be God who put out my fire – who saw me dripping and half naked, screaming into an empty fire bucket. Not the sort of thing I'd intended at all. Evidently he never spoke about it, though. He had tactfully withdrawn by the time I emerged from my room, my crowning glory, or what was left of it, wrapped in a light blue toque.

Montreal was something of a relief after that. Mother seemed better, although the doctors were still unable to diagnose the trouble. When her illness had been at its worst, two months previously, Father had written her a letter, and I like to think that the things he said were solely to cheer her up and encourage her to get well.

'Dear and Only,' he began. 'How I wish you were well again. There is so much happiness in life for you and me if you will get strong. . . .

'For myself, I have many faults. But I love you. If the expression of love is full of faults, the defects spring from a wilful and wayward past. But so far my love is constant and fixed, you are the object of it.

'In time I will become easier and I hope better to deal with. You must give me now companionship and encouragement. You must show me how to bring back the happy days of our youth. . . . And I declare that you are the only permanent love in my bad and wicked life. So come back soon and get strong too.'

She was trying. And when we returned to stay with Chip for our last few days in Canada, both he and I thought there were signs of a permanent recovery. But Dex, who had come to know her so well, kept her opinion to herself, saying only that it might be a good thing if Mother could remain in Montreal for a while longer before returning to England. This was typical of Dex. When she felt deeply about something, she always hesitated to say anything until she was sure in her mind it was exactly what she believed and nothing more. When she announced her intention to get married to Mr Rennie, the butler, she had obviously thought about it very hard. The year was to be 1926. And so it was. We were so happy for both of them, although in our heart of hearts we felt that no one could ever be quite good enough for Dex.

As for me, I was more than usually apprehensive about seeing Jacques again. I was still suffering from the after-effects of shock at what, but for the grace of 'God', could have been a terrible injury. In places, my singed hair was ridiculously short, even by the bobbed standards of the time. Jacques had so many friends, a lot of them girls who vied for his attentions quite openly. Now, for some reason, I felt unable to cope. I was still seventeen, and knew, thanks to the navy, that men found me attractive. But after the car crash, the appendicitis and the fire, I was beginning to feel the need of some reassurance. Jacques gave me that, and more. We spent every day together. I don't remember what we did except that we laughed a lot, and wherever we went it was as if there were just the two of us, separated from all others by the barrier of our youth behind which we could enjoy the intimate warmth and excitement of each other's company.

When it came time to return to England, I was in despair. How could such a thing end with no more than a casual farewell at the railway station? Surely it meant more to us than that? Jacques must have felt this, too, because half an hour out of Montreal *en route* for New York he suddenly appeared in our compartment, having jumped on the train as it left the station. Mother was enchanted. She saw my obvious joy and welcomed Jacques as if she herself had been a fellow conspirator. She bought him a return ticket and paid for his hotel room that night, after treating us both to dinner at one of New York's best restaurants.

The final parting came next day when our liner, the SS *Majestic*, inched away from the wharf and I watched his waving figure grow smaller as the great ship glided out into the Hudson river and so to sea. My cabin was filled to the brim with flowers from Jacques, and I could not stop the tears. First love is like that; a fragile, beautiful thing that knows no past, no future, only the end of the beginning.

*   *   *

We reached Southampton on a fine spring morning. My father, both brothers and Aunt Helen were there to meet us. 'Father's gone all musical,' said Peter in a low voice when the hugging and kissing had stopped. 'You'll see.' Peter was thirteen now, frustrated at not being allowed to go to Winchester, and angry at being sent to Westminster with Max, whom he seemed to want to get away from. My favourite younger brother was beginning to show signs of withdrawing into himself, a form of self-protection manifesting itself in a couldn't-care-less attitude towards anyone in authority, particularly Father. But he worshipped my mother and spoke to me, as he always had, about the few things that really mattered to him. I was so pleased to see him again, and to hear about his success in junior tennis. But even that seemed to give him little satisfaction.

Max was his usual buoyant self, following in Father's wake, imitating his moods and mannerisms. Father had evidently ensconced Jean Norton as manageress of the New Gallery Cinema in Regent Street. She was already a close friend of Edwina Mountbatten's and would very soon be a successful hostess in her own right, entertaining Douglas and Mary Fairbanks and introducing them to the Prince of Wales – no mean feat in view of the Prince's innate boredom and elusiveness. I heard from Aunt Helen that Tallulah was still in good form, shocking the West End to an even greater extent in a play called *Scotch Mist*, made still more popular and successful as a result of having been condemned by an outraged Bishop of London.

My main preoccupation in the weeks that followed our return

from Canada centred on my presentation at court, due on 1 May, and my 'coming out' party two weeks later. These things were taken very seriously in 1926. Our days were spent in London at Stornoway House, so it wasn't until later that I discovered the meaning of Peter's remark about Father 'going all musical'. Mother and I set out on a hectic round of buying clothes, calling on friends, making and acknowledging invitations. Father, who was there much of the time, insisted that I ride with him in Hyde Park every morning at eight thirty. I think he did this to keep me to some extent under his own control, and to impose himself on our feminine activities in which he could otherwise play only a minor part. He insisted on this awful routine for years, whenever I was at Stornoway House, knowing that I couldn't refuse because of my professed love of riding; always a bone of contention between us.

The first of May, the great day, came. I was dressed in a three-quarter length Chanel creation of silver lamé, with three rows of lace on the skirt. Coloured flowers were sewn to the side of it. A lace train, six feet long, hung down my back on to the floor. They fixed the traditional three Prince of Wales feathers in my hair and placed the required ostrich fan in my hand. I wore high-heeled shoes with pointed toes, and an expression of rather nervous pride. 'You both look very beautiful,' observed Father from his study doorway. 'We will dine later at the Savoy.' I thought Mother was looking far more glamorous than me. She wore her clothes and jewels with such unconscious elegance. Together we climbed into the back of the big, black Daimler. I was already having trouble with the three feathers. They kept falling over my eyes.

We queued in the Mall from four o'clock in the afternoon. It was a question of first in, first out. Three hours later we entered the palace. Liveried footmen in red and gold with white knee-breeches, stockings and gloves, ushered us into a vast, ornate waiting room with three hundred gilded chairs in lines on each side. Here we waited for another hour, watching more debutantes arrive, some of them friends of mine, accompanied by their superbly dressed and bejewelled mums.

At last the call came. 'Lady Beaverbrook presenting her daughter, the Honourable Janet Aitken, to their Majesties!' The King and Queen sat, like graven images, in gold chairs on a dais. Were they real? They didn't move. He had an enormous nose. She appeared to be looking down hers. Both were magnificent. I curtseyed as low as I could, trying to blot out Max's parting quip: 'And remember, Jan, not on *both* knees, like Laura Corrigan!' Laughter now would be fatal.

King George V's eyes stirred. So here was the hard-nosed man who had three times tried to block Father's advancement. First the baronetcy, then the peerage, then from being Chancellor of the Duchy of Lancaster. He had lost the first two and won the third. So it was 15–30.

The King very slightly inclined his head. I straightened up. Thank God the feathers were still in place. Had Queen Mary smiled? I think so. Maybe they didn't disapprove of us too much after all. I took away with me an impression of two very regal people who seemed to say, 'We don't *enjoy* this either. And *we've* got another two hours of it.' I was to be presented to them again a few years later, and later still to their son, King Edward VIII, at a garden party.

Breakfast next morning was something of an anticlimax. A lot of coffee was consumed in silence. No one felt much like eating. 'They'll do it,' said Father finally. 'They'll strike.' More silence. Two weeks earlier, my indignant protests would no doubt have included phrases like, 'But the invitations have been *sent out*. It's not *fair*!' But that would have been before I went to south Wales with Father.

He spoke to the miners at the coalfields about pay and productivity. He told them he was already backing their demands for more money. He also told them to ignore their union leaders and call for arbitration. Any other road, he said, would lead to sure defeat. Above all else, he urged them: '*Do not strike!*' He was alternately booed and cheered by the hundreds of grim-faced miners staring up at him. But this time they knew they had power. They knew they could bring about a general strike throughout the country.

On the journey to Cardiff I had been preoccupied with thoughts about my 'coming out' party. This trivial, although to me at the time all-important occasion, was to be the ball of the season. To cancel it was unthinkable. The arrangements were made. Mother and I had worked so hard, and Duke Ellington was already on his way from America to provide the music. Now everything was threatened. How *could* they? I glared at them. It was not the first time I had seen workers *en masse*, having been present when Lloyd George had harangued a cheering multitude. Workers were from a different world, a world of smoke and grime, undernourishment and hard slog. The whole thing was unjust, but they were different. They were none of my business. Now, suddenly, they were affecting me personally, so what they thought and did mattered. This was no blinding moment of social awakening, but the first small pinprick of a social conscience that I was both slow and reluctant to admit.

The General Strike of 1926 lasted only nine days, but for the first time since the war it brought the 'them' and the 'us' together again. The fact that this time it was in conflict, one with the other, would cause an antagonism that has continued ever since. We fought the strike, of course. In the name of 'patriotism', we played trains, bus-drivers, canteen-workers, delivery people and policemen. It was 'us' against 'them'. But the niggling conscience persisted. Mother worked in the canteen at the *Express*, while Jean Norton and Edwina Mountbatten manned the switchboard. Mary Holmden and I delivered quires of newspapers to our agents in Surrey, and even Diana Cooper employed her immaculate fingers folding newspapers. Everybody did something.

My party had been cancelled. Duke Ellington came and went. Father had his famous row with Winston, who had started his *British Gazette* and wanted Father's newsprint. He didn't get it and their fury with each other was spectacular. Then the strike petered out. The miners hung on for another six months before they too had to admit defeat, returning to work with longer hours and even less pay. But was it a defeat? In practical terms it was. But the country had been shaken up.

We returned to Cherkley when it was all over, to regroup and gather our scattered wits before plunging into the social whirl of

74

the London season. My party had been rescheduled for 18 June, so the long crinoline dress of pale green tulle with the deep plunge-line at the back had to remain on its peg for a further month. At Cherkley I found out what Peter had meant. Father's 'musical period' was in full swing. It seemed to centre round Gwenn Francon Davies and the London production of *The Immortal Hour*, at that time enjoying enormous success.

Apart from the undoubted charms of Miss Francon Davies, a small woman with a beautiful voice, Father had also succumbed to the oboe. This difficult instrument was a mandatory inclusion in all musical weekends, on some occasions performed within an entire orchestra brought from London for the occasion; at others, as a solo piece which seemed to satisfy Miss Francon Davies as an accompanyist, and Father in his enjoyment of *The Immortal Hour*. And it didn't stop there. Other music and players of a very different kind also attracted him. Among them were Paul Robson, Harriet Cohen and Chico Marx. He couldn't stand opera. The prime mover in all this was no doubt Captain Mike Wardell, already well established in society and shortly to be employed by Father on the managerial side of his fast-growing press empire.

This engaging personality introduced Father to Malcolm Sargent, who was promptly requested to assist in the formation of a private orchestra of four or five pieces 'to be available at any time and to stay as long as desired. I want the music to go on like a gramophone or hurdy-gurdy, no matter what I do or where I go.' Malcolm Sargent gave him a price for all this, his mind no doubt boggling at the thought of wandering minstrels following Father about the streets in broad daylight. The idea was modified. A quintet of young players, on a retainer of £10 a month each, was employed to play for him as required, either at Cherkley or Storno-way House, in the evenings.

I remember one such musical evening at Cherkley when a furious row broke out between Winston and his son Randolph. The climax came when the music stopped. To my horror, Randolph rose from the table, walked round it and hit his father full in the face. This, or something equally violent, happened quite frequently. Randolph was always the aggressor, yet Winston always forgave him. On this occasion their reconciliation was eased by the orchestra, who quickly started playing again.

But if music calms the savage breast, it had only a limited effect on Father's. For those who repeatedly criticized him and his way of life, he nurtured a very special and long-lasting dislike. Writers like G. K. Chesterton and Hilaire Belloc were either ignored or openly attacked, while for Dorothy Parker, the tough gossip-writer for the Hearst empire in New York, he reserved a deep-seated hatred. No one quite knew why, but her name was never mentioned in his presence. William Randolph Hearst himself, however, his wife Millicent and their two sons John and Bill were welcome visitors to Cherkley. With their father away much of the time chasing the beautiful Marion Davies, I often found myself alone with John or Bill. I liked them both. Their mother, a hand-some, junoesque lady from the deep South, seemed to take a remarkably philosophical view of her husband's dalliance. For when the ubiquitous Valentine Castlerosse, having evaded a recent challenge to a duel, sped gallantly to her rescue, ready and willing to provide solace and companionship, she instantly welcomed him with open arms and that beautiful smile for which she was already famous.

Hostesses were finding Valentine irresistible. Apart from the power he wielded with his 'Londoner's Log', they feared his barbs of acid wit which, though never wantonly cruel, could readily prick the balloons of their pretentiousness. He ridiculed English and American hostesses alike, yet became friends with them all. When Elsa Maxwell lumbered on to the scene, he invited her to his Irish ancestral home, then called her a 'wicked hag' for not getting up to go to church. He was certainly someone to be reckoned with in society in the twenties and thirties.

Hostesses were much on my mind when Mother and I returned to London. They were a formidable lot. 'Circe', the Marchioness of Londonderry, sat at the top of the heap, unassailable despite her tattooed ankle. Their magnificent home in Park Lane was to con-tinue to host balls and parties until long after the Second World War when it was pulled down to make way for the London Hilton. The Londonderry children were all nice, particularly Robin, who, unknown to me at the time, would turn up as best man at my wedding in the following year. But we had to behave ourselves at Londonderry House.

Wimborne House was my favourite. It stood next to the Ritz Hotel and featured an enormous and very beautiful ballroom which, like the rest of the house, was lit entirely by candles in magnificent chandeliers. Lord and Lady Wimborne were both charming and popular, in spite of the former's relentless pursuit of Diana Cooper. Their champagne, caviare and lobsters were superb. Their son, Ivor Guest, who like me would one day be a pilot, became my regular escort and greatly valued friend throughout much of the season. I met many famous hostesses during that first season in 1926. Most of them, alas, I have now forgotten, but some names and faces still linger on in my memory. I lunched with Lady Maud Cunard, in love with Thomas Beecham, hating her daughter Nancy, and changing her own name to Emerald. I also met Lady Colefax, and the remarkable Mrs Ronald Greville who drew royalty to her like moths to a candle. I was to meet her again in rather embarrassing circumstances a year later.

I remember the Americans too; Mrs Brown, her daughter, Charlotte Wilson Young, Laura Corrigan and Elsa Maxwell. But they are only names now; their faces, though not their reputations and the anecdotes linked to them, dimmed by the mists of time. Except Mrs Brown, who rented a house next door to Stornoway, and became a very close friend until the day she died in 1964, and Tanis Guinness's mum, whom I wanted so much to like because Tanis had been my friend since Paris.

Tanis, Leslie Campbell and I were together a lot in that first year. Old friends like George and Mary Holmden cropped up from time to time, as did Duck Pugh and his sister Sylvia. Prince George, still in the navy, was now joined by Dick Coleridge and Ian Fleming. The former was the poet's grandson and the latter rather boring, ruminating perhaps too much on the future adventures of James Bond. There were many other newcomers too, among them Benny Rogers and Dereck Morley, whose best friend, Ian Campbell, I had heard about but never met.

I remember Leslie liking Dick Coleridge rather a lot, until she married Dereck Morley in 1930. Prince George was often seen with Poppy Baring on his arm, long before he met Princess Marina and married her in 1934. Tanis seemed happy with no one in particular, until she met a man called Drogo Montagu and married him three years later. I liked Benny Rogers, an American undergraduate at Oxford with a huge sense of humour and a penchant for fast cars, including a Lagonda and a Hispano-Suiza. In friendly competition with him was Francis Pierce, who drove a silver-coloured racing car.

If I have linked names, it means no more than that. We were all so innocent, intent only on our fun. We lived in a whirlpool of balls, dances, dinners and social events, taking each as it came with that same furious pace that prompted the *Daily Mail* to dub us the 'Bright Young People'. Sometimes we would go to two or three parties in the same night. Wimborne House was the exception. Here, Ambrose and his Band, together with the marvellous food and drink, would hold us till dawn. Otherwise, Leslie, Tanis and I, together with our escorts, would rush from one party to the next. We were all invited. We were on the 'list'. A quick 'Hello' and we were on yet another dance floor, rotating wildly to the charleston or the black bottom, often picking up where we had left off with the same tune.

We danced, and we danced, as if stopping would make us suddenly grow old and die. We scarcely noticed the ring of mums sitting round the edge of each ballroom like elders at a tribal gathering. And we laughed at the vicar who publicly prophesied a 'permanent distortion of the ankles' as our punishment for such sinful behaviour. We never behaved badly until supper. This was at midnight and, wherever we were, it always ended in the traditional bun fight. Bread rolls would be a more accurate description of what was thrown, followed by pats of butter, cushions and the odd spoon. If the party had been really dull, plates and even chairs might follow. Bun fights were never dull. Most people gauged the success of their party by the extent of the shambles next morning.

When the eighteenth of June came and it was my turn, I remember Father and Winston standing at either end of the table hurling cream cakes at each other, while bespattered guests, including

Duke Ellington, joined in the fun. Breakfast at 3 a.m. was usually a more decorous occasion. We were just too tired to even fling an egg. And there was no riding in Rotten Row at eight thirty after *my* party. Father seemed suddenly to lose his enthusiasm for it.

Evelyn Waugh appeared on the scene at about this time. My memory of him is that he always seemed as though he feared people, as if he would not be accepted. He shouldn't have worried. When we had finished Scott Fitzgerald's *The Great Gatsby*, we were all to reach for *Decline and Fall* and then, in 1930, the newly published *Scoop*. He was one of us.

The parties continued, becoming even more frequent towards August and the end of the season. Leslie and I were inseparable, sharing our secrets and our hidden likes and dislikes of the many new young men who entered our lives each day; some to become friends, others whom we would never see again. We had built up a system of mutual protection and would call on each other for help when a relationship seemed to be getting out of hand. No doubt the modern generation would have described us in most uncomplimentary terms, but things were different then. Kissing was accepted. Anything more was simply 'not on'.

We went to Oxford for the 'Commem. Ball' and stayed at the Mitre, although we never slept there. We didn't sleep anywhere, but spent the warm, silent hours of the dawn in a punt on the misty river, listening to the soft laughter of others further downstream, the clink of glasses and the occasional splash of somebody falling in. Then more laughter and again the silence, until the first, small sounds of the morning chorus told us it was time to be gone.

London, Oxford, Henley, Hurlingham . . . a fast car was essential for any young man on the social scene. In London, there was a very special need for one. I think it was F.E.'s daughter Eleanor or Loelia Ponsonby, or maybe even the Jungman sisters, who invented the midnight treasure hunts. These legendary young ladies had established the rules when they were leaders of the 'Bright Young People' a year or two earlier. We would meet at somebody's house; about twenty of us in ten motorcars, most of the best ones being two-seaters. Envelopes containing the 'clues' of things to be found were handed round. Then, on the stroke of

2 a.m., we would be off, tearing open the envelopes as we went.

'The Palace!' I would have to shout against the wind. 'It says, "gold-leaf from the railings"!' Help. Switch off the torch. How on earth . . .? Hyde Park Corner, Constitution Hill, then a gentle skid to a stop under the trees. A glimpse of Benny Rogers scaling up the railings as the great Lagonda waited, engine burbling, like a cat about to spring. Policemen smiling . . . half-hearted attempts to catch him . . . sentries staring straight ahead.

'Next?' Benny would still be half way across the road, a sliver of gold-leaf clutched in his fingers.

'The Kit Cat. The doorman's hat. Or the Embassy first, if you like. A knife and fork!' Down the Mall, left into St James's. Gosh, there's Stornoway. Hope Father . . .

'Steady, old fruit, you're doing sixty!' Deserted streets, wind in my hair . . . mustn't lose the gold-leaf.

'There goes Dick.' His car, with Leslie waving, crosses in front of us down Jermyn Street. Piccadilly, Bond Street, more stops, scuffles, laughter, money changing hands . . . Francis Pierce in the silver racer going the other way.

'Here, grab this!' Off again, the gold-leaf in the doorman's hat. Knife and fork rattling about on the floor . . . my God! Was that Valentine? No, couldn't be.

'Let's see that list.' We would stop, maybe in Curzon Street, And in the silence, peering at the list, we'd hear the roar of other engines echoing down the well-loved streets, round Berkeley Square and further, into Grosvenor Square, and away. The town belonged to us.

And so it would go on; a madness of wind and sound until at last we had got all the clues, or maybe *nearly* all, the live goose from that farm near Maidenhead having defeated us. Exhausted and happy, we would tell each other of our adventures far into the morning. We were like children, and life was a new toy to be played with until it wore out, like the cars we drove. We wanted to go faster and further than anyone else. But was a Lagonda *that* much better than a Bentley?

5

The fun and frolic of my first social season was punctuated by some bad arguments with Father, resulting in a heavy, brooding atmosphere at home. I wasn't the only one to row with him. And I wasn't the only reason for the awful scenes that occurred at Stornoway, or indeed Cherkley at weekends. To start with, he tried to put a curfew on my evening activities, insisting that I be home by midnight. This was plainly ridiculous. Many parties didn't really get going until then. Mother and I won that one.

Mother insisted I had a night-chauffeur to drive me home after late parties. This caused another outburst from Father, until she pointed out that the main reason for having one was to save me from the amorous attentions of young men who would otherwise have to drive me. We won that one too.

The morning rides in Hyde Park were often carried out in total silence. Father rode his horse with a kind of clutching obstinacy; all grip and no balance. I could see the grin on his face, knowing I was dying from lack of sleep. However, our ride would sometimes be enjoyable. If the weather was fine, and I had not been late home the night before, he seemed to relax a bit and treat the outing as recreation rather than retribution. On these occasions he would talk, mostly about Arnold Bennett, who, now that Rudyard Kipling had gone and Tim Healy was still in Ireland, had become his closest friend. He seldom spoke of Valentine Castlerosse, unless it was to reveal the source of his secret knowledge about my nocturnal doings. That was when the rows would start.

'I know you were there. You were *seen*!'

'You're *spying* on me!'

'Time you stopped gadding about. Develop a sense of responsibility.'

'Responsibility! To whom? Mother? What about *you*!' Grim silence. We'd been over this ground before and he knew it was dangerous. So he would change the subject to Peter, whose welfare he knew was a constant source of concern to me. Poor Peter. He came in for so much criticism. Why couldn't Father see he was different? He was like Mother, with his own values in life, trying to go his own way.

And that's exactly what Mother herself did, or very nearly. She bought a small house in Brook Street to get away from it all; from Father, Jean Norton (still very much in evidence), and loneliness. She also wanted to provide a home, or a refuge at least, for me and my brothers; a place to come to, to be happy in. I know she loved Father, and continued to do so all her life. She loved him with constancy, indulgence and unselfishness, and would react instantly to the smallest show of affection on his part. But the long periods of neglect were too much for her. So was Jean Norton.

Mother never actually moved into her house in Brook Street. I think Father suddenly realized what was happening and talked her out of it. Theirs had always been a hot-and-cold relationship, but towards the end of 1926 they managed to draw closer to each other. As if in response to this, and in some way to help build bridges, I became interested in politics. 'A sense of responsibility' Father had said. And I remembered Lloyd George's remark about every politician having to have *some* sense of altruism before he could even start.

One evening at dinner, I found myself sitting next to Stanley Baldwin. 'And what,' he asked, 'do *you* do?' What a ridiculous question! I turned to him and thought again how much he looked like a cross between a bookie and an undertaker.

'Do you have any suggestions, Prime Minister?' Stanley Baldwin was no fool. In fact he was probably one of the best political in-fighters ever to have graced the House of Commons. With a few well-chosen sentences, he not only persuaded me that one day I could be a Member of Parliament, but then proceeded to tell me why and how. The 'why' obviously had to do with patronage in general, and Father in particular, and the 'how' concerned a crash course in political education involving the London School of

Economics and the Bonar Law School of Speech and Elocution. I was hooked.

My term at London University, studying under Harold Laski, was both rewarding and stimulating. I loved the man. He had spent much time in Canada and knew several of our relations there. Apart from this, he seemed to sense in me that small spark of social conscience that had been born in Wales at the time of the General Strike. But after only one term, Father intervened: 'Tim's back,' he said one Sunday morning as we clomped round Rotten Row. 'We're all going to Spain.'

We went by train via Paris. I think there were twelve of us, including Dex and the valets. Apart from Tim Healy, weary from his job as Governor General in Dublin and badly in need of a rest, my mother, Arnold Bennett and Sir Thomas Horder, the dapper little doctor already enjoying an enviable reputation among his own profession for his ability to keep sick and ancient aristocrats on their feet, came too. Father thought the world of him and, with typical thoroughness, had invited, or perhaps engaged, him to watch over all of us, particularly Mother.

We assembled at Victoria Station on a cold morning in spring 1927. I remember seeing Dex, sitting rather primly I thought, surrounded by the gentlemen's valets in their own section of the Pullman. They supervised the loading of mountains of baggage and then we were ready to leave. It was great to see Tim again. He was over seventy now, but hugged me as he had always done, the laughter sparkling in his eyes made huge by the thick lenses of his glasses. Arnold Bennett arrived in a shabby hat and a suit two sizes too big for him. Father continued to glare at me until I went up and said 'Hello. So nice to have you with us,' or something equally trite. To my surprise, he actually smiled at me, then sat down and mopped his forehead with a coloured handkerchief. He looked exhausted. Sir Thomas just made it, quickening his rather mincing steps to climb on at the last minute. I rather wish he hadn't. Even then, I wasn't sure I liked him very much.

Paris was, as Paris always is, wonderful. We stayed at the Ritz and shopped in the rue de Rivoli. I managed to keep Tim with me as much as I could. He told me about his life and work in Ireland;

the land, and the people, he loved so much. Then he would listen in turn to my reminiscences of Paris a year earlier. I told him about Michael Arlen, of whom he thoroughly approved, and wherever we went and whatever we did, I was never once conscious of the fact that my laughing little white-bearded companion was fifty-four years my senior. Tim never grew old.

After three days, Father prised himself and Arnold Bennett away from the red plush and gastronomic delights of the Ritz, and led us on to another train bound for Madrid. The Kingdom of Spain under Alfonso XIII was, to me, a land of amazing contra-dictions; a country steeped in tradition, still moving slowly and painfully into the twentieth century. Peasants and an emergent middle class seemed determined to speed things up, while a hide-bound aristocracy dragged its well-shod feet. The Church, locked in its own self-interest, appeared to be looking right and left to see where the greatest danger lay.

Obviously it was Tim, Irish Catholic Tim, who helped form any worthwhile impressions I may have gained of this complex nation of hard, friendly people. For, unlike the Parisians, the men and women of Madrid seemed genuinely and naturally friendly. But the contradictions were there: a deep love for all children, for instance, whether their own or somebody else's, seemed at odds with their apparent contempt for all animals. Like most Anglo-Saxons, this bothered me, until Tim pointed to the poverty, the very real poverty, that surrounded us on all sides. 'If an animal helps them to survive,' he said, 'they will look after it, indeed cherish it. They do not understand pets.'

I listened to their voices, some soft and lisping, others harsh, as if forcing the words out through lungs half filled with dust from the south. From a street near the Plaza España, I saw a fat man in a tight suit singing in a bar, accompanied by a guitarist holding his instrument almost vertically. I would have passed on if Tim had not stopped me. I'm glad he did, for that man's voice had the quality of angels. At one moment it was strident, almost brutal, the next so pure, so filled with tenderness and compassion, I could hardly believe it was the same voice, the same song. This was my first experience of true flamenco singing, so different from the modern equivalent served up for package-holiday tourists.

When we walked back through the crowded streets to the hotel I couldn't help staring at their faces. Some were white and soft, forever shaded from the sun, while others were so hard and strong the bones seemed to be pressing outwards through the deep-brown skin. Then Tim took me to the Prado. He told me afterwards that when we entered the very first room, my footsteps slowed, my words faded in mid-sentence, my jaw sagged and my eyes bulged, until finally I just stopped, stood there and gawped. I think he exaggerated, but it was a moment that changed my whole life. Titian . . . Murillo; each masterpiece a world in itself. Goya . . . Velázquez . . . El Greco; shape, light, shade, colour and movement. No words could express the excitement I felt. We went from one room to the next. I was like a child who discovers a bag of sweets, then eats the lot and is unable to remember the taste of a single one. There was just too much.

I returned to the Prado every day during our stay in Madrid. In the end I got it right. Stay in one room, relax with it, grow to love the beauty of a single painting more and more. Then leave and return later, perhaps to the same one, perhaps another. For when Rembrandt rubs shoulders with Rubens and Jan Brueghel, the eye of the beholder can become confused and unable to cope.

On one visit, Father came with me. On the surface he seemed unimpressed, perhaps because I was so obviously deeply affected by what we saw. But it might have lit a spark in him too, for later on he spent much time and money establishing his own art gallery in Canada, filling it with the best pictures he could acquire. The spark it lit in me was to last and increase in intensity all my life. For I, myself, became an artist and ever since, through failure and some small success, I have remembered, and in a way gained strength from, those first moments of blinding revelation I experienced when Tim took me to the Prado.

We reached Seville in time for Easter. Here, the full panoply of Catholic pageantry filled the streets. Religious processions, led by gilded images and golden crosses, passed before us in a seemingly endless river of colourful humanity. Priests, monks, acolytes and choristers. Guards in medieval costume, mounted captains, bands and fanfares. And the people, always the people. Many were walking, some on horseback; proud, controlled, yet ready to smile or wave to a friend in the crowd.

To begin with, I had half expected to see the dreaded Inquisition pass; black-hooded monks on caparisoned mules, driving the unfortunates before them. But they had long disappeared. I looked for the flagellants too, flogging themselves and each other towards a gory absolution for their own and the world's sins. They were not there. So I continued to watch the people, fascinated, until the last man passed; a horseman mounted on a fine Andalusian stallion, capering it sideways with the slightest touch of fingers and knees, upright in the saddle, well forward on the horse's back, in that unmistakeable Spanish style.

Tim touched my arm. 'Care to go to church?' There was a smile as usual in his eyes. The cathedral was magnificent, the service impressive. A hundred choristers sang in a world of gold and silver, ornamental effigies, Latin incantations, pomp, tradition and a thousand candles. Not understanding a word of what was being said or sung, I stared upwards, lost in wonder once more, at the great paintings of Murillo and El Greco which adorned the massive walls. Around me, the congregation of men, women and children; young, old, rich and poor, stood, sat or knelt; sang, prayed or were silent in conditioned response to their age-old ritual of worship. This was *their* way, what *they* wanted, just as the beautifully simple Presbyterian service of my childhood was mine. It was a wonderful experience.

When we returned to the hotel Father was truly angry and, thinking of John Knox, he shouted, 'How dare you, Tim!'

'Gently, Max.' Tim's beard jutted out. 'There was no harm in it.'

'No harm? A papist plot. No *harm*?' Father turned away, his face red with anger, and stumped out of the hotel lobby. John Knox would have been proud of him.

I took Tim's arm. 'He'll get over it. Give him twenty minutes.' And so it was. Father came back and we were all friends again.

When we were invited to the bullfight, Father accepted for us all. Easter in Seville is one of the greatest fixtures in the bull-fighting calendar. Three of the most famous matadors of the day were to take part, including the great Juan Belmonte. This was to be my first *corrida*, so I was justifiably excited. Only Tim held back. He seemed to do so for my sake rather than his own. I asked him why.

'There's a part of it you won't like,' he said unhappily.

'Killing the bull?'

'No,' he replied slowly, 'I think that the only people who can legitimately criticize that part of it are vegetarians who have been to an abattoir.' At the time, I wasn't quite sure I knew what he meant by that. None of us were vegetarians, so we all went.

The setting was superb, the parade both brave and colourful. Matadors, their assistants, picadors on horseback, *banderilleros*, each in a gleaming 'suit of lights', crossed the circle of smooth ochre sand to salute the President in his box high up in the stands. The crowd roared. The music gave way to a single trumpet. A gate opened somewhere and a magnificent black bull charged into the ring. He charged everything, the bright pink capes of the assistants, one after the other, even the wall – the *burladero* they hid behind. Then he charged the picador's horse.

What followed sent me weeping and retching down the steps, through the tunnel and out of the Plaza de Toros for ever. The light of my new-found love and understanding of Spain was suddenly dimmed. I didn't wait to watch the speed and daring of the *banderilleros* or the swirling majesty of a 'veronica' by Juan Belmonte. In fact I just made it out of the gates before being violently sick. I know the muscles of the bull's neck must be weakened, and I know that the horse's flank is now protected by a large matress. But even though his entrails no longer spill out on the sand as they did that day, he is still forced to stand there, blindfolded, trusting his rider, until a furious black animal weighing half a ton and travelling at 30 m.p.h. hits him in the side, blasting air from his lungs and lifting him off the ground, often to crash sideways against the barrier and from there to the sand. I've even heard it said they cut his vocal chords to stop him screaming.

The *corrida* is half ballet, half theatre, all drama and no sport. I have read Hemingway and Tom Lea, and tried to come to terms with it – one man's battle, not with the bull but with himself, his courage and skill, or lack of it. This part I understand, as also I understand the graceful art of the *rejoneador*, the mounted bull-fighter. *Their* horses never get hurt, or very seldom. They're worth millions. The picador's horse may be worth only a few pesetas and already destined for the knacker's yard after a lifetime of pulling a cart or carriage.

Back in Madrid the party split up. Mother decided to return to England with Tim and the others. Her health was still a worry. She had kept her headaches a secret from us, but Dex told me about them, adding that Horder's only proposed treatment was rest and freedom from anxiety. Father and I drove northeast, out of Spain and into France, to Mimizan in the Landes, south of Bordeaux. Here we were to be the guests of the Duke of Westminster. 'Bend Or', as they called him (a nickname derived from his grandfather's famous Derby winner), was a good deal larger than life. At forty-eight, he was between marriages, having divorced his second wife the year before. Three years later, in 1930, he was to marry Loelia Ponsonby, one of the stars of our treasure hunts.

Bend Or owned most of Mayfair, all of Belgravia, square miles of Cheshire, mansions, houses and hovels from Scotland to The Wash. All were his. He also enjoyed a very long-term relationship with the beautiful 'Coco' Chanel, at that time joining Lanvin to transform us from flat-chested, low-waisted, bobbed-haired 'boys' into something more attractive and feminine. He was friendly with Arnold Bennett and not at all friendly with the King, having been ostracized by him for marrying a divorcee. He was restless, easily bored and bad tempered, yet displayed immense charm when he felt like it. I thought he was a bit mad at times, an opinion I evidently shared with Osbert Sitwell when it became known that he had sold his beautiful Gainsboroughs, including *The Blue Boy*, to America. I suppose he just got bored with them.

So this was the man who invited me to join the boar hunt the next day. Father declined as gracefully as he could, no doubt having decided that his host's acres would provide a rather less agreeable ride than Hyde Park. Our host's acres, and there were many thousands of them, were in fact densely covered with closely planted pine trees. Beneath them the undergrowth had been severely discouraged by lack of light. Having borrowed some suitable clothes, I mounted a chestnut cob and prepared myself for a gentle hack through the woods behind the Duke and his hounds. We started decorously enough, then suddenly they both gave tongue at the same time – the hounds with a deep call somewhere between a moan and a grunt, the Duke with the words: 'Head down, Janet.'

We were off. Down a slope and into the trees. Going rather fast, I thought. This would never do in the 'shires'. Collect him, gather him up and make your own pace. It was a good idea but the cob had a mind of his own – flat out and avoid the trees. He did what he'd always done and in the process turned my initial exhilaration into near terror. We hurtled through a stark and forbidding underworld, dodging tree trunks as if taking part in some sort of demented slalom. When a projecting branch, little higher than my chin, nearly decapitated me, I decided to lie low on the cob's back, grip like crazy and leave the rest to providence.

We thundered on, my mount bobbing and weaving like the veteran he was, his hooves thudding on the carpet of pine needles. We were going faster now. Left, right, and right again. Downhill? No, up! Could he see in the *dark*? My hat was gone a mile back . . . never find it now. A shout from somewhere. Bend Or thundered out of the gloom, going left to right. He passed, inches away. Obviously, like me, he couldn't stop and wasn't looking. I saw their rumps disappear down another line of trees and decided to follow. But nothing would dissuade my cob from his chosen course. He wouldn't stop, let alone turn. Should I jump? I had visions of this going on forever. Where would we come out? Paris? I was beginning to shake all over. *I* wasn't hunting. The *cob* was.

I had almost given up hope of ever seeing family, friends or even the light of day again, when I heard an indescribable racket coming from ahead and slightly to the right. The boar was down. A few more unbelievable swerves, and the cob had arrived. I was still flat on his back, eyes closed. I opened them long enough to see a great brown, butting, biting animal surrounded by hounds. A second later, the huntsman, a diminutive man in a green coat, darted in like a ferret and slit the poor brute's throat.

'In at the kill, eh? Have a snort!' Bend Or was offering up his flask. I gulped at it gratefully, hoping my deathly pallor did not betray my feigned indifference to death – my own or the boar's. He looked a bit shaken himself.

'Good sport,' I murmured. 'Nice little cob.' Then I fell off. Bend Or was kindness itself during the hack home. They must have steered by compass. He never referred to my suddenly collapsing muscles and brain, saying only that to dismount quickly eased a horse's back that much quicker. I liked the Duke of Westminster – he had such great panache. Rather like his cob.

6

Le Touquet was becoming popular in the twenties. The British, for there were almost no French visitors, had put the place firmly on the map. It was easy to get to, had an airfield, a golf course and a casino. We could hunt there too; over pretty countryside on adequate horses. A delightful contrast to the Bend Or experience. Mother, Max, Peter and I arrived in the summer of 1927 after another hectic season in London. Dex and a trained nurse came with us, their orders to ensure that Mother had a complete rest following a bad relapse of her illness a month earlier. There was still no diagnosis. Her headaches and dizziness persisted. Father arrived later *en route* to Berlin, his entourage following in his wake. This included Valentine, Arnold Bennett, Jean Norton and Lord and Lady Weymouth.

Mother was charming to Jean, and, in spite of my deep prejudice, I was beginning to realize what a very nice person she was. We all stayed in the two best hotels, the Westminster and the Hermitage, and later, with Father gone again taking Max with him, there were still many people to see and things to do. Benny Rogers, down from Oxford, was still much in evidence, as were other friends, many of them from Whites club who had flown in to play golf, and gamble.

So it was inevitable, I suppose, that sooner or later I would meet Ian Campbell . . . in the casino. I had heard of him before, but only because he was Dereck Morley's best friend. His reputation, however, had preceded him. In most London homes he was known as a devastatingly good-looking 25-year-old, long on charm but short on judgement at the gaming tables, notably backgammon. One day he would inherit an ancient Scottish title from his cousin.

I remember looking up and seeing him watching me from the other side of the roulette table. It was a moment I shall never forget, the sort of magic that maybe happens to all of us once in a lifetime, if we're lucky.

'My name is Ian Campbell,' he said. 'I know yours.' I blinked and watched him as he threw another gaudy plaque on the table. Seconds later, the croupier scooped it up. 'Can I get you a drink, Janet?' So this was the famous Ian Campbell. He knew who I was, which didn't particularly impress me. He also knew how to make me feel like an adult, which did. I was just past my seventeenth birthday and, being under age, had been forced to sneak into the casino in the company of older friends. Now here I was, hours later, drinking Dom Perignon, feeling marvellous and at ease, laughing with someone who put flowers in my hair, kissed my cheek and whispered exciting things to me as we danced our way into a rose-coloured dawn.

Looking back on that night I am still enchanted by the memory of it; Cinderella and her Prince Charming. The clock struck five and we ran back to the hotel. Infatuated? Swept off my feet? What's the difference? I neither knew nor cared. I was in love. And when Prince Charming's slipper arrived in the form of ten dozen red roses at my bedside, I was certain he loved me too. So that was that.

Mother was sitting propped against the pillows looking pale but beautiful. She smiled as I blurted out the full story, ending with an impassioned plea for her understanding and approval. 'Darling Janet,' she said gently, 'I'm so happy for you.' The pain was always present in her eyes now. Trying once more to hide it, she gestured for me to sit on the edge of her bed. Then came the warning: 'Be very careful, darling, please. Ian Campbell is a gambler, like his father. And his father spent over a year in jail . . . perhaps because of it.' I don't think it would have made any difference if she had told me he lived on a diet of frogs and slept standing up. A girl in love is not to be reasoned with. I was already exhibiting much of Father's independence of spirit. But I had always loved Mother more deeply than anyone else. And I later had cause to remember the heartfelt warning she gave me, born solely of a desire to see me happy and secure. I knew this. What I did not know was that she was dying.

*　　　*　　　*

I met Ian for lunch. 'Why do you call me "Efelant"?' I asked. His answer was something to do with elephants being his favourite animals and me being his favourite girl. I let it pass. I was in love with the most handsome, intelligent man in the world who loved me in return. I wasn't *too* happy with my nickname, though. But it didn't matter, nothing did. We spent the whole of that evening together, and the following day. Then he told me he had to fly to London and would be back in a week.

The next five days were a nightmare. Not because Ian had left, but because Mother's illness had again become suddenly worse. The nurse, Peter and I took turns to sit with her. Dex never left her side. It was heartbreaking to see her fevered struggle against unbearable headaches, punctuated by vomiting that racked her whole body. I felt so helpless, and when Father eventually phoned to ask how she was, I pleaded with him to send a doctor from London. Horder arrived in France soon enough and having examined her once again, pronounced his usual verdict – nerves. Then to my astonishment and fury, he said it was probably my fault because she was worrying about me. Horder and I loathed and distrusted each other from that moment. He simply would not listen. 'I'll send you another nurse,' he remarked, and left for London. He had been with us for exactly thirty minutes. No doubt his bill came close to four figures.

Father and Max arrived two days later, Father carrying a large box of violets, her favourite flowers, which he proceeded to scatter on her bed. As I watched her warm smile of welcome, and the way she held up her arms to kiss him, I was overcome by a sudden, un-reasoning anger. I think now that it was probably jealousy that prompted it, jealousy of Father who could behave so badly to her yet always be loved and welcomed on his return. And I resented Mother's weakness towards him too; her undying love and the way she seemed to forgive and forget his infidelities. At that moment I was ready to hate all men. They left shortly after-wards, Mother's health having miraculously improved, or so it seemed. They went on a two-day trip to the war graves and battlefields of Flanders. When I kissed her goodbye, I could see she was trying hard to hide the pain.

Then Ian arrived and all my indignation and resentment evaporated. I couldn't wait to see if the magic of our first moment was still there. It was. The next two days were among the happiest of my life. I believed I was getting to know him a bit, too. He spoke with easy confidence about the famous people he had met and the fascinating places he had visited in a short hectic life. And all the time there was this wondrous feeling of warmth and excitement between us, a feeling so hard to explain yet known to everyone who has ever been in love.

He had brought Dereck Morley with him; a quieter, taller and possibly even better-looking version of himself. And I think it was he who first told me of Ian's love of books and his thirst for the knowledge to be gained from them. He was right, but, as I was beginning to find out, Ian's love of books came a poor second. We visited the casino every night and because it had become impossible for me to continue to bluff my way into the gaming rooms, they took turns to drink and dance with me and go to the tables. I was deliriously happy, and when it was Ian's turn to go, I found myself searching the doorway with my eyes, longing for his return. It was on one of these occasions that Dereck fixed me with a look, torn between loyalty and concern, and asked gently: 'You do know what you're taking on, don't you?'

Monday morning dawned dark and blustery after a night of rain. The short runway glistened like silk under a leaden sky, the grass beyond boggy and uneven. Ian had ordered a small aircraft to take him and Dereck back to London, having delayed his return to give us one more evening together. They climbed into the back seats and I watched anxiously as the fragile Fox Moth taxied on to the runway. The engine roared, and soon they had left the hard surface and were bumping and lurching across the grass into the wind. Some way from the wire fence and sand dunes which bordered the airfield, the plane stopped and sank. The pilot revved his engine, extricated his wheels from the bog and taxied back to the tarmac. I watched with relief. Even my untutored mind told me the thing would never have left the ground before it hit the fence.

Then, to the horror of everyone watching, he swung his plane into the wind again and headed for a second try.

'Ils sont fous!' someone shouted.

'Ils sont Anglais,' muttered someone else, by way of explanation. I stood dumb with fright, scarcely daring to look as the plane once more gathered speed into the wind. This time they made it off the ground, rising the few feet necessary to clip the top of the wire fence. The plane hit the sand dune with a sickening thud, ploughed on and turned over. I was running, while all around me sirens blasted and people shouted 'Fire!'. When I reached the sand dunes, I saw three figures staring at the wreckage from which petrol gushed on to the sand. Somehow there was no fire.

I turned away almost sick with relief, blotting out the fearful image of broken, charred bodies. They were safe. Then a hand touched my shoulder. 'This'll give us another day together, Efelant.' His voice was quiet, his eyes smiling. Oh God, I loved him. Then the pilot spoke: 'Sorry I tripped you up.' The man was actually laughing. I wished the ground would swallow him up, beside his smouldering engine with its crumpled prop.

I was still a bit shaky when Father and Mother returned that evening. But after much prompting from me, and a little help from Peter and Max, they agreed to meet Ian for the first time at dinner. Father's initial reaction was typically enigmatic. He fired questions that had no simple answers and sometimes let the conversation hang in a silence pregnant with distrust. Mother's disapproval was hidden to all except me. She treated Ian with the same warmth and friendliness she extended to all my friends. But I could see that she didn't like him, and this hurt. I understood my mother, and knew that her feelings about Ian were prompted solely by her love and concern for me.

Father was different. At times he seemed to enjoy Ian's company as they set about charming each other. But I could see there was a conflict in that complicated brain of Father's; suspicion and jealousy on the one hand, and admiration for Ian's intelligence on the other.

Father left shortly afterwards and almost immediately Mother's condition deteriorated. The local doctor advised me to take her

95

home as soon as possible. We drove to Boulogne and boarded the steamer for Folkestone with Dex, the nurse and a doctor. The crossing was a nightmare. Mother became violently ill and lay moaning in her bunk as the ship stood on its nose, lurched and rolled in the heavy seas. The doctor and nurse hung miserably over the guard rail while Dex and I held Mother's hands, certain she was going to die. The nightmare only ended when at last we arrived and she was on her way by ambulance to Stornoway House. Father met her at the door and, deeply shocked at her appearance, sent for Horder.

This remarkable charlatan arrived forthwith and once again diagnosed nerves: 'Peace and rest is the only cure.' And so it seemed, strangely enough, because Mother rallied once more, allowing me to spend every spare moment with Ian. Father made no objection. He was being uncharacteristically philosophical about it all now.

So, on 15 November 1927, with my parents' written permission, Ian and I announced our engagement to marry. I was eighteen. Presents and letters of congratulation began to pour in. They included one from Tim. I have treasured it ever since. 'Nice child,' he began, 'I am contributing Louis XIV's dressing table, made of ivory and bone . . . Your old romp, Tim.'

It was then that I met one of the nicest people I have ever known – Princess Louise, daughter of Queen Victoria. She was also the widow of Ian's uncle, the 9th Duke of Argyll, who had been Governor General of Canada. She wore Victorian clothes with a high lace collar, hated me curtseying to her and was utterly charming. 'Come and have lunch with me,' she said on the phone. 'I have a wedding present for you.' After a rather heavy meal served by a butler and two footmen in royal livery, Aunt Louise presented me with a large jewel box and told me to open it. I did so, and saw, in the rather dim light of Kensington Palace, a magnificent tiara of diamonds and emeralds glittering on a bed of blue velvet. 'It comes apart,' she said, 'to make a necklace and brooches if you wish.' My open-mouthed astonishment gave way to a spontaneous show of gratitude and affection. Unable to find the right words, I put my arms around her and kissed her. Aunt Louise was to become a

My mother with my two brothers, Max (in a sailor
suit) and Peter, and me.

My father, going off to Flanders to join
the Canadian army.

Winning at Richmond Royal Horse Show on my pony
Baby, when I was just thirteen.

RIGHT: My mother and myself dressed up in Spanish
costume with Arnold Bennett in Seville, 1927.

FAR RIGHT: A photograph of me when I was a debutante.

LEFT: Ian Campbell, future Duke of Argyll.

BELOW: My wedding dress. I married Ian on 11 December 1927.

RIGHT: A hug from my eldest child, Jeanne Louise, born in 1928.

With the rich and famous Michael Arlen, author of *The Green Hat*.

Proud owner of the Vega Gull, a fast, good-looking aeroplane.

Marriage to Drogo Montagu,
son of the Earl of Sandwich, at Caxton Hall.

The 1936 Berlin Olympics: the crowd rose to greet
the Führer and the noise was deafening.
I was introduced to Hitler a few minutes later.

Jean Norton.

Father and I playing golf at
Walton Heath.

I went to Egypt with
Caroline Condon, where we
got to know some of the officers
from the Camel Corps.

warm and understanding friend. I saw her whenever I could. Having no children of her own, she took a touching interest in me – a very personal relationship. I'll always remember her parting advice to me on that never-to-be-forgotten first occasion: 'Don't pluck your eyebrows, Janet. I admire thick eyebrows.'

It was mid-November when Father sailed away in his yacht, *Miramichi*. His entourage no doubt included the usual raft of beautiful ladies and their witty, intelligent escorts. His first port of call was Deauville. Beyond that, it was anyone's guess. Mother's condition worsened as usual, almost from the moment he left. Max, Peter and I spent hours sitting by her bedside. Horder was now in daily attendance. Each evening I would dine with Ian at the Berkeley, but I always tried to be home by midnight. And it was at midnight precisely that the nurse rushed into my room. One look at her face was enough. A few seconds later I was on the telephone to Horder. 'I'll be along in the morning,' he said, in his best and most expensive bedside manner.

'Now!' I yelled. He hung up.

I ran into St James's Street, found a taxi and gave the address: Horder House, Harley Street. He came to the door in his nightcap and nightshirt, with eyebrows raised. The sight made me hysterical. Half crying, half pleading, I told him Mother was dying. He didn't believe me. I would have dragged him with me if I had been able to. But he disentangled himself long enough to get dressed, and we were on our way.

After a quick examination on arrival, he admitted Mother was extremely ill. He suggested I contacted Father, and called in a second opinion. His name was Wilson, one of the kindest doctors I have ever known, who later became Lord Moran, Winston Churchill's personal physician. His opinion was unequivocal: Mother had a tumour on the brain and death was imminent.

My memories of the days and nights that followed are etched in my mind as sharply as ever. The pain is there too, though softened by the passing of time. We found Father in the end, after leaving a message with the harbour master at Biarritz. He called that night, his voice faint over the wire, anxious, enquiring. 'She's dying,' I told him. There was no need to say more. He arrived by private

1st Dec:/27-

KENSINGTON PALACE.
W. 8.

Poor dear Janet
I am so terribly grieved for you in your great sorrow in the loss of your dear Mother. It is so unspeakably sad for you, & Josh at this time, when a Mother's love & help means so much - You have all my sympathy - I am sure Jan will do all he can to comfort you -
Please express

plane via Paris and Croydon and went straight to her bedside. When she smiled weakly up at him, I saw the tears streaming down his face. I left the room, closing the door quietly behind me. This time I felt no anger, no resentment; only a profound sadness.

She died on the cold, grey morning of 1 December at the age of thirty-nine, and in doing so brought her family closer together than we had ever been before, or ever would be again. I shared my grief with Max and Peter. From then on each could prop up the other, and did so without question. My father looked stunned, as if for the first time in his life something had affected him too deeply for him to comprehend it. 'My harbour has gone!' he said. The tragedy of it seemed to mystify him. Then, 'I loved her so much but she was too good for me.' He kept saying it, over and over again.

Her brothers, Victor and Chip, arrived for the funeral, which took place in the serene old Saxon church of Mickleham at the foot of the Cherkley drive. They joined Father, Max and Peter to help *my sympathy to your father for him in this great loss — & to your Aunt Mrs. Fitzgerald please also tell her how much I feel for her — This time which was to be all happiness for you has indeed had a sad cloud drawn over it. Luckily she knew of your engagement & she will have blessed you entering so soon in your new life — All my sympathy is with you in your trouble Yours sincerely Louise*

carry Mother's coffin to the grave. The service was beautiful in its simplicity. By the time it was all over, the short winter day had come to an end. The mass of flowers on her grave shone in the light of many lanterns.

> No sun, no moon. No morn, no noon,
> No dawn, no dusk. No proper time of day.

I saw Chip watching me and my heart went out to him. The Drury family had been very close.

It was Leslie who took me away that night. She just grabbed my arm and insisted. We climbed into my little Talbot and didn't stop until we reached her home in Beaconsfield where her parents, Sir Nigel and Lady Campbell, were waiting. And it was there, in the company of my closest friend, that I read the obituaries. They came from some of the greatest in the land, among them F.E., now Lord Chancellor of England. Of the many hundreds of letters I received, I think the one from Princess Louise touched me most.

On returning to London, the sight of familiar places and people only served to intensify my sense of loss and, above all, my loneliness. Ian, who had not come to the funeral, arrived like a being from another world – a world into which I could escape, not only to find happiness and excitement, but also the sort of caring love I had always received from Mother. I think I was too young to see the desperation in his eyes, or perhaps I just misinterpreted it, because when, after saying all the right things, he begged me to marry him, I accepted. I remember Father saying, 'If you think it will make you happy, darling. But never forget that I disapprove.'

So I married Ian Douglas Campbell at the Presbyterian church of St Columbas in Pont Street on a wet December morning just ten days after my mother's death. I wore a white wedding dress with a beautiful train of Brussels lace that both my mother and grandmother had worn before me. In silence, for there was to be no music, no hymns, I went up the aisle on Father's arm clutching a small bouquet of violets. Ian, magnificent in full Highland dress, waited beside his best man, Robin Castlereagh, while scattered about the big church stood my brothers and a few friends. No reporters, no flowers, no reception. Father had made sure of that, as I had asked him to. But when it was all over, the best man gave us cold fish and champagne in the back of his Rolls Royce. I had always liked Robin. As the eldest son of Lord Londonderry, he lived in undisguised splendour and dispensed genuine affection to all who knew him. We were to meet again often; a tall, broad man with a weakness for Pernod and the strength to meet his own personal tragedy when it came.

Ian and I were to spend the first night of our honeymoon in a small country cottage before flying to Paris the next day. On the way out of London, I suddenly, inexplicably, burst into floods of tears. The next thing I knew the car had stopped and I was being shaken so violently my teeth rattled. 'Stop snivelling! God, I hate women who blub.' His furious expression changed again. He put his arm round my shoulders and hugged me to him. And that is the way we slept that night, thankfully, as I knew nothing whatsoever about making love. It was the same for a lot of us, in 1927.

In Paris we checked into the Ritz, ate a superb dinner of oysters, lobster and champagne, then went out for a night on the town. The thought that my present happiness could in any way belittle my feelings for Mother was not for me. Those feelings would never change. So we would dance the night away. Or so I thought. Arriving at a fine house, we were met by a somewhat overdressed lady who planted a kiss firmly on my husband's cheek and ushered us inside. I was still looking around excitedly for the orchestra and dance floor when my attention was drawn, rather crudely I thought, to a large double bed. 'Now watch this, Efelant. You've got a lot to learn.' One look was enough. A scantily clad couple emerged through a glass door and were climbing between the sheets. Out on the street, I lashed out at him with my fists and called him every name I knew. A bordello . . . on our honeymoon! I swiped at him again, cutting his cheek with my engagement ring. The rest of our short stay in Paris was spent in moods ranging from outrage to prolonged truculence. In the end we made it up. I just got tired of shouting.

I had already had a row with Father because he had not allowed Peter to accompany us to New York, our next stop.

'He's coming with me and that's that.'

'But I *need* him! We'll all arrive at the same time. He *wants* to come.'

'He's coming with Max and me. There's an end to it!'

Was he *still* jealous? Peter and I had always been very close and now, if ever, was the time we needed each other most. But it was not to be. The three of them sailed from Southampton on the *Leviathan*. Ian and I followed a day later from Cherbourg on the German liner *Bremen*. It performed like a submarine at times, ploughing through Atlantic winter gales, but the furies outside could not touch us now. For the few short days it took us to cross the Atlantic, we were in a world of our own. And we were very happy.

Max and Peter met us in New York and together we drove to the Plaza Hotel to find that our rooms had been filled with flowers. America was an exciting place in the twenties; prohibition, Chicago gangsters, talking pictures, jazz, Hemingway and Scott Fitzgerald . . . Later I would have found the nearness of any one of them fascinating. The fact that I remember nothing indicates the degree to which a teenage bride can blind herself to everything that is not her immediate concern. I spent a good deal of my time alone in my room being bored, while Ian met friends and relations, Father invaded Wall Street, and my young brothers became glassy-eyed from going to one cinema after another.

In the end I managed to get Ian to myself, and together we took a banana boat to Jamaica. The still, blue waters of the Caribbean were reached only after more violent storms. Our tiny cabin was a shambles of overturned suitcases and scattered belongings. In an effort to get things straightened out, I decided to repack everything, and in the process I opened my jewel box. It was empty. The fabulous tiara had gone. I stumbled blindly about the cabin, turning things over, yelling for Ian, the steward, the captain. Then I burst into tears. 'Stop the ship!' I screamed. 'Search it! Search everyone in it!'

The cabin door shut firmly behind me. 'Efelant. There's something I've got to tell you.' We stood there, staring at each other. It was like one of those Hollywood movies when, after a dramatic pause, the girl whispers: 'You bastard!' And that's exactly what I said, except that I didn't whisper it.

'There were these debts you see. In London and New York. Some of the cheques I paid . . .'

'You *stole* it!'

'I took it. Or I would have gone to jail.'

'Like your father!' I bawled.

'Yes.' It was a sobering thought. Wife of a jailbird! What on earth would Father say? What would Aunt Louise say? What would *everyone* say? 'I'll get it all back for you. Don't tell anyone. Trust me, Efelant.' What else could I do? Like all movies of the time, it had to come out right in the end.

But Kingston didn't help. I found it noisy and overcrowded. Men in shorts and girls in gaily coloured dresses whistled and sang to a strange form of music they called 'calypso'. My mood was as dark as the bottom of the hotel swimming pool, so after one night we motored across the Blue Mountains, through fields of sugar cane and forests of banana trees, to Port Antonio. Here, everything was white sand, palm trees, oleanders and hibiscus. Humming birds and butterflies swooped and hovered in the gentle breeze, which made the blue waters of the Caribbean beyond ripple and glitter in the hot sun.

I spent my days on the beach, sunbathing, swimming and trying to come to terms with the truth. It was a lonely and depressing experience. I loved Ian, and often he would respond with the warmth and affection I so desperately needed. I could go on loving him for that, but I could no longer trust him. The words of warning from Mother and friends like Dereck Morley came back to haunt me. So that's what he'd been doing in New York. Gambling! And in London too, while Mother was dying. And, God perish the thought, that was why he was in such a hurry to marry me. He was in debt up to his eyebrows and I was to bail him out . . . me and my money. But I *had* no money.

My mood got blacker and blacker. I would talk to him again. Furious anger, resentment, reassurance, appeasement – it went round and round. Meanwhile, he was rushing about with a large net, catching butterflies for his collection. I felt sick. The doctor told me I was pregnant.

*   *   *

'Have a drink, Efelant. Do you good.' We celebrated on rum punch. In my new-found happiness I got completely drunk for the first and last time in my life. I wept, laughed, and was sick, as the bedroom ceiling swirled about and the walls shook. The only witness to all this was that nice Mrs Greville; friend of kings and princes, who owned magnificent houses, and whom I had met in London as one of the top hostesses on the social scene. I often wonder what she thought. The hangover was something I'd prefer to forget. All I wanted was to go home and find a good doctor for me and my unborn baby. I begged Ian to pay the bill and buy our tickets.

'No money, Efelant.'

'You mean you've spent it *all*?' He told me he had, and went on to say that you couldn't get blood out of a turnip. So I cabled Father, who had given me a large number of shares as a wedding present, and asked him to cash some of them now. Eventually the bank in Kingston called, and a few days later we were on our way.

All I remember about the journey is my longing to get home. On arrival, Stornoway House looked solid and indestructible, a refuge and a home. I hugged Father and watched a wide grin spread across his face. It spread even wider when I told him he was to be a grandfather. He didn't ask many questions about our trip to Jamaica, nor did he say anything about my sudden request for money. But when at dinner he looked up and asked Ian for his opinion of the wine, I caught his eye and sensed he knew more about my husband than either of us was prepared to admit.

A few days later Ian took me to Scotland, to the Highlands and the home of his widowed aunt by marriage, Lady George Campbell. Her house, Strachur Park, nestled amid glorious scenery on the banks of Loch Fyne. I loved the place from the moment I arrived, and when I met Lady George, I loved her too. She had an old-world charm that was quite irresistible, and a cook who made real scones. Her daughter, Joan, was a warm and friendly companion to me whenever I went there. I got to know her well and liked her enormously, but as Ian's cousin and childhood friend, her loyalty to him was such that I never dared to ask her opinion about the things that troubled me.

Living at Strachur Park was like stepping backwards in time. The peace in that house was unbelievable. And when on occasion their neighbour, Lady Malcolm, came to tea, the scene might have come straight from a novel by Walter Scott or one of the Brontës. Lady Malcolm herself made a great and lasting impression on me. Her name was Jeanne, and people said she was even more beautiful than her mother, Lillie Langtry. She lived in a fine house, Pol-talloch, had exquisite taste and an adoring husband. I loved talking to her because, although older, she treated me as her equal. And that, for a nineteen-year-old living in the twenties, made her truly exceptional.

On the other side of Loch Fyne stood the grey forbidding mass of Inveraray Castle, the hereditary home of the Dukes of Argyll. It was inevitable, therefore, that sooner or later I would have to go there to meet Ian's cousin, Niall, from whom my husband would inherit the whole estate, lock, stock and dry rot. Ian rowed me over there in a boat. Even in late April, I believe the place was colder inside than out. We clattered through a vast banqueting hall, hung with magnificent tapestries, and along endless corridors, preceded by an ancient butler and followed by an icy draught. Echoes were everywhere, making an endless repetition of everything we said.

So I was not a bit surprised when, on rounding a corner, the cousin met us with the words: 'Quickly, quickly.' He scuttled into one of a hundred small rooms and sat down. We followed, whereupon the same ancient butler presented each of us with something inedible on a plate. I don't think the cousin ever knew who I was. And I'm not even sure he knew who Ian was. He had never married – which didn't really surprise me, as he would probably never have remembered who it was he had asked!

After a while I began to feel sorry for him. He was quite alone with his butler and his ghosts. Both, I understood, terrified him. 'Quickly, quickly,' he said as he led us once more into the great hall. 'Now you must go . . . must go, go . . . go.' He was always in a hurry it seemed, the 10th Duke of Argyll. But it was to be twenty-one years before he finally got where he was going.

$$* \qquad * \qquad *$$

Persistent asthma is one of the more insidious afflictions to have emerged from Pandora's box. But when, as on this occasion, it is combined with pregnancy and a bad kidney infection, things get serious. I was rushed to hospital in Selkirk and confined to bed for a month. During this time, Ian came and went, as did the doctors. Then Father appeared. As usual, in times of trouble, it was as if he had been waiting in the wings, watching to see how I would cope. He stood by the bed, grinning from ear to ear. I was never more pleased to see anyone. He told me I was going to Bowlands, the estate belonging to Aunt Laura and her husband, Douglas Ramsey, to recuperate.

Aunt Laura was wonderful, just as I remembered her as a child. She was always smiling and wore her dark hair parted in the middle.

I hardly saw her husband until, one day, he came and told me I had to leave. He had a large shooting party coming for the weekend and he needed every room. He was rich, very dour and lived for his shooting and his hundreds of lowland acres. Laura fought as hard as she could, but to no avail. I had to go. Poor Aunt Laura. Her love of Scotland was so deep. Perhaps that's why she married Douglas in the first place. I can think of no other reason. I never even saw him smile. Years later, when she knew she had cancer and was dying, she came to say goodbye, and once again asked my forgiveness. Of course, I answered. What was there to forgive? She had done nothing wrong. But I don't think she ever quite got over seeing me leave Bowlands in an ambulance.

I recovered eventuallyand returned to Stornoway House with Ian. Father was delighted to see me, and gave me the good news that he had found a house for my baby to be born in. It was situated on Coombe Hill near Kingston, with a garden and a nice view over the golf course. Here I would be safe and secure to have my baby in peace. Ian was working, or so he said, and Mother had left me all she possessed; her jewellery, fur coats – everything. I had still not told Father about the tiara. Ian had promised me that his inheritance, 'a large amount of money', would be forthcoming very soon as he had now 'reached the right age'. He would then redeem it, he said.

Time passed, the asthma persisted and with it my sense of foreboding. I did not have long to wait. 'I need cash, Efelant, now! Give me your mother's jewels. Give me *some* of them.' In a last despairing effort to hang on to the jewellery, and the relative tranquillity of the past few months, I wrote another letter to Father, This was his reply:

My little lamb,

I have received your letters. Don't bother any more. Your husband's complicated financial affairs should not concern you in any case. Look after your own money and keep it safe for your middle life. In old age, the poor house is just as agreeable as a palace. Some other day, when you are in London and well and strong, I will talk with you about your baby boy or girl. But I think it would be better if I, too, avoided any dealings with your husband in money matters. It would make for better relations all round. So we will agree not to discuss money with him – or to discuss his money or the want of it with each other.

Your loving Father.

So I was going to have to make it on my own. I hid my mother's jewellery and waited, trying not to panic.

The baby was born on 10 December 1928, and it wasn't easy. I came to on the floor, fighting for breath, and having haemorrhaged. Then, when at last the doctors and nurses were sure I would pull through, they put a beautiful little girl into my arms.

Max was the first to arrive, followed by Peter. Both brought great armfuls of flowers and, young as they were, seemed genuinely pleased at the sight of their new niece. Ian was happy too. I watched him holding the baby in his arms and hoped with all my heart she would change things for us and, above all, give him a sense of responsibility. But it was Father I wanted to see now. Where was he? I kept looking at the door, listening for his footsteps. When the phone rang, the nurse answered it. He had been in a car crash on the way to see me and was badly shaken but not seriously injured. He never did get to Coombe Hill.

Two days later I was lying in bed still unable to move. They told me that if I did, I might bleed to death. The baby was next door with the nurse, so I was alone when Ian burst into the bedroom.

'I've got to have those jewels, Efelant. Now.'

'We've been through this before,' I said, 'and the answer is no.' Instead of shouting, he turned and closed the door, then came to my bedside, staring down at me. I had never seen a glint of desperation in anyone's eyes before, and it frightened me. So did the silence.

'I need a thousand pounds,' he said quietly. 'If I don't get it, I'll do something stupid.'

'I don't *have* it.' I was beginning to cry.

'The *jewels* then.'

'No.'

Again the awful silence. This time his expression was one of sadness, almost of pity. 'Then I must kill myself, Efelant,' he said. 'There is no other way. Maybe it will be best for everybody.' He turned away abruptly, opened a drawer and took out a revolver. At the sight of it I screamed. God, he was serious! I shouted at him to stop, and screamed and wept as he left the room, without looking back. I couldn't *move*.

I was still screaming, struggling to sit up, when the nurse rushed in. '*Quiet*, madam. You'll wake the baby.' She was pushing me back against the pillows. 'Now, what's the *matter*?'

'My husband,' I blubbered through streaming tears. 'He's going to shoot himself!' Then two shots rang out, from the garden, close beneath the window. I became hysterical, thrashing about on the bed, trying to shake her off me. Suddenly she slapped me and when I stared at her in disbelief, I saw she was actually smiling! 'It's all bluff, madam. As long as he hasn't woken the baby.' She moved to the window, threw up the sash and looked down. Then she straightened up, closed the window and turned. '*One* shot would have been quite enough, madam. Now if you'll excuse me . . .' She was gone, back to her baby, and the serious things of life.

But for me the damage had been done. I lay in the cold aftermath of shock, scarcely able to look up when Ian came back and stood at the foot of the bed. 'Take them,' I said dully. 'Take them all if you want to. But don't ever do that to me again . . . please . . . ever.' So he took them and went to London, and paid his gambling debts. And still I didn't realize that his own sickness was far more serious than mine. His was incurable.

*   *   *

Three weeks later I motored to Stornoway to see Father. He was lying on the sofa in his library, as pale as a peeled walnut. 'I think I'm going to die,' said Father. 'Nice of you to come, darling.'

I walked towards him, carrying the baby. 'Meet Jeanne Louise.'

'Why those names?' he asked. I told him: Jeanne after Lady Malcolm, and Louise after the Princess. He grunted and stared at his grandchild. I watched and saw the first flickerings of an interest in her which was to increase steadily and last all his life.

When the conversation turned to Ian, I said nothing about

Mother's jewellery, and still nothing about the tiara. I just couldn't tell him. Father fixed me with a baleful look and said, 'We gotta get him to work.' And we tried; Father, Lady George, Aunt Louise and I. We tried.

At times we thought we had succeeded. In May he agreed to stand for Parliament, and Princess Louise wrote him an encouraging letter. When that failed through lack of interest on his part, Father offered him a job on the *Evening Standard*. He walked out at the end of a week without a word of explanation to anyone. Why? What made Ian Campbell what he was? He had charm, wit and intelligence. He was an avid reader of books on a variety of subjects. He was interested in almost everything, except sport of any kind. And people liked him. But, in spite of this, he was lazy, often getting up at noon and with a hint of that same desperation in his eyes that I had seen once before.

By now I was twenty, but had I, and the world, been a little older, something might have been done for Ian, for the answer was staring us in the face. When he said he needed money to gamble, he meant it. His needs were as compulsive as those of an alcoholic or a drug addict. But in 1929 these things were little understood. People only dealt with the effect. The cause, if seen and recognized at all, was usually swept under the carpet. Ian was *addicted* to gambling; an addiction he was compelled to satisfy.

Perhaps Father understood Ian more than most. Perhaps Father's pursuit of power was an addiction too? In the summer of 1929 he wrote a letter to Lady George Campbell that revealed to me the extent of his understanding. I was staying at Strachur at the time and she let me read it. In later years, she let me keep it.

Dear Lady George,

Many thanks for your letter and remarks about Ian . . . I will do everything I can (for Janet) except give her more money than would be good for her! . . . she can have the tiara back, and all her mother's jewellery if she wishes. I give her £4000 a year less tax, which brings it to about £3000 per year.

Yours sincerely,
Beaverbrook

So he had been watching in the wings. He had bought back the jewellery, all of it, and had said nothing. He had welcomed Ian to his home, laughed and joked with him, without ever once giving either of us the slightest inkling that he knew. Did he do it for my sake? For Ian's? Or did he do it because he enjoyed his secret knowledge, knowing the power it gave him over my husband? Of my father's many biographers, most would seem to opt for the latter. I'm not so sure. In any event, Father had had enough. We were banished to the south of France in an effort to put distance between Ian and White's, the venue for most of his gambling. This was to be his last chance.

Things went well for a while. With Father's help, we bought an old farmhouse at Auribeau, which had a waterfall and a glorious view over terraces of jasmine. Then, having recovered from another bout of kidney trouble with the help of a French doctor (one litre bottle of Vitel water every morning before breakfast), I bought two Arab stallions, imported from Algeria and destined for the knacker's yard, for the equivalent of £20 each. So while Ian read and watched over our daughter, I could indulge my passion for riding once more. And this I did, over the hills and round the endless fields of flowers.

At that time, Cannes was not popular in the summer. But I could see the changes coming. Already it was becoming fashionable due to the arrival of several rich families, among them the Guinnesses, who were building houses in the area. I wrote articles about this, and the changing face of the Côte d'Azur, and sent them to the editor of the *Express*. One or two were used.

Among the families we met were the Clews. They were American, and lived in what can only be described as a 'mock castle' at La Napoule. They were very rich. Their daughter, Louise, although not beautiful, was tall and attractive. I enjoyed her company on many occasions but could never quite understand why she allowed all her friends to call her 'Oui Oui'.

They were happy days, but when the end came, as was inevitable, things happened with amazing rapidity. Ian, drawn to the casino like a moth to a candle, had lost, lied and been found out. In an agony of bitterness and resentment I decided to leave him. Having phoned Father, I fled by taxi to St Raphael and, clutching my baby, boarded the Blue Train to Paris. It was a shattering experience because I knew that once Ian realized we had gone, he would do everything he could to stop us. As indeed he did, for having been born in France of a French mother, he knew we were subject to French law. And the law, as Father had pointed out to me on the phone, would, and could, stop us leaving. So when, after hours of hiding Jeanne under rugs and trying not to look anyone in the face, we arrived at the Gare de Lyons, I was little more than a nervous wreck, alone and scared.

Then I saw him; the small figure in the black hat, blue suit and brown shoes, grinning at me across the platform. My father. I hugged and kissed him.

'Get in this car,' he said gruffly. 'It'll take you to Calais. Then get on the steamer. You'll be met.'

'And you?'

'If you come with me, you'll be caught. They're watching the airport. Goodbye, darling.' Everything went as he had planned it. Passport Control at Calais was a nightmare but nobody stopped us. And when at last I carried Jeanne through the doorway of Stornoway House, Father was there to meet us. 'They searched my plane,' he said angrily. The next day I made Jeanne Louise a ward of court.

*   *   *

Although I was to meet Ian Campbell again some years later under very different circumstances, there is an unhappy postscript to the story of our few tumultuous years together. Walking one day in St James's Park, I felt a tap on my shoulder and heard a familiar voice behind me: 'Let's talk about it, Efelant, for all our sakes. No need to be bitter – to fight.' So talk about it we did, in a room at the Park Lane Hotel. I wanted so much to believe him, this one last time. But soon his pleading turned to bitterness, then to a white-hot fury I never knew he possessed. Suddenly he was someone else, a man who kept shouting and hitting me, breaking a rib, a cheekbone, and bruising my whole body. When they got me home, I couldn't open my eyes.

Mistakes are made by both sides in most, if not all human relationships. I must have made my share of them with Ian. The picture of our time together is clearer now, uncluttered by emotion, made more easily understood by the passing years. And anyway, we remember the good things, and there were plenty of them.

7

Life at Stornoway House with Father in 1929 was often a frustrating experience. He seemed to ignore the fact that I was now a married woman (although seeking a divorce) and a mother. His watchfulness, and the disciplines he had imposed three years earlier, were renewed and if anything increased. Once again I found myself riding in Hyde Park at eight thirty in the morning and being forbidden to stay out after midnight. I know he feared that I would be compromised into giving grounds for a divorce action and, as it turned out, those fears were justified. It nearly happened twice.

The first time was an appealingly worded phone call from a 'friend' in need, summoning me to a flat where I had to fend off the suddenly amorous attentions of an almost total stranger. The next was a similar happening in a car, having accepted the offer of a lift to a weekend house party in the country. I knew Ian was having me watched and Father's network of society gossips kept him fully informed about me and my friends.

So I stayed at home most of the time, enjoying the company of my one-year-old daughter for whom I had engaged a wonderfully efficient nanny. Miss Davis was a Scot, of whom Father approved, so I had doubts as to where her true loyalties lay. I think they were with Father, as she asked too many questions. There were obviously evenings when I felt the need for youthful company, and, to avoid the detective whom I now knew was following me, I would go down one staircase of the tube and dash up the other side, putting him right off my trail. I would then meet friends and dance the night away.

Sometimes the Prince of Wales would wander into Stornoway House when he had nothing better to do. He would walk up from St James' Palace and arrive without warning. He usually came alone, but sometimes he brought his girlfriend, Mrs Dudley Ward. He was good company and he was interesting to talk to because of his wide-ranging interests. I remember him as a marvellous-looking, deeply sensitive person, though very egotistical. Seeing us both as prisoners in our own different ways, I developed a good deal of sympathy for him. He was bored and he was looking for something. But whenever he came, I wished he wouldn't drink *quite* so much. Sometimes our butler had to escort him home. Freda Dudley Ward herself didn't make any mistakes that I know of, but her successor, Thelma Furness, did. She introduced him to Mrs Simpson.

We were all a bit bored in 1929, I'm afraid. Ramsay MacDonald had defeated Baldwin in the May general election and the resultant Labour Government looked duller than most. Augustus John was painting Tallulah's portrait (an event of singular unimportance to Father) and Lord Inverclyde married the beautiful June. I watched Father with increasing apprehension. Times of inactivity caused depression and restlessness which in turn could bring about sudden and dramatic changes to our lives.

I wasn't surprised when he sold his racing stables, Kelvin Lodge, which he had inherited from Sir Edward Hulton. Racehorses had never really interested him and he didn't understand trainers and jockeys. But I was intrigued when he suddenly sold his cinema interests. Admittedly he made a huge profit from the deal but I couldn't understand why he was content to lose his considerable foothold in a business I knew he loved. He followed this up by selling almost all of his vast holdings in Canada. He said the time was ripe, and it was. It was as if some sixth sense had warned him, for when the great crash came, and some, among millions of ruined men, tumbled from their office windows to a messy death on Wall Street, Father remained rich and apparently untouched. I, on the other hand, lost what little I had.

'Black Tuesday' they called it. Four hundred banks failed within five days, as did thirteen hundred more a year later. Fourteen million Americans were unemployed. I think that the Wall Street Crash was only one of the things that galvanized Father into the furious action that was to follow. He knew that the American tragedy would have serious effects on England in the years to come, but there were other considerations too; the effect on him of Mother's death, the long recovery from his car crash, boredom and depression, each played a part. At one point he had even offered his newspapers for sale to Lord Rothermere. But I don't think he meant what he said when he wrote: 'I have retired and intend to spend the eventide of my life far·from the quarrels of Fleet Street.' He was only fifty and I told him so.

He went to Russia with Jean Norton, Arnold Bennett and Edwina Mountbatten and seemed as morose and preoccupied on his return as he had been when he left. Evidently the visit was something of a non-event. He was the first ex-cabinet minister to visit Moscow since the Revolution, but he and the Russian leaders were mutually unimpressed with each other. On his return he had little to say. Europe, Russia, the United States – war, revolution, economic catastrophe . . . the past spoke for itself. With an uncanny instinct he forecast another war with Germany in ten years time.

Father had often spoken of the need for tariffs on foreign imports while allowing a free flow of goods, both raw and manufactured, within the British Empire. For him this had always been a progressive concept, aimed at bettering the lot of Britain, her colonies and dominions, particularly Canada. But now, with misfortune and chaos on all sides, there was the added need to close the ranks, to isolate the Empire from the dangerous happenings in the outside world and at the same time create a system of benefit to all her peoples inhabiting a quarter of the world's surface.

One morning at Cherkley, Father and I were sitting in what we called 'the Italian Garden' when suddenly he folded his newspaper and spoke very deliberately: 'If there was ever a right time for the Empire, it is now.' I knew that Empire Free Trade had been a dream close to Father's heart since he had first set foot on English soil, perhaps even earlier. For as long as I could remember, I had heard him expounding his arguments for it. But until now they had been only generalized theories, lacking a detailed plan of action. He had always been a man of broad-brush ideas, often great ones. Having launched them, he would then stand back and allow others to carry them through while he remained ready to advise and, when necessary, contribute.

On 24 October he published a manifesto under the title of Empire Free Trade. The theories were clear. The Empire Crusade had been born. Father now looked round for friends, for support, and for people of like mind. A few were forthcoming; young men with bright futures, like Harold Macmillan and Robert Boothby, but they seemed to be motivated more by disenchantment with their leader, Stanley Baldwin, than enthusiasm for Empire Free Trade. Perhaps they wanted a lever. Indeed it has been said that Father's prime objective in all this was to unseat Baldwin as Leader of the Conservative Party. This I do not believe. But I can remember his fury and frustration when Baldwin, together with Neville Chamberlain, whom Father liked and to some extent compared with Bonar Law, used every trick in the political book to outmanoeuvre him and to confound his aims with false promises of cooperation, delaying tactics and, in the end, outright violent opposition. They must have been very scared.

If the Empire Crusade was only a romantic dream born in Father's mind, then he pursued it with single-minded tenacity to the end. It was sad that Rudyard Kipling, the one old friend who might have given him the moral support he so needed, was now lodged firmly with his cousin, Baldwin, in the opposing camp. There was nothing revolutionary about Empire Free Trade. As a policy, its aims were kept flexible, open to modification and compromise. Lloyd George had already proposed something similar, as had Oswald Mosley from within the Labour Party. 'Obsolete, impractical and mischievous,' said Chamberlain, however. He said it with Baldwin's approval, no doubt to protect their own entrenched positions as leaders of the Opposition. After all, if Empire Free Trade, even in a modified form, were to be adopted as part of official Conservative policy, Father as its architect could be a very real danger to them.

The faults of the policy were many. The details needed sorting out. I think Father had always planned to find someone with real political power, such as Churchill or Earl Birkenhead, to head the movement. But Winston was a 'free trader' and that meant trade with anyone, anywhere, and F. E. Smith, my childhood friend, opposed it at first, then died soon after the campaign got into its stride. R. B. Bennett, for so long Father's close friend and at that time Prime Minister of Canada, also opposed Empire Free Trade. His reasons, Father said, were purely those of internal politics. In spite of his profound disappointment, he seemed to understand. But it was a bitter blow. For him, Canada *was* the Empire.

So he was alone, or almost so. James Dunn rallied instantly, helping to drum up money for the cause, but from the Dominions only Sir James Parr, a former High Commissioner for New Zealand, and Senator Elliott of Australia, spoke up for it. Father had another ally, however, a powerful and unpredictable one – his neighbour. Lord Rothermere was a law unto himself and his motives in supporting Father's Empire Crusade were suspect. He made no bones about the fact that he wanted to unseat Baldwin. At the same time, he nurtured an obsession about India, bigoted and prejudiced beyond reason.

I would watch the two of them together, each trying to steer the attention of the other back to his particular interest. Father was content to leave Baldwin where he was, provided he kept his promise to include some at least of the major points of Empire Free Trade in official Conservative policy. They had little in common except massive power through their newspapers until, in the end, Baldwin was forced into the open and showed his true colours. Then they were both against him. Father formed the United Empire Party on 18 February 1930 and mounted the famous red emblem of an armed crusader on the front page of the *Daily Express*. Baldwin was rattled, Rothermere delighted.

So the Empire Crusade now had a political party. Father offered its leadership to several prominent political figures including Chamberlain. None accepted, so he threw his own hat into the ring and went to the polls. There were six by-elections during the next twelve months during which the Empire Crusade progressively gained ground until, at the last, it became of such burning importance it threatened to split the Conservative Party, bring down its leader and in consequence give Labour a clear run at the next general election.

It all happened, Father said, because Baldwin kept breaking his word. Had he not done so, a significant part of Empire Free Trade policy could have been absorbed within the Conservative manifesto itself, and all would have been well. Foreign food taxes, tariffs, Empire preference; each could have been the subject of compromise. Father was willing to do just that. 'Empire Free Trade is like liberty, something to be striven for. Men strive to be free. They never *wholly* succeed.'

He didn't field candidates at the first three by-elections. In contrast to Rothermere's outright condemnation of Baldwin, he still wanted to cooperate and knew that at least two of the Conservative candidates were sympathetic to Empire Free Trade. So he supported them wholeheartedly, speaking at gatherings throughout their constituencies, and he threw the whole weight of his newspapers behind them. Two out of the three candidates were elected.

By now I had become totally committed to the cause. I watched Father struggling alone for the things he so passionately believed in, and listened to his hopes and his disappointments far into the night. He was no longer just the man of ideas, pulling powerful strings in the background. He had accepted the challenge to put forward those ideas in the forefront of the battle. He had to. He was the crusade.

At the fourth by-election in October, he decided to propose Vice Admiral A. E. Taylor as the first candidate to represent the United Empire Party. It was the only way he knew to ensure that the policies of Empire Free Trade would be correctly presented to the electorate. Baldwin was already playing a double game. To Father's satisfaction, Admiral Taylor was in fact adopted by the local Conservative association at South Paddington, forcing Baldwin out into the open and to oppose him with his own candidate chosen by central office.

It was a wild time. I remember how everyone, staff, friends and relations from Cherkley and Stornoway House, converged on Paddington, canvassing from morning to night in support of our candidate. After studying with Harold Laski and the Bonar Law School, I already had some political knowledge and experience in public speaking. Father, who had confided in me from the start, now gave me the biggest ward in the constituency to canvass and organize. Young helpers were flocking to the cause in ever-increasing numbers. At last I could be of real help to him. I preceded him at many meetings, hurrying from place to place, hoping he would arrive while I still held the stage and the interest of the audience. He always did.

Excitement was intense as the results were declared. Admiral Taylor won. He beat the official Conservative candidate by 941 votes and was elected to parliament. Father was exultant. He followed up by getting himself on the wireless, despite protests from just about everybody, including the governors of the BBC, who all complained that it would be a party political broadcast, which in a way it was. He succeeded at the third try and expounded Empire Free Trade to a nation of listeners who, already faced with mass unemployment and economic depression, were ready to hear anyone who made constructive suggestions as to how the country's troubles might be alleviated.

Now there was a groundswell of public interest in the Empire crusade. It came from groups of restless young MPs, both Conservative and Liberal. Letters flowed in, among them one from a newcomer named Brendan Bracken who, although he disagreed with much of Father's policy, as did his mentor Winston Churchill, expressed his admiration for his 'force and resource'. All the time, Father was striving for facts; precise, detailed facts with which to answer the hundreds of questions put to him each day.

Having committed his newspapers to the crusade, necessitating the exclusion of some news coverage through lack of space (much to the chagrin of his editors), he was more than ever determined that it should be presented as a positive, constructive policy of the utmost importance and seriousness. His great and colourful neighbour, however, blasted away on the subjects of the Empire, Baldwin and India in uncompromisingly abrasive terms, heedless of the consequences. 'Rothermere came in like an elephant, messing up my campaign by running it in other directions,' Father later said.

He was a Conservative and always had been. He told me he was concerned that each time the United Empire Party contested a seat, it could bring about a dangerous situation which he would be powerless to prevent. The next by-election was to show exactly what he meant. It happened at East Islington, a Labour seat, on 19 February of the following year, 1931. When the poll was declared, the United Empire and official Conservative candidates had split the opposition count between them, allowing Labour to hold the seat on a minority vote. For Father, the result was a hollow victory, for, although his candidate had polled more votes than Baldwin's, overall success had been sacrificed.

For his part, Baldwin was now on the point of resignation. Rothermere was jubilant. Chamberlain, who stood to inherit the leadership, was known to be far more sympathetic to Empire Free Trade and, as always, ready to compromise. The Empire Crusade had reached its zenith. Then, before anyone could do anything to resign or inherit, the stage was set for the last and final contest. It was a straight fight, this time, between Baldwin and Father. St George's, Westminster, was a safe Conservative seat. No Socialist or Liberal contested it. I think perhaps the fact that Father decided to field a candidate at all served to stiffen Baldwin's sagging resolve and draw to him those disaffected supporters who, badly shaken, were now concerned only with the unity of their party. After two well-known Conservatives had refused him, Baldwin found a candidate in Duff Cooper, who, although sympathetic to Father, remained loyal to his party.

So it was a strange and rather sad line-up, made more so by the fact that the United Empire candidate, Sir Ernest Petter, was cast in a mould designed by Lord Rothermere, whose sabre-rattling outbursts on the subject of Baldwin and India he so exactly echoed. We were all a bit jaded after the previous effort, but once battle had been joined, the rough and tumble of the hustings was fierce and frightening. This was a battle royal – Tory against Tory, un-inhibited by class considerations.

Once again I ran the biggest ward. Early in the campaign, while canvassing, I received a violent shove which sent me sprawling down some steps and landed me with a broken ankle. This was set in plaster at St Mary's Hospital, where Father had recently donated £60,000 for a new nurses' wing, and soon I was back in the front line, wielding crutches when things got too rough and wearing a red wig to avoid further recognition. I must have looked a sight.

Whenever I was needed, I stood in for Father in halls and meeting places, expounding on Empire Free Trade and the benefits foreign food taxes would bring to our farmers. Sometimes I likened the Empire to the United States of America, a close-knit federation designed for the good of all states and individuals, safe from the political and economic dangers of the outside world. I think I gave the hecklers as good as I got. When Father arrived, a bit breathless from his last meeting, I would again watch him with loving admiration as he caught and held the attention of his often unruly audience by the power of his personality and undeniable sincerity.

It was stirring stuff. We fought all the way. Father's own newspapers backed us to the limit, while Rothermere's blasted out headlines of awe-inspiring irrelevance. I suppose he meant well but soon it became obvious that our powerful and erratic ally was cutting his own furrow. On the eve of the poll, I was at the Queen's Hall, complete with crutches and red wig, already hoarse from heckling, when Baldwin arrived to speak. He was a desperate man, trapped by his own deviousness, now fighting to reassert himself as leader and preserve the unity of his party.

As the air outside reverberated to the thunderous headlines of a hostile press, Baldwin spoke. Without naming names, he inferred that the newspapers conducted by Lord Rothermere and Father were:

> . . . engines of propaganda for the constantly changing policies, desires, personal wishes and personal likes and dislikes of two men. Their methods are direct falsehood, misrepresentation, half truths . . . suppression and editorial criticism of speeches which are not reported in the paper. What the proprietorship is aiming at . . . is power, but power without responsibility – the prerogative of the harlot through the ages.

Rudyard Kipling had struck, providing his cousin with a moment of rhetorical genius which, more than any other single event, swung the fight in his favour.

For me it was just too much. Was Baldwin calling Father the harlot of Fleet Street? Power without responsibility? I *knew* how deeply Father felt, how passionately. I yelled my protest in furious anger; a sudden outburst that caused pandemonium throughout the hall. I shouted and kept on shouting as stewards converged on me from all sides. *Baldwin* said that? Baldwin, who couldn't keep his promises? The uproar increased as other voices joined in, many of them in my defence as I successfully wielded my crutches to save myself from being thrown out. When they got behind me, I was done for. My wig fell off and the yelling increased as many recognized who I was. In the end I was bodily carried away, still shouting my anger at the injustice of it, leaving behind me a roar of conflicting protest. The proceedings had been held up for ten chaotic minutes.

The next day, Duff Cooper won by 5710 votes and was returned to parliament. Father blamed himself for the defeat at Westminster. 'It was wrong to fight on India and the leadership . . .,' he wrote, without once referring to the Rothermere emphasis. His generosity surprised me. He had always insisted that Empire Free Trade was the issue and had been determined to keep it that way. I had been with him every day throughout the campaign and knew how hard he had tried.

Chamberlain saw a lot of him afterwards. I think they both knew that now Baldwin felt secure again, he was willing, indeed anxious, to adopt some of Father's policies. Together they drew up an exchange of letters which were published; a kind of truce document that Father always referred to as the 'Stornoway Pact'. It promised nothing and by then, I'm afraid, Father wouldn't have been very impressed even if it had. The campaign for Empire Free Trade was over although the red crusader continued on the front page of the *Daily Express*. They put him in chains when Britain became committed to join the Common Market and released him again on the day Father died. He is still there.

*   *   *

Cherkley became our refuge once again in 1931, providing the same tranquillity and restfulness for both mind and body as it had three years earlier after the General Strike. We were lucky. In August, the financial crisis caused a major upheaval in the well-ordered lives of many still fortunate enough to be unaffected by the Depression. Even the King broke off his holiday, returning to London to persuade Ramsay MacDonald to head a Nationalist government. He then offered a substantial reduction to the royal purse, whereupon the Prince of Wales did the same – to the tune of £10,000 a year. There was no crash and there was no panic, but I remember income tax rising to five shillings in the pound, the dole being cut by 10 per cent and the country abandoning the Gold Standard. Then, in October, the National Government was returned to power at a General Election.

It had been an exciting year, and in many ways a sad one. Arnold Bennett had died, much missed by Father and, to a surprising extent, by myself. Looking back, I wasn't really old enough to enjoy the company of this talented man to the full. But the greatest shock of all had been on 31 March, just twelve days after the Empire Crusade's final battle, when the news reached me that my beloved Tim Healy had died. I couldn't say a word. I remember walking out into the yew forest where I unashamedly wept. So much time had been wasted when I could have spent at least some of it with him. The black pony, the tree house, Paris, the Prado . . . memories came flooding back. I missed him for a very long time.

But there had been happy events too. At least we all thought so at the time. While I had been hiding at Stornoway House between forays on behalf of the Empire Crusade, Leslie Campbell had married Dereck Morley, Tanis Guinness had married Drogo Montagu, and the great Bend Or had waltzed down the aisle with Loelia Ponsonby – then proceeded to banish from the country his brother-in-law, Lord Beauchamp, who happened to be a Knight of the Garter, the Lord Warden of the Cinque Ports and the Leader of the Liberal Party. Bend Or must have been very cross about something.

While Rothermere continued to fire sporadic broadsides at Baldwin (now Deputy Prime Minister), promoting a strong line on India, Father adjusted his political sights to concentrate on foreign food taxes and help for our farmers. He felt keenly the deaths of his two old friends. As a result, he drew closer to Castlerosse and Mike Wardell. But both Valentine and Mike worked for him, so somehow it was different. He went everywhere with Jean Norton and I was beginning to think, indeed hope, that one day they might marry.

In December I took Jeanne, now three, to her first big Christmas party and watched her being enthralled by a Punch and Judy show in the company of other children of her own age, including Caroline Thynne, the eldest of the Weymouth children, Billy Wallace and John Julius Cooper, Lady Diana's son. The party was given by the second of Bend Or's rejected duchesses.

*   *   *

My memories of 1932 are fragmented. Some things were ending and others just beginning. Some turned out to be important, others trivial. The country itself seemed to be going left and right at the same time in a confusion of extreme political sentiment, influenced no doubt by the emergence of nationalism and communism abroad in the face of continued Depression and hunger marches at home.

Max and Peter were still at Pembroke College, Cambridge, from where they were both 'sent down' for one term for outrageous behaviour; a fairly typical happening for undergraduates of the time. Max, however, had already won a Blue for both soccer and golf, while Peter continued to collect trophies from whichever tennis tournament he chose to enter. The universities mirrored the national confusion of political thought among the young and privileged. Whereas a few years previously, the pursuit of pleasure and fun came first, the youth of the thirties, of which I was still a part, inclined towards a quest for political rather than social change, and if, in so doing, one shocked one's parents, so much the better. But even I was shocked when, a few months later, the famous Oxford Union debate took place, carrying the motion that 'This House will in no circumstances fight for King and Country'.

There was, however, another, quite different side to university life, the importance of which few of us at the time could even guess at. Young men like Max were learning to fly.

For the literary intelligentsia it seemed that nothing short of a revolution of the proletariat could solve the nation's problems. Karl Marx was their cult figure. So it came as not too much of a surprise to me when I heard that Leslie Campbell had left Dereck Morley and run away with a communist.

I had met Sir Oswald Mosley several times. The most notable occasions were at Winston's party for Randolph in June, and again at another party, given by Mrs Bryan Guinness for her sister, Unity Mitford. Winston was not the only political commentator who said that if Mosley hadn't been quite so overtly ambitious and self-opinionated, he might have made an outstanding prime minister. He was an attractive personality, never mean and obviously very intelligent. But to jump from socialism to national socialism in order to get one's point across was to swerve through the full spectrum of political thought. And although Mussolini was being hailed by many as a champion against communism, Mosley's British Union of Fascists was a bit suspect from the start. His ambition had landed him, looking faintly ridiculous, in a black shirt and boots.

The right and the left congregated separately in many of the great houses, but to some extent it was still part of the social scene and not yet to be taken too seriously. In some houses, such as that of Lord Redesdale, the political polarization occurred within the family itself. Unity Valkyrie Mitford avowed her intention of getting to know the emergent Adolf Hitler, while her sister, Jessica, simply said she would marry a communist. They both did exactly what they said they were going to do. At Cherkley, the confrontations were sometimes explosive and often hilarious. Father, from his position at the centre of the table, would encourage friends of various political persuasions to air their differences after first mellowing them with abundant offerings of good wine.

Aneurin Bevan was about to occupy a very special place in Father's and my affections; a place he was to maintain until he died in spite of his future wife, Jennie Lee, who from the date of their marriage in 1934, tried to stop him seeing Father or me ever again. I thought this was a bit unfair, particularly as Father had helped Miss Lee with various introductions earlier in her political career. But anyway, I think that as wife to Nye, Jennie was the red under the bed rather than in it.

At the time, Nye was free to do as he liked, and one of the things he enjoyed most was bating Brendan Bracken. I was present at the dinner party when Brendan, who had a pretty short fuse, rose from the table, ignoring the protests of Winston and Father, strode round it and shouted in Nye's ear: 'You're nothing but a champagne Bolshevik!' He then went on to castigate poor Nye for accepting the hospitality of a rich man's table while nurturing dreams of bloody revolution. Winston told him to sit down. Nye winked at me across the table. It remained a joke between us for years: 'Ah yes, the revolution,' he would say. 'Well, remember this now, Janet. When we go to the barricades, your father will be the first to hang from a lamp post.' Dear Nye. I think he loved Father as much as Father loved him. Often he stayed at Cherkley for long periods at a time. For a while it was more or less his home.

Brendan was something of an enigma. No one much minded his unspoken claim to be Winston's illegitimate son. Winston himself seemed amused by it, and Randolph, who fought with Brendan, as indeed he fought with everyone sooner or later, sometimes referred to him as 'the half brother'. It was all a smoke screen put up by Brendan for obscure reasons of his own. In the end, his humble Irish origin, which would have further endeared him to most people, was discovered by Percy Hoskins, the *Express* crime reporter, at Father's instigation and with Valentine's help. Having done so, Father promptly forgot about it. But I must admit there was something about Brendan that didn't ring true. It was as if he was hiding something else, even from himself. But whatever it was, it didn't detract in any way from the immense contribution he later made at Winston's right hand during the war.

Winston himself was writing his *Life of Marlborough*. Father evidently considered him something of a spent force politically, saying that although the Tories had forgiven him for deserting to the Liberals, they'd never forgive him for coming back. Lloyd George, another spent force and now very much an elder statesman, was writing his war memoirs and Father, who, after the Empire Crusade, considered himself to be in the same category, was publishing his own book, *Politicians and the War*. I wasn't writing anything except letters, seeking to renew friendships with people I had known before my marriage and to relieve the tedium of my incarceration under Father's watchful eyes. At Stornoway House, things got to a stage where I was forced to come in through the front door, clump up the stairs and past his bedroom door, making as much noise as I could, then tip-toe down the back stairs and out again to rendezvous with my date who would be waiting in his car at the back of the house. It was all ridiculous, as indeed were the unavoidable rides in Hyde Park after my late nights.

My dates in 1932 were mostly with Bobby Sweeny, an American, who became the amateur golf champion and whose brother, Charles, was about to become engaged to the beautiful Margaret Wigham. Bobby, even better-looking than his brother, had been in London long enough to know almost everyone and be invited almost everywhere. He taught me to play golf, which I picked up fairly quickly, having a natural aptitude for most games. I never considered myself a particularly good athlete but these things came easily to me. Soon I think Bobby was enjoying it too, instead of just having to walk round coaching a novice. We played at Sunningdale, Walton Heath, Gleneagles and other top courses up and down the country. I remember playing with Henry Cotton and Rex Hartley, another amateur champion, and when I wasn't playing, I would walk round with Bobby on one of his competition days.

At night we would go dancing at the Embassy, Victors, the Kit Cat or the 400, where the bands, big or small, held sway over all of us. The musicians, perched on a dais like sacristans round an altar of drums and symbols, responded to their leader, who stood before them, all coat tails and slicked-down hair, conducting them to an ever increasing, ever more popular, demand. Between dances, the air around us would be thick with cigarette smoke and small talk:

'Of course she shot him!'

'Who, Elvira Barney? What makes you think so?'

'She said so in the Café de Paris.'

'She was acquitted. Why should she say that?'

'He had a thousand girls!'

'Who? The man she shot?'

'No, silly. The sexy rector.'

'Harold Davidson? They defrocked him.'

'Wouldn't mind doing that to *her*!'

'Don't be common, Charles.'

'Isn't that Unity Mitford?'

'She's got a pet snake, y'know.'

'. . . then he just passed out.'

'Who, the snake?'

'No silly. Augustus John.'

And so it would go on, between gulps of champagne and sudden lunges on to the dance floor every time a favourite number was played. We were all subject to gossip because we had nothing much else to talk about on these occasions except each other. We talked about Douglas Fairbanks and Mary Pickford breaking up, and about Diana Churchill and John Bailey getting together. We talked about Henley, Hurlingham, Ascot and Lords, dinner at Cliveden and lunches with Lady Cunard; what was amusing and what was a shattering bore in a life that must have seemed to others a long and never-ending charade.

So the Fairbanks were breaking up, were they? A pity this, but so what? Then someone told me that he had heard from a friend at White's Club, that Tanis and Drogo Montagu were also separating. All so petty – all such a waste of time. So what indeed!

8

My interest in flying dates back to 1927 and Ian's somersault at Le Touquet. The crashes themselves filled me with horror, but the apparent ease with which people flitted between countries, and even continents, fascinated me.

My first flight was with Imperial Airways to Paris and back, eight hours for the round trip, made longer on the return journey by the pilot who, having had 'one over the eight', circled the greyhound stadium at Brighton to watch the racing. When we finally arrived at Croydon he was arrested, but I had enjoyed every moment of it, sitting back in what can only be described as an airborne drawing room, sipping drinks and gazing out of the window at the scenery passing close beneath us.

I now found myself reading about fliers and their feats of skill and endurance – Lindbergh, Mollison, and the grand old Duchess of Bedford who, at sixty-four, had piloted her own Spider plane to Cape Town and back in twenty days. A year later, Amy Johnson flew to Peking, then in 1932 did her epic return trip to Cape Town in a Puss Moth. Even the 'mad' Major Draper intrigued me, flying his plane under Tower Bridge. I read about them all. The accidents were terrible, some of the victims being known to me personally. In 1930, the airship R101 had crashed, killing forty-six people, and in the same year, the Marquess of Dufferin and Ava, together with his friend, Viscountess Ednam, mother of Peter Ward, died when their plane disintegrated on a flight back from Le Touquet. Everybody knew someone who had an exciting story to tell about flying. And in those early days, most of the stories were true. I shared my interest with Max who, at twenty-three, was already a pilot with London's 601 (Auxiliary Air Force) Squadron having graduated from the University Flying Club. But in 1933 both he and Peter were intent on racing cars, so when the three of us went to Brooklands in the summer of that year, they went to thunder round the track – Max in a Jaguar and Peter in an ERA – and I went to see Duncan Davis, the most knowledgeable and experienced flying instructor of his time.

'Why do you want to fly?' he asked. This shook me a bit. I thought he'd just take the money and get on with it. I was twenty-five now, and most men seemed quite pleased to have me around, even instructors. Golf, riding, flying – it was all the same, one had to learn. 'It's the fastest way to go. Everybody's doing it these days.' He eyed me closely for a minute, then told me to be back in the morning at nine o'clock sharp.

Cherkley wasn't far from Brooklands so I had no trouble being there on time. I arrived in a pure white flying suit with helmet and goggles. He indicated a rather ancient-looking biplane, a Puss Moth, standing on the apron. 'Climb in the front.' I did as I was told and prepared for the 'off'. But he seemed to take ages fiddling with the two shoulder straps of the safety harness, which struck me as being a bit ominous. Then he indicated a voice pipe. 'Talk if you want to.'

The engine roared, a quick lurch and run and we were up, climbing higher every second. As the ground fell away beneath us, I experienced for the first time that feeling of joyous freedom I have never been able to explain; a sort of release from all earth-bound pressures, both mental and physical. Feeling rather like von Richtoven patrolling the Western Front, I pointed downwards to identify Cherkley below and to the right. 'My home!' I shouted into the voice pipe.

'Pull your arm in,' he replied. I did so. Then the world went mad. A sickening drop and the earth was revolving round me in a blur of woods and fields as Cherkley itself shot up over the top of my vision and disappeared from sight. We were spinning earthwards at a terrifying rate. I was preparing myself for my inevitable doom when we levelled out at what could only have been a few hundred feet above the trees. I felt myself shrinking into the seat as we gained speed and shot skywards again. In desperation I concentrated my eyes on the instrument panel in front of me.

We seemed to be level again but now the earth was over the top of it. We were upside down.

'Stop it!' I yelled. However, we then levelled off and descended in a gentle circle while I shut my eyes again and tried to adjust everything into its normal position once more, particularly my stomach. We landed. I felt a couple of bumps and that was all. He switched off the engine. I looked up. We were in a small field with high trees on all sides. He was climbing out.

'I'll walk home from here,' I said, hating the sight of him standing there grinning at me.

'Still want to fly?' he asked.

'Not like that.' I was already struggling with the harness. 'How dare you do that to me!'

'Still want to fly?' he repeated.

'Yes!' I shouted at him. 'I want to fly. But safely, from one place to the other. Not like *that.*'

Slowly the grin left his face. 'Then I'll teach you,' he said. 'You looked like one of those fast ones. Out for kicks. I was wrong.' He explained there and then about a lot of things; about the plane itself, which stalled at around thirty m.p.h. and had been built to withstand the sort of pressures he had just subjected it to. He explained where we were, how we would find our way back to Brooklands, and how long it would take. Then he turned the plane and took off from the impossibly small field to rise effortlessly, well clear of trees and hedges, and fly sedately home. By the time we got there, my fear had evaporated and my confidence had returned. I really did want to learn to fly.

When Father heard what his children were up to at Brooklands, his reaction was unequivocal. I was banned from flying, and my brothers were banned from racing cars. It was as simple as that. Our own reactions were typical. We each of us behaved as we always had when Father laid down the law. Max, who had crashed his Jaguar on the track, agreed to call it a day and concentrate on flying. Peter completely ignored the ban and went his own way, in the process winning a major race at Donnington. I argued. Nothing was going to stop me flying and I wanted to make Father understand how important it had become to me. In the end I moved out of Stornoway House and into a flat at Grosvenor House with my nanny and baby. I did this to stop the arguments and to gain at last that degree of longed-for independence. But I agreed to continue to ride with Father each morning in Hyde Park.

Father was very upset, because not only did he miss me, but he also knew that I would now be vulnerable to Ian's detective. For these two reasons, he thought he would bring me back by cutting off my allowance. In the old days he would no doubt have taken my ponies away, but he gauged quite rightly that money now, or the lack of it, was the ultimate sanction.

He could be generous with his wealth, but this depended on his mood. It was as if he was never quite sure if people liked him for himself, and this insecurity could make things very awkward. Jean Norton, for instance, received £6000 a year (a not inconsiderable sum in those days) and a cottage at Cherkley. But even for her there was always a degree of uncertainty. It depended on whether or not they had had a row. To each of his much-loved and trusted lady friends, such as Sibell Lygon, Daphne Weymouth, Diana Cooper and June Inverclyde, he gave a present of £100 at Christmas and on his birthday. This was a gesture of pure affection. There was never a need to play safe with them. To the men he would offer valuable advice on the stock market. I know that hundreds of gifts, both solicited or not, were sent out to people he wanted to help. He gave to the arts, charities and foundations, seldom spoke about it and never expected anything in return.

As for me, I was broke. I was also a bit angry. I sold a string of my mother's pearls to Billy Bethel which enabled me to continue my 'circuits and bumps' at Brooklands and to maintain a car with which to pay visits to Cherkley to see my horses. In London, I ran up large bills all over the place and had them sent to Father. Not long after this, my allowance was resumed.

Bobby Sweeny returned to America in 1933, leaving me feeling depressed and alone. It wasn't that I didn't have friends. Perhaps I had too many. London can be like that; surrounding you with people and leaving a gap in the middle. My only close friend at that time was Jean Norton, whose company I sought whenever I could. We spent many happy days together at Cherkley, our conversation often revolving round Father whom we both loved deeply but with whom we were frequently exasperated. In London, she and Father were part of a 'set' I suppose. They called it the 'Mountbatten set' because Edwina and Lord Louis were at the centre of it whenever they were in England.

Although seven years younger than Edwina, I found her a fascinating, wilful person, highly intelligent, who seemed determined to live her private life to the full, regardless of the fact that she was married. Lord Louis appeared to view her indiscretions with amazing tolerance, inspired perhaps by a deep love and understanding on the one hand and, on the other, a frank recognition of his own promiscuity.

Father's relationship with Edwina was, if nothing else, protective. Four years earlier he had helped squash a threatened divorce action in New York in which Edwina had been cited as co-respondent. Thereafter, his affection for her, and in later years his admiration, remained undiminished until her death in 1960. For her husband, however, Father developed a lasting antipathy which grew with the years and became known to both press and public as a deep, personal feud. Three things caused it, all of which took place during or just after the Second World War.

The first, the most publicized and the least important, was the 'No War This Year' headline on the copy of the *Daily Express* seen floating in the sea from a torpedoed merchant ship. It was featured in Noel Coward's *In Which We Serve*, a film on which Lord Louis was technical adviser. The second was Father's anger and resentment at the tragic loss of so many Canadian lives during the abortive raid on Dieppe which took place while Lord Louis was Chief of Combined Operations. The third, and in my view by far the most likely reason for their feud, was that Father found a stack of passionate love letters Lord Louis had written to Jean Norton.

One evening I was dining at White City with General Critchley, chairman of the Greyhound Racing Association, when a stranger approached our table. On being introduced, I found myself shaking hands with the second son of the Earl of Sandwich.

'So *you're* the person who married Tanis,' I said.

'She talked about you a lot,' said Drogo Montagu. My first impressions were not favourable. Drogo had too much of everything; tall, good looking, rich, fair and charming. In 1933, he was every girl's ideal. He was good at all games, rode well and was a first-rate pilot. I found out about this from Max who flew with him in 601 Squadron. That first evening, however, was a total disaster. When it was time to leave, the racing over and the crowds long gone, he kept me back, saying there was something rather special and private he wanted to tell me. I waited, thinking it might be news about Tanis or even Max. It wasn't. A few seconds later, I had to make a run for it, with what I can only describe as a sex maniac chasing me all over the deserted stadium. He raced after me down terraces and over rows of seats with a lustful exuberance I would have found amusing, had it not been so insulting and undignified. I was quite a fast runner.

'Wait, Janet! I didn't mean it!' Like hell he didn't. I ran on, vaulting obstacles, trying to keep as many seats and barriers between us as I could. I could hear Drogo floundering along behind me.

My God! A groundsman was watching! Did he have a camera? Visions of Valentine's gossip column flashed before me – 'Satyr in pursuit of Nymph!' Not that I was much of a nymph. Doris Castlerosse had already observed that I ought to have a passionate love affair to lose weight. But not with this maniac behind me. I heard a crash, stopped and turned round to look. He had disappeared between two tiers of stands. I walked back to find him sitting, leaning against a concrete wall. He was laughing. 'We ran a full circuit,' he said.

'Look, Drogo, you may be all things to most girls, but you're nothing to me.'

'I don't blame you,' he said.

'And I don't blame Tanis, for leaving you.'

'Neither do I.' He was climbing painfully to his feet. I backed away. 'Sorry,' he said. 'I behaved like an absolute cad. Won't happen again.' And it didn't. Strangely enough we were laughing when we left the stadium.

He wouldn't leave me alone after that. Flowers arrived at the flat every morning and, on one occasion, a gramophone. He was amazingly frank about himself, telling me about Tanis, who was just 'too good' for him, and about their son, Dru. I don't think I ever heard him say a bad word about anyone, including Tanis, and, at the time, he was behaving impeccably. 'Everything's different with you, Jan.' When, at last, he met Father, they got on wonderfully together. I think perhaps it was largely due to Drogo's enormous sense of humour, his ability to make people laugh and his undying optimism. He and Father would sit happily over the port, gossiping like fishwives. Between them, they knew everybody.

To be loved is to be given great power. As time went on, the power Drogo gave me increased to the point where I thought I could change his errant ways forever. His reputation in society as a womanizer only increased my determination to prove them all wrong. Where gossip was concerned, it was us against them. We had to be very careful. Already, the word had reached Bobby Sweeny in New York (probably from a member of White's). Drogo showed me the letter: 'I thought you were one of my best friends,' Bobby wrote, 'but all you do when my back is turned is steal my girl.'

Well, I wasn't Drogo's girl; not yet. For although his divorce from Tanis had now come through, mine from Ian had not. So we were friends – riding, flying and playing golf together, without giving anyone a clue as to our real feelings. For by now they were real, as slowly, indeed reluctantly, I found myself responding to all the patience and loving attention he showed to me. It is hard sometimes to resist these things. And even if, on occasions, I found him flirting with, or even kissing, another girl, I could persuade myself that it was only a final fling on his part and that, once we were married, I could change him for good.

I knew what sort of a pilot he was the first time I flew with him. 'Damn. I forgot to fill the tank.' He would then execute a perfect landing and do so. In the air he was brilliant, manoeuvring a light aircraft with a seemingly subconscious coordination of mind, hands and feet. Years later, the great Brian Kingcome, one of the foremost aces of the Battle of Britain, was to remind me of this: 'You don't just *fly* a Spitfire,' he said. 'You *wear* it. Pull it on like an overcoat, then go where you want to.' I think it was a bit like that with Drogo. He was good at the rest of it too; radio communication and flight planning. But he was always forgetting to fill the petrol tank.

In 1933 and 1934, we flew all over the place together; Le Touquet, Deauville, Lympne – anywhere where the members of White's had decided to fix up a golf match. White's was a sort of second home to Drogo and his friends, a hub from which they could base their lives and plan their activities. We flew to Lympne a lot, either to play golf or as a jumping-off place for the continent, and spent many happy weekends with Sir Philip Sassoon in his beautiful house nearby. Philip was a great gardener and a man of exquisite taste. He loved to share his beautiful things not only with his many friends, but also with the public for whom he opened his gardens once a week. I remember the entrance hall best. It contained murals by Rex Whistler and seemed to typify the beauty and informality of the whole place. Sadly, Rex was killed in the war, and Philip died just before it started. I often wonder what happened to those wonderful murals.

Weekend parties in Lympne were memorable. All sorts of people would arrive, including many of my own particular friends, such as Jean, Edwina and, of course, my beautiful Aunt Helen, now married but with whom Philip was still hopelessly in love. Noel Coward was always there because he lived close by, as did Mr Harold and Lady Dorothy Macmillan. At one time, Robert Boothby rented the French House, situated within the grounds. I never found it easy to talk to Noel Coward. Whenever I met him, in London or at Philip's, he was either sitting at a piano, or looking around for one. He would strum away for hours, improvising and making up topical lyrics as he went along. Entertainment was his world, so if you were no part of it – and a girl – there was little you could say that was of interest to him.

On one occasion at Philip's, however, he became very animated, as did all of us who knew what had happened. Lady Dorothy Macmillan had absconded with Bob Boothby. It was to be the scandal of the month, affecting everybody one way or another chiefly because we were so fond of them both and didn't want anyone to get hurt. But grey hairs sprouted overnight amid scenes of near apoplexy when the news reached London. I remember Philip's desperate efforts to get things back to normal again. I suppose they never were *quite* normal. The reverberations of this social earth-quake were felt far and wide, the tremors spreading out over the years to touch people who were nowhere near the epicentre when it happened.

Things did quieten down eventually, and before 1933 was over Father and I, catching the general mood of reconciliation, made our peace with regard to my flying. I think that both Drogo and Max put in a good word. Not long afterwards, he invited me to join him on a trip to Berlin. We went with Jean, Valentine and Lord and Lady Weymouth. I'm not quite sure why we went, unless Diana Cooper had recommended that we should go. She and Duff had been there in August with Diana and Unity Mitford. It is not easy to describe Berlin in 1933. Visconti's great film, *The Damned*, gives a fair portrayal of it. We stayed at the Adlon, from where we sallied forth to witness the city's squalid night-life which rivalled that of Sodom and Gomorrah, with homosexuals, child prostitutes and transvestites openly propositioning all who came near them. Valentine appeared to be in his element, and no doubt enjoyed luring me successfully into a brothel and watching my outrage when I discovered, as I had done once before, that what I was watching was no normal cabaret. When I left, however, he came with me. It wasn't safe to be on the streets alone.

By day, though, there were interesting things to see if one could tear one's eyes away from the bare-footed children and the thin, haggard people pushing wheelbarrows full of banknotes – enough to buy a loaf of bread. Some of the architecture, influenced by Walter Gropius's Bauhaus theory which had been in vogue since the twenties, showed neat, colourful houses of modernistic design. I became fascinated by the Bauhaus. Encompassing architecture, design, painting, writing, music and even acting, it seemed to me that Walter Gropius had established something very profound. Soon it was to be swamped by a wave of National Socialist-approved taste, as banal as it was ugly. But I'm glad I caught a glimpse of Germany before Hitler's thugs were in complete control.

*   *   *

'Now listen, Max,' said Nye Bevan, fixing Father with one of his penetrating Welsh looks, 'it's time you gave something to your daughter. Something of substance, you see. Money's not enough, now is it?' We were standing in front of an old, oak-beamed, house near Henfield in Sussex. The three of us had driven over from Cherkley.

'Oak beams take too much cleaning,' said Father who was fast running out of objections. He had already complained that it was too big, too old and above all, at £14,000, too expensive.

'For a house, three cottages and sixty acres?' I asked, astonished. Father mumbled something and turned away. Nye gave me a look which said, 'Leave this to me', and walked after him, leaving me to gaze longingly at the house and the beautiful farmland that I hoped with all my heart would be mine. 'She needs a home, Max,' the soft voice persisted in the background, 'somewhere for her daughter, too.'

Father could be obstinate. He and Nye had had some terrific arguments in their time. But when we got back into the car for the drive home, I could sense that Nye was gaining ground. What an orator! He answered Father's objections with the same gentle passion and undeniable logic that contributed so much to his success in government later on. I listened, fascinated.

'Billsborough!' said Father. 'What an awful name.'

Nye gave me a slow wink. 'What would *you* like to call it, Max?' he asked gently.

'Anything but Billsborough!' He was staring out of the window at the passing fields.

'Billsbottom?' suggested Nye, artfully. Father snorted.

'Something Canadian.' It was the first time I had spoken.

Father swung round. 'Tracadie!' he said.

'Ah, yes.' Nye spoke as if he knew – which he didn't – but might have guessed – which he had – that it recalled a river or mountain or something in Canada. 'Very good,' he smiled, magnanimous in victory. I kissed Father with love and much gratitude. I had a real home of my own at last.

Tracadie came to mean a great deal to me over the years, almost as much as Cherkley had in the days of my childhood and growing-up. As soon as it was furnished, warm and comfortable, I moved in with Jeanne, now six, and Dex, who continued to be such a help. Drogo, Max and Peter all came and went at regular intervals. I had moved my horses, and a pony for Jeanne, from Cherkley, and began to look around for some stock for the farm which included some fine barns and piggeries.

'Buy a cow,' said Peter.

'No money.'

Pass the hat then.' Thus the 'cow box' was born. We inscribed it with the words: 'Please help Janet. She wants a cow', and bribed Father's butler to place it in the middle of the dining-room table at Stornoway House to attract, we hoped, the largesse of the high and the mighty, the rich and the ambitious, who dined there nightly when Father was in London. I know a lot of people contributed to my cow; two cows in fact, because with three weeks I had collected £100. I was told that, much to the amusement of Father, Winston had dropped a banknote into it, as had Lloyd George, Chamberlain, Randolph, Brendan, Valentine, Mike Wardell, Nye and Joachim von Ribbentrop who had arrived in London as German ambassador. Unlike his rather large and vulgar wife, he wasn't rich, but he could be charming. Soon afterwards, Peter went to Canada and courted a Canadian girl, Janet MacNeill. His marriage to her a year later caused a further rift between him and Father.

The news that so-and-so had been to tea with Hitler became quite a talking point over the next few years. Leading this unusual pursuit was, of course, Unity Mitford, who at last achieved her ambition in February 1935, having tried for months to catch the man's eye. Mosley followed her two months later, then, a year after that, they both took tea with Hitler again when Sir Oswald married Unity's sister in Dr Goebbels's drawing room. Father went next, and in 1936 Lloyd George sampled the brew, no doubt inspired by the Prince of Wales's 'Stretch forth the hand of friendship . . .' bloomer. After that, the Prince, by then demoted to Duke, went to try it for himself, taking Wallis with him. Poor Neville Chamberlain, after his three sessions at the Führer's teapot, might well have done himself a lasting injury by the time he returned home waving his bit of paper. Hitler's tea was strong stuff.

Before all this started, however, news came that Ian had at last agreed to a divorce. My immediate reaction was, 'Who is she, and does her father have millions?' Of course he did. The lucky girl was none other than Louise Clews, our friend from the south of France. I wished her luck. Both she and her father's fortune were in for a bit of a battering.

Having made his first 'advances' at White City, Drogo chose Stamford Bridge for his next. But this time it was different. We had been flying a Puss Moth from Shoreham on a roundabout course to Walton Heath, taking aerial photographs of London's West End along the route. Suddenly, the engine coughed and we started to lose power. This time it was *not* through lack of fuel. Unperturbed, Drogo dropped the nose to maintain flying speed. 'We'll have to put her down,' he said.

'Try Hyde Park!' God, I needed a cigarette. I'd just given them up.

'Too far. This'll do.' We were circling down towards a patch of green the size of a postage stamp, the engine spluttering intermittently.

'But it's too small! It's . . .' We skimmed over the roof-tops and cleared the outer fence and the stands by a few feet. Then we dropped, side-slipping, righting ourselves, to thud on to the turf of the Chelsea Football Ground about ten yards short of the centre circle. We ended up staring into the net behind the far goal posts. I climbed out. A groundsman was running towards us. 'Got a cigarette?' I asked him. He fished in his pocket and offered me one.

'You nearly scored,' he said with a weak smile, nodding at the nose of the Puss Moth which had stopped a few inches short of the goal line.

'Yes,' I said, taking his matches and lighting up. 'We did, didn't we?'

Drogo was studying the height of the stand roof and the length of our tyre marks on the grass. 'Could have done better than that,' he said.

'And worse,' said the groundsman. 'What if we'd had a match on?'

Drogo didn't seem to hear him, still calculating his achievement which, by any standards, had been a remarkable piece of flying. We had no brakes in those days. 'Come on, Jan,' he said finally. 'Let's get married. You're making me nervous.'

So we got married, on 5 March 1935, in a registry office. It was a second try for both of us. We chose Scheidegg for our honeymoon and left for Switzerland by train, taking Max and his current girlfriend with us. This was Drogo's idea. Both he and Max were keen skiers. They shared many other interests too, and instead of a romantic sojourn on the sunlit slopes (I could ski pretty well myself), things turned into a bacchanalian orgy of epic proportions.

When we arrived at the hotel and caught our first glimpse of the rich and beautiful people staying there, I stole an apprehensive glance at my brother's girlfriend and wondered just how much control she had over him. Her name was Toto Coopland, an outstandingly attractive Eurasian, half Javanese, and the daughter of a top executive with KLM. Having been ditched, surprisingly I thought, by Alexander Korda, Valentine and Father in turn, she had arrived on Max's doorstep with no trace of mental or physical wear and tear. Apart from her devastating good looks, Toto was a quiet, shy, and very nice person who had come to love Max deeply. Beneath his youthful and rather brash exterior, I believe that Max, at twenty-five, felt the same about her. But Father didn't. He threatened to cut Max out of his will if he took the relationship any further. In another place, and at another time, I think they might have married. But to be Eurasian in 1935 and expect society to take you seriously was like crying for the moon. Society had yet to grow up.

Our honeymoon night was like something out of a French farce. Both Toto and I had gone to bed, tired after our long journey and the champagne we had consumed *en route*. We expected our men, and in my case my brand-new husband, to put in an appearance after 'one last nightcap' in the bar. Two hours later, Drogo was still missing. There had been times like this before, at parties. I would find him upstairs with a girl, or in the car park, the summer house, somewhere, looking rather flushed. He would greet me on these occasions rather as I imagine an alcoholic would greet a friend from Alcoholics Anonymous arriving in the nick of time to save him from the dreaded booze. 'Thank God you came, Jan,' he would say as I led him meekly away. 'If it hadn't been for you, that girl . . .'

'What, Drogo? What would she have done? Raped you? Come on. Time to go home.' And off we'd go, Drogo immediately regaining his composure and good spirits. Only once did he look back. But that came later.

'Just a whisky and soda,' was his favourite expression. 'Nothing important. It'll all change when we get married.' I had promised myself it would indeed. So I waited, a new and very angry bride, until I couldn't wait any longer. The first person I went to see was Toto. I found her sitting up in bed crying. Max had also gone missing. We searched the bar, lounge, dining room, dance floor, card room, billiard room, garden and terrace, without success. Only the bedrooms remained. We approached the desk. 'Nous cherchons son frère, Monsieur Aitken, et son ami,' said Toto hopefully. Pursed lips and a few shrugs. The fact that they insisted on speaking German didn't help. So I went back to my room and returned a few moments later, armed with a good supply of what it takes to loosen tongues. Suddenly they all spoke French, some even English. Drogo's whereabouts proved expensive; Max's less so, being one of the cheaper rooms at the back of the hotel with no view of the Eiger.

A hurried consultation with Toto, and we went our separate ways, watched rather apprehensively by the concièrge and his minions, each of whom were now several hundred francs richer. As I picked up the fire extinguisher and positioned myself in front of the door, my anger and desire for revenge were to some extent tempered by a grudging admiration for Drogo's taste. The suite had been booked in the name of Baroness von Thyssen, quite one of the most stunningly beautiful women I have ever seen, before or since. We had noticed her during dinner when for one electrifying moment she had graced us with her presence and, in the process, turned every head in the room. I tapped discreetly on her door. 'Drogo?' My tone was soft and honey sweet.

From inside came a sudden urgency of whispering, then a noise like someone emptying a bucket of potatoes on the floor. A few more whispers, scuffling sounds, then the crash of a chair overturning, a subdued oath, more scufflings, and a light appeared under the door. Another, inner, door slammed. I waited. A key turned. Drogo, flushed as usual, emerged. 'Thank God you came . . .!'

I got him dead centre, then went on spraying until I had finally run out of foam. He just stood there, wiping it from his face. 'That put out the fire, Jan.' He was actually *grinning*. What could you *do* with the man? I turned and walked away before he could see the beginnings of my own helpless laughter.

The rest of our honeymoon was spent in an atmosphere pregnant with distrust, interspersed with moments of pure hilarity. For when Drogo and Max got together, nothing was impossible, nothing too outrageous. Toto never discovered what Max had been up to that first night. When he had finally emerged from the room at the back of the hotel, he said he'd been playing cards. Toto didn't believe a word of it and threw a bucket of water over him just in case she was right. Years later, Max admitted she had been.

When eventually we had made our way back to London, Drogo and I moved into a new house built for us in Chelsea Square, then called Trafalgar Square. It was a delightful house, sadly to be totally destroyed by one of the first bombs to be dropped on London in the war. Before long I bumped into our near-neighbours who turned out to be none other than Ian and Louise Campbell. To my surprise and pleasure, we slowly, cautiously, established a warm, uncomplicated relationship that in the end made me look forward to our times together. I spent many hours talking with Ian, who, now that all emotion was spent, I found interesting and likeable.

With Drogo working in the City, life at Chelsea Square began to return to normal, or as normal as life with Drogo could ever be. He was a marvellous companion, always cheerful and never boring. Perhaps that's why Father enjoyed his company so much. Our weekends were spent at Tracadie whenever possible, and at Hin-

chinbrook, his family's beautiful Charles II house in Huntingdon-
shire.

Drogo's mother might have been an invalid. I never knew for
sure. She was seldom if ever seen by visitors, or by her family, for
that matter. She remained in her suite all the time and never came
downstairs. When I met her husband, the Earl of Sandwich, I
began to think that her room was, perhaps, the best place for her.
Sandwich was a bit weird, especially to the girls. But his collection
of modern art was memorable. I liked Drogo's elder brother, Lord
Hinchinbrook. He married twice, his second wife being Lady
Dorothy Macmillan's sister. Then he became a Member of
Parliament and, alas, deteriorated rather fast. They were an unusual family, to say the least. But I loved their beautiful house and
looked forward to our visits there.

Towards the end of 1935, Drogo and I bought ourselves a
present, which we had to order four months in advance. It was a
Vega Gull, arguably one of the best light aircraft ever made. With
dual controls, wheel brakes, a range of 630 miles and a cruising
speed of 150 m.p.h., it meant we could go to any place in Europe
that had an airfield – and one or two that hadn't. I was particularly
pleased about the brakes. On our last trip, Drogo's unhappy knack
of taking off without first checking his fuel gauge had landed us in
a French village on our way to Biarritz to play golf. My main duty
was navigation and I had not yet learned to double-check the all-
important fuel supply when flying with Drogo.

With his usual skill he had put our Vega down in an impossibly
small field, and had then gone looking for help. He found it in the
form of several cans of petrol and around thirty French villagers
who seemed intent on celebrating the occasion with quantities of
their excellent new Bordeaux, fresh from the vine.

'Why all these people?' I asked.

'They're the brakes,' was Drogo's reply.

We turned the plane and pulled it back to the furthest extremity
of the field, where its tail-skid rested on the edge of a drainage
ditch. This done, the villagers – men, women and children –
crowded round it expectantly. Many seemed to have brought
their lunch.

'What's the French for "hang on till I tell you"?' asked Drogo, pouring petrol into the filler pipe.

I addressed myself to someone wearing a blue suit and bicycle clips who looked rather important: 'Quand nous sommes prêts,' I said, 'tombez votre mouchoir.' It worked. He produced an enormous red and blue handkerchief and practised dropping it on the grass. After a few rehearsals we got it right. The children had been cleared away from the front of the aircraft while everyone else hung on behind at carefully selected places. The blue suit with the handkerchief stood to one side, his arm raised.

Drogo started the engine, whereupon two ancients holding the tail-plane were blown into the ditch. Amid hoots of laughter they were pulled out and the cast reassembled. The engine roared once more. The plane, its tail now raised horizontal, strained to move forward against the combined drag of twenty windswept villagers. 'Now!' yelled Drogo. The blue suit dropped his *mouchoir*, the villagers let go, and we were shot forward with enough speed to take us up and away. We circled once to wave 'good bye and thank you', then set course once again for Biarritz. I have always liked the French. They're wonderful people when you get to know them, especially the villagers.

We did one more trip abroad before the year was over; again in the Vega Gull. We flew to Cortina in the Italian Dolomites. The skiing was marvellous but the moment I remember best was the arrival in the hotel dining room of Mussolini's daughter. As she made her entrance, the orchestra stopped and we all expected the Italian anthem. Instead, and to the visible fury of Il Duce's daughter, they broke into our own 'God Save the King'. Drogo smiled. It must have cost him a packet. But we all felt better now. Italy had just invaded Abyssinia.

9

My first son, William Drogo Montagu, was born on 9 February 1936. Three weeks earlier, King George V and Rudyard Kipling had died within two days of each other, both aged seventy. It saddened me that Father had not seen Rudyard Kipling once more before he died. Father may have tried to heal the breach, but I don't think so. I know I did, however, and Elsie Kipling tried too, but perhaps both our fathers were content to let the memories of their long friendship rest in happier times.

On the occasions when Father came to Chelsea Square to see his grandson, I was able to sit with him and talk – a thing we had hardly done since the days of the Empire Crusade. It was like old times, and I loved it. He would start with a bit of gossip, then, when I asked him, which I always did, he would tell me about the things that were important to him. He said he was opposed to an alliance with France, and opposed to the League of Nations, both of which would, in his view, drag us into war. He had met Hitler and Mussolini and disliked them both, but thought it inevitable that once she was strong enough to do so, Germany, at least, would right the wrongs done to her at the Treaty of Versailles.

Father wished, even if he did not believe, that it was none of our business to interfere. He had worked hard, with Sir Samuel Hoare, to devise a peace settlement with Italy over Abyssinia, and had failed. Mussolini was master of Addis Ababa; the Lion of Judah, no more than a refugee, was living in some style in an English country house. My father's beliefs were simple, and in many ways consistent with the Empire Free Trade policy of recent years: collective security within the Empire, friendship with the United States, rearmament without provocation, isolation from European affairs.

But he wanted to meet and talk with Ambassador Ribbentrop and Count Grandi, his Italian counterpart. Appeasement would be too strong a word with which to label Father's endeavours. Restraint might be more applicable. But without strength, even the smallest degree of friendly persuasion was impossible. He welcomed Ribbentrop but saw little of him once he became Ambassador. Dino Grandi, whose views on Mussolini and the excesses of Fascist ambitions were, to say the least, mixed, became a close friend of Father and remained so all his life. Father's views on Russia were such that, although he didn't like communism, he considered no war in Europe feasible unless she was on our side. So when Nye Bevan introduced him to the Soviet Ambassador, Ivan Maisky, and his wife, they were immediately invited to Cherkley; an invitation repeated and accepted many times. Father said they didn't talk politics much, but simply became friends.

To my delight, Father had at last decided that the aeroplane was the best means of European travel. Perhaps my own activities had influenced him a bit, although he would never admit it. He had always hated flying, except in the direst emergencies, and shared his views with Valentine, who had long nurtured a horror of flying and admitted the whole idea scared him silly. Now that Father had changed his mind and flew everywhere, Valentine either stayed behind, left early or struggled to catch up.

Max and Drogo were now flying seriously with the AAF and would frequently arrive at Chelsea Square with others who were doing the same: businessmen from the City, barristers, and young men of many other professions – some with money, some without. Most had been to Oxford or Cambridge, and all shared the same great interest in flying. Among them was a South African, Paddy Green, a friend of Max's, who skied and 'bobbed' for England and was, according to Drogo and Max, a superb pilot as well as a natural leader.

Drogo was up to his tricks again – that I knew. His 'whiskies and soda' were taken discreetly enough, but a certain Peggy Hamilton, one of the 'Dorchester cabaret girls', who kicked up their heels for the delight of the customers, had begun to crop up in the conversation rather too often. I tried to shut my ears to it, hoping that either the problem or Peggy Hamilton would just go away. Father, perhaps sensing something of my frustration and unhappiness, suggested I join his party for the Olympic Games. I accepted with alacrity.

It was high summer when we arrived in Berlin. We flew direct from Croydon in Father's private plane, leaving Valentine to follow by boat and train. Our reception at Berlin's airport was impressive. Obviously the word had gone out that the British press lord and his entourage were to be treated like visiting royalty. A fleet of gleaming black Mercedes cars whisked us away to the Adlon where obsequious managers, white-coated bellhops and maids in attractive ginghams catered to our every wish. On our hurricane trip through the city, I had noticed a marked change from my last visit only three years before. Gone were the street vendors, the prostitutes and the vagrants; gone the hopeless poverty, the dirt and squalor. People seemed to walk erect and with a purpose now. A new hope had been born.

But there was a sinister side to it too. I saw swaggering groups of young men, each with a swastika armband, standing on street corners. Brown uniforms were everywhere. I also saw strange notices about Jews not being allowed in certain shops, or if they did so, they entered at their own risk. Father had become increasingly quiet during our trip across the city. He knew that the reception we were being given owed much to his newspapers' policy of outward friendship towards the Third Reich and his outspoken optimism for continued peace between Germany and Great Britain. If Winston had been in the party, things might have been very different. For Winston alone shouted his distrust of Hitler, his warning of things to come, and a call to arms. For that reason he would not, could not, be there to see and evaluate things for himself. There was no need. He had already made up his mind.

Amid much bowing and clicking of heels, Joachim von Ribbentrop arrived at the hotel soon after we had settled in. He brought flowers for me, and an invitation for the whole party to lunch with him and his wife at their country house the following day. I watched him closely. Was this vain, arrogant man, surrounded by his posturing sycophants, the same charming person I had danced and laughed with at the 400 nightclub in Leicester Square not so long ago? Obviously it was, and I didn't like the transformation. When he left, however, everything seemed even more awkward and alien. The sycophants in uniform wore high, polished boots and carried holstered pistols. They strutted and laughed, posing as if aware of their Ayrian good looks, a quality for which they had no doubt been chosen.

'You will see the Olympic Games, of course?'

'Of course,' we chorused. Father kept silent. He was starting to look bored. I had never been particularly pleased to see Valentine at any time, wherever we were, but on this occasion the sight of his vast and familiar bulk advancing towards us through the red-plush furniture filled me with pleasure and relief. He greeted Father, then the rest of us, seeming not to notice that there were others present. 'Lord Castlerosse,' said Father, by way of introduction.

Valentine's enigmatic stare was supreme. As the uniforms postured around him, he removed his cigar long enough to say: 'Ah yes. How d'you do?' It was as if his attention had been drawn to an unwelcome delegation of his Irish tenants who had been waiting for a week. The sycophants wavered and fell silent. Valentine had a bad habit of staring over people's heads. 'They're fêting Chips Channon,' he said, turning to Father, 'as if he were the Second Coming. D'you think perhaps he is?' Laughter. We all knew how the vastly wealthy and socially successful American-turned-Englishman felt about Germany; on the surface anyway. Recently, his eulogies had known no bounds. The uniforms laughed too. And then the whole thing became funnier because obviously they didn't know what on earth they were laughing about.

The Ribbentrop country house was splendid, with parkland gardens stretching down to a lake. We had arrived in the now familiar fleet of official cars after another hair-raising drive, this time through undulating countryside with rivers and forests. The house itself was furnished with heavy, Wagnerian sofas, chairs and tables, on one of which I noticed photographs of a smiling Adolf Hitler holding a scowling Adolf Ribbentrop, our host's young son.

Ribbentrop and his wife had met us at the door. 'So nice of you to come.' How very English. Lunch was served on a long, narrow table in a long, narrow dining room. Father and I were placed on either side of our host. Butlers, footmen and maids, all blond, hovered at discreet distances while we enjoyed the good food washed down by the very best hocks and Moselles. Valentine was obviously impressed with the latter, for Frau Ribbentrop's father was the largest exporter of fine wines in Germany. Her husband had once been their salesman in London.

As before, the conversation hinged round the Olympic Games. Would we be going every day? We must, of course. These would be the greatest Olympics ever. The Führer had set his heart on it. German athletes, and English of course, were bound to do well. I looked at the faces of the German guests. All of them spoke perfect English, and all of them seemed anxious for us to be at the games, all the time. 'No,' said Father, 'but I'd like to see the opening ceremony.' A moment of consternation, then our host turned to me and caught my own look of disappointment. He was smiling. 'But *you*, Janet. Would you not like to see the athletics?' I admitted I would. 'Then stay with us! We will go together and see them. Shall we do that?' I paused, seeing Father's furious glare in the background. Why not? It was a chance in a million. While they were all languishing in the hotel, I would be at the centre of things; where it was all happening.

'Yes,' I said, 'how kind of you. I'd like that.'

'Settled then!' He looked up at his wife. 'We'd be delighted to have her with us for a few days, wouldn't we, my dear.' Frau Ribbentrop nodded and beamed her approval. Father's face was as black as a storm cloud.

When morning came, the warm sunshine that flooded into my bedroom dispelled all the nervousness and apprehension I may have felt the night before. Soon, a breakfast of bacon and eggs, fruit, cheese and coffee arrived on a trolley decked with roses, among which nestled a gold-bordered card requesting me to be ready to leave for the stadium at 11 a.m. I took a shower and dressed in gay colours, then finished my coffee by the window, listening to the birds in the beautiful garden below. It was all so friendly, so reassuring, so very peaceful.

Whenever I try to describe my impressions of the 1936 Berlin

Olympics, I remember again the confusion of conflicting emotions I felt at the time. It started with our cavalcade of black Mercedes cars moving rapidly through the countryside while the Ribbentrops chatted away happily. When we entered the outskirts of the city, however, they fell silent. We slowed to a snail's pace and glided forward down a seemingly endless avenue of cheering crowds, before which two lines of men in brown shirts, with red and white swastikas on their arms, gave the Nazi salute. They were the SA, forty thousand strong, many of them middle-aged and rather portly. They didn't look too warlike. But in fact they were still a formidable, bullying lot, well fed and powerful, like their leader Ernst Roehm; big men in boots, until they had got too big for them. Many were later murdered, cut down by Heydrich and his SS Blackshirts on the 'night of the long knives'. The SS were the elite of the future war. There was one of them sitting in the front beside the driver; a tall young man who, in my innocence, I thought rather attractive, with his ready smile and his efficient, courteous way of handing me in and out of the car.

We were in the Olympic village now. On either side of us were well-constructed buildings designed to accommodate the world's athletes with the maximum comfort and convenience. The black-shirted army were predominant here, saluting and waving us through, their movements quick and watchful as we swung towards the tunnel leading into the stadium itself. When our Mercedes, flying the swastika, emerged into the vast central arena, we were greeted by the deafening roar of 150,000 spectators, rising to their feet in welcome. Was this for Ribbentrop? It must be. I glanced quickly towards him. He was smiling up at them, his arm raised in a half-salute.

It was an awe-inspiring sight. The crowded stands of the great stadium seemed to stretch into the sky; a solid oval of tremendous sound, while, in the foreground, SS guards, some smiling, some tight-lipped, guided us towards steps leading up into a special box reserved for the Nazi hierarchy. Flowers were everywhere, a bouquet of them being handed to Frau Ribbentrop by a slim, blond girl in a white dress. The noise was so great I couldn't hear anything else. We seemed to move on waves of it, buoyed up by an invisible blanket of sound that blotted out all reality. I saw people moving close to me as if in a dream, mouthing at each other, and found myself among a group of high-ranking officials, one of whom escorted me to a comfortable seat with a perfect view over the entire arena.

Suddenly the roar of the crowd became ear-splitting. Something was happening below me and to the left. Then the roar became a song, and the song became 'Deutschland Über Alles', followed by that strangely beautiful, hideously corrupted, music of Horst Wessel, the Nazi anthem. The crowd went wild. Shouts of 'Sieg Heil!' battered the ear-drums and I realized that everyone was standing, peering excitedly to our left. The Führer had arrived, miraculously it seemed and with precision timing, to acknowledge the great ovation that awaited him.

Like everyone else, I smiled and craned sideways to catch a glimpse of him. But all I could see was a bustling group of immaculate uniforms, armed SS and a sprinkling of their handsome, if dowdily dressed ladies. Then Ribbentrop was beside me. 'Come,' he said, 'I would like you to meet him.' His eyes were very bright. Things had quietened a bit by the time I was ushered into the Führer's box. He sat hunched in his chair, gazing out across the arena, his head and rather plump neck appearing curiously out of place above the uniform tunic. Ribbentrop had the 'honour of presenting' me. Hitler paused, then rose and turned, offering his hand. It felt boneless, like a piece of wet meat, clammy and soft. I towered over him. 'How do you do?' I said. He took his hand away. There was nothing there; no warmth, no voice, not even an awareness. The eyes were unfathomable, the jaw strong enough, but the man himself seemed totally lacking in any sexuality; without substance, inhuman. He turned away and sat down again. I had ceased to exist. Someone touched my arm.

As we were leaving the box, a great roar rose from the crowd once more. The Hindenburg airship appeared like some bloated phantom over the Olympic column, high above the stands. It hovered there as the roar rose to a crescendo and a German athlete, blond and striking, ran into the arena with the Olympic torch. The flame was lit. Young Richard Strauss conducted the Olympic hymn that day, a hymn he had himself composed.

When it was over, the vast crowd again bayed for their Führer: 'Sieg Heil! Adolf Hitler, Sieg Heil!' I watched, fascinated, as he rose to his feet. Gone was the apparent lethargy, the slackness; the inhumanity. His body was alive now, ten feet fall, gesticulating – every fibre of it vibrant with emotion as his voice crashed out, thundering across the stadium: 'Germany needs *peace!*' he raged. 'Germany *desires* peace!' The harsh, gutteral words were thrown out through ten microphones and a hundred speakers, to be picked up and relayed across the world. And the world tried to believe him, because it wanted to. I turned away, anxious for the games to begin.

Leni Riefenstahl, that politically unsavoury but gifted film-maker, produced the official Nazi version of the 1936 Olympics. They called it *Triumph of the Will*, and it became in its way a film classic. In it, Miss Riefenstahl, whose undoubted talents were further augmented by every facility the Party could provide for her, faithfully recorded some, if not all, of the Führer's disappointments. For Hitler, believing in the physical superiority of the Ayrian race (of whom, it was rumoured, he himself was but a doubtful member), walked out in fury when the black American, Jesse Owens, carried off the major gold medals.

I saw some of those events but not all, because after three days Father insisted I rejoin him at the Adlon. 'We're going home,' he said.

I didn't argue. There was outrage in his face. 'Because of me?' I asked, 'I'm sorry.'

'No,' he said gruffly, 'you had nothing to do with it.' His face softened. He looked tired. Without knowing why, I suddenly felt very close to him. He didn't tell me his reasons for leaving. I didn't ask him. I think it was Valentine who told me in the end. Hermann Goering had visited Father in his hotel room. Having delivered an unusually boastful monologue, he carefully placed a reel of recording tape on Father's table and suggested with a fat smile that he might like to hear it. Father did so, and heard himself. His room had been 'bugged' since the day he had arrived.

On our way back to the airport, I saw again how clean everything looked. It reminded me of Ribbentrop's smile when he had said goodbye. Something was beginning to feel all wrong. Berlin had been ruthlessly cleaned up, purged of all 'undesirables', to leave a bland, white-washed exterior for foreign visitors to admire and delight in.

*   *   *

Miss Wallis Warfield, who became Mrs Spencer, who became Mrs Simpson, who then became the Duchess of Windsor (having nearly become the Queen of England), won her second divorce on 27 October 1936. King Edward VIII (as yet uncrowned) was a very impatient lover. The events that followed have been written about many times. For as long as they lasted, they almost totally eclipsed the sinister happenings in Germany and embroiled the nation in a domestic row which threatened the very foundations of the monarchy. Father saw it coming. 'I'm going to Arizona with Valentine,' he told me on the telephone. I wished him luck and didn't think much more about it, chiefly because I was having an appalling problem with Drogo at the time. His 'whiskies-and-soda' were beginning to seem more like a full-blooded binge.

Father, whose feelings towards the monarchy were warm but not euphoric, took the view, in accordance with his Presbyterian faith, that divorce was acceptable though regrettable, and that any other view was reminiscent of Rome. Marriage was a contract, not a sacrament. He didn't get far on his way to Arizona. The King telephoned him in New York and requested him, urgently, to come back and give him some advice. Clearly he wanted Father to help try to control certain elements of the press which seemed intent on the King's – and Mrs Simpson's – destruction. I know Father liked King Edward, perhaps because he had seen so much of the world and revered the Empire. He also knew that Stanley Baldwin was one of the King's chief opponents and the chance to settle an old score was just too good to miss.

So Father came back, and telephoned the King on the day the Crystal Palace burnt to the ground. He then geared his newspapers to persuade the British public to accept their monarch, warts and all, and asked the King if he would please be patient and wait a bit. Father wasn't alone in all this. Winston and Lord Rothermere were already on the King's side, fighting hard in parliament and the press, while Esmond Harmsworth found himself lunching with Mrs Simpson, endeavouring to explain to her the full implications of the word 'morganatic'. Ranged against them were Stanley Baldwin and the most powerful elements of church and state, including *The Times*, which, under Geoffrey Dawson, was being unusually venomous towards Mrs Simpson.

The battle lasted ten days (Father had told me they would need twenty), during which time the Rothermere and Beaverbrook presses were in full cry and public opinion began to swing in favour of the King. Then, on 11 December, exhausted with the whole business, the King ran out of patience. Having agreed to the idea of taking a wife but not a queen, he told Baldwin to accept that much, or else. Baldwin would not accept it, and the King abdicated. I was with Father when King Edward telephoned to say goodbye, and I could see that he was deeply moved.

George VI was crowned five months later. The British had unexpectedly found a man of such great personal courage and integrity that, as the years dragged on and we struggled through the worst and most dangerous war of our time, he became much admired and loved; possibly more so than any other English king in history. The Abdication Crisis was over. Baldwin had won again, but Father found at least one consolation: 'It was good to fight *with* Winston for a change,' he said.

Immediately afterwards, he renewed his trip to the United States. In New York he bought a Lockheed 12 and engaged a professional pilot to fly him the rest of the way. Although the dry air was good for his asthma, the dust storms were not. So he altered course for Miami. But at least he had decided to spend his winters abroad, and to that end he started looking round for a home in the sun. He investigated both the Bahamas and Jamaica and liked what he saw. Then, a bit later on, he bought La Capponcina from Captain Edward Molyneux, the dress designer. It was a lovely house at Cap d'Ail, near Monte Carlo, and he was to spend much of his time there in later years.

Father wasn't the only one in search of the sun. I arrived home at

Tracadie one cold winter's evening and, having checked that Jeanne and Bill were safely tucked up in bed, went downstairs to find a note from Drogo propped against the mirror over the mantlepiece: 'Gone to Jamaica, darling, with Peggy. Back in a month.' That's what *he* thought! I decided I'd had enough. I moved my things out of Chelsea Square and rented a flat in Dolphin Square for the days I wanted to be in London. I didn't feel particularly hurt, sad or lonely. Drogo was Drogo. I thought I could change the leopard's spots, but I was wrong. I felt defeated at the time, though, as if I had failed in some way. But I soon got over it. I missed the laughter most of all.

They were strange times, those years immediately before the war; a sort of inbetween time. Nothing seemed really secure any more. So people played just that much harder and did things on the spur of the moment that they might otherwise have thought about more carefully. Max and his friend Paddy Green came to Tracadie one day, from the 601 Squadron's weekend base at Shoreham. They suggested I join them at St Moritz where both were competing in skiing competions. I said that I would. Then Father returned. Like Max and Paddy, he seemed to know all about Drogo's behaviour and asked me to go with him to Nice, and bring Jeanne with me. Winston would be there, he said, and of course Jean and Valentine. He was obviously trying to take my mind off things.

Apart from listening to some fascinating badinage between Winston and Father on the subject of 'Rearmament and European involvement' versus 'Isolation and Empire security', it was Valentine who provided the highlight of my trip. We were staying in the Negresco and, having successfully lured me into yet another brothel (for the second and last time), he retired in triumph to take a bath before dinner. When he turned on the taps, all that appeared was green sludge. The great Negresco had a plumbing problem. So Valentine ordered twenty crates of Vichy water (charged to Father) and bathed in that. When Father returned from inspecting his alterations to Capponcino, he pretended to be furiousbut couldn't keep a straight face. No matter what you thought about Valentine, the man had style.

After a few days I left for St Moritz, taking Jeanne with me. She was nine now and developing into a very independent little person; a fact that was to cause a few problems later. She was a lot of fun to be with, and when we joined up with Max and Paddy I was happier than I'd been for a long time. In the evenings, while Max became the star of the après-ski, Paddy seemed content to stay with me. He told me a lot about their 601 Squadron, the terrible lack of planes, equipment and armament, and the enthusiasm of the young men who were taking part. I heard many names for the first time; names like Roger Bushell, also South African, and Michael Peacock, Jimmy Little and Willie Rhodes Morehouse, all weekend pilots who, with Max and Drogo, would be in the forefront of the air battle if one ever took place. We talked about the Spanish Civil War and Jessica Mitford's elopement with Esmond Romilly, who had been fighting with the international column for the Republicans against Franco. We also talked about her sister, Unity, who had had the temerity to appear at a Hyde Park Corner Labour rally, sporting a swastika badge and had narrowly escaped being thrown into the Serpentine as a result. And we talked about ourselves a bit too; our hopes and our fears at a time when everything seemed crazy, as crazy as Hitler who, in the words of Willie, his ubiquitous, English-born nephew, was a 'peaceful man'.

It was over all too soon and once again we had to exchange the blue and white Alpine skies for the drab grey of an English winter. I might have known what to expect when we got to Tracadie. Drogo looked bronzed and fit. 'You can't stay here,' I said. He didn't argue. He didn't try to explain, nor did he even say he was sorry. Drogo seldom did the obvious. I was expecting something, nevertheless. I didn't know what. Some mention, perhaps, of his tireless propensity for the Peggy Hamiltons of this world and his inability to resist them.

'Do you want to see Bill?' I asked.

'I've seen him.'

'What are you waiting for, then?'

'I wanted to see you, too.'

'All right, you've seen me. Now you can go.' So he went.

The next day he came back. 'How's the Gull?' he asked. I told him I didn't know. I hadn't been to look at it. We talked about aeroplanes then. I couldn't help it. He said he wanted to do a flight to Venice and asked me to go with him. When I didn't answer, he plunged into great detail about the flight-plan he had been working on. In the middle of it, he suddenly broke off to say, 'I'm sorry, Jan. I care about you a lot.' Then he continued about the flight-plan, using the same tone of voice as he had before. He talked about stop-overs, refuelling points, times, altitudes, cruising speeds and the rest of it. As I listened to him I realized that if there was to be any future for us at all, its basis was twofold, no more. There was no denying our shared love of flying, nor, indeed, the greater love we shared for our son. But it would never be the same as before. Too much damage had already been done. I waited for him to finish.

'I think one can get a divorce in France on the grounds of stupidity,' I said.

'Stupidity?'

'Yes. Allowing yourself to be found out.'

Drogo looked quite shocked. 'Never really thought about it before,' he said, 'but I take your point.'

So that's the way it was with Drogo and me; a sort of 'on-off' relationship that thrived when we were together and died when we were not. I asked no questions, dreaded gossip and hoped for the best, for I knew that the next time would be the last. When I drove over to Cherkley to explain to Father that Drogo and I were going to try again, he seemed to take a rather lofty view of it all: 'You're old enough to cope with things like that,' he said, referring to Drogo's past philanderings. Old enough? I remembered he'd said that once before, and on a not too dissimilar occasion. It was at Warwick Castle, where we had been invited for a weekend house party. After a prolonged evening of dining and dancing, I had gone to my room to sleep through what was left of the night. I emerged from the bathroom and began to climb into bed, only to find a grinning Mr Hore Belisha already in my bed, waiting for me! I remember running to take refuge with Mike Wardell in the next room. 'I've hardly ever spoken to the man!' I raged. But how old does one have to *be*, to 'cope'?

On the drive back to Tracadie, I thought about Father. Sometimes it seemed as if he didn't care. So often he had appeared just to stand back, offer no advice and let me work things out for myself. I couldn't talk to him, discuss problems as I had once done with Mother. It was at times like these that I missed her most of all. And yet, in reality, Father did care, very deeply. I knew this, because he had never once failed to help or at least try to do something constructive whenever I was in trouble. He had done so with Ian, then when I needed a home, and now with Drogo. 'Watching in the wings', I had called it. And he was still doing the same thing. When I was making a mistake, he let me get on with it. When I realized it myself, he would help me put it right. But sometimes I wondered. He always did things in his own way.

When I got home, the phone rang. 'I want you and Drogo to come to California with me.' Valentine, who was in the process of getting a divorce, came with us, as did Jean Norton and her daughter, Sally. We sailed for New York, and then went our separate ways to California. Father took Drogo and the others in his own plane, the Lockheed 12. Valentine went by train, and I followed a day or two later by Constellation, which made two refuelling stops on the way. The Abdication was still a hot news item on the day I arrived alone in Los Angeles. At the airport I was astonished to find myself surrounded by reporters all asking the same questions: What did I think of Mrs Simpson? Did I like her? 'You have a very fine airline,' I replied. 'The Constellation is a beautiful aircraft.' This seemed to me preferable to 'no comment', which I was well aware could be interpreted in any way an editor wishes. So I repeated myself time and time again.

At last I got away and joined Father at San Simeon, where William Randolph Hearst and Marion Davies had invited the two of us to stay the night. It was dark and gloomy, with carpetless corridors that echoed, and it reminded me of Inveraray Castle. This was hardly surprising, since much of San Simeon itself had been a castle, uprooted from Europe and transported, stone by stone, to California. At dinner our host talked about dachshunds, and one in particular which slept in his bed. While I struggled to say awake, Father looked bored and Marion Davies concentrated on the wine. It was not a very jolly evening.

Having slept fitfully in an enormous and rather lumpy four-poster, hemmed in by heavy curtains, I awoke to find that, almost without exception, the newspaper headlines screamed the same story: 'Lord Beaverbrook's Daughter Says She Hates Mrs Simpson.' According to the papers, I disliked her so much I had once walked out of the room when she entered it. Reactions at breakfast were mixed. Father was furious until he checked my own story with one of the reporters who had been at the airport. Our host, who owned most of the newspapers anyway, merely shrugged, while Marion poured another hair of the dog that had bit her the night before. She wasn't a bit interested in newspapers, or Mrs Simpson.

If Orson Welles, for whom our host nurtured a lasting resentment, had indeed found inspiration for *Citizen Kane* in San Simeon and its occupants, I think he might have included the private zoo. For unlike Kane, William Randolph Hurst really did love animals. Years later, his granddaughter, Joanne Hurst, told me that when it was reported to him that mice had eaten the candle wax, his only concern had been for the mice. Thereafter, food was to be left out for them.

Father and I left soon after breakfast. We joined the others at the Lodge Hotel at Pebble Beach and from there flew all over the place to play golf, bathe in the sea and enjoy the mountain and desert scenery. We stayed at the El Mirador in Palm Springs, then flew to see the Grand Canyon and the Hoover Dam.

Valentine felt rather left out of things, but when Sam Goldwyn invited us to a party, he made sure he was there on time. He was not disappointed. A bevy of beautiful starlets mingled with the guests. They wore brief and colourful swimsuits, high heels and glamorous smiles. On entering the vast, floodlit swimming pool, however, their swimsuits then their smiles disintegrated on contact with the water. Valentine was delighted. Father laughed. Drogo smiled, perhaps a little wistfully. I thought it was all rather vulgar. Then Drogo and I flew back to New York in the Lockheed, while Father and the others travelled by Constellation. Valentine took another train. We had been in California three weeks, during which time Drogo had behaved perfectly, apart from one temporary lapse over a missing swimsuit. But I didn't think it was his fault.

After the exhilarating three-thousand-mile flight across the United States in Father's Lockheed, Drogo and I arrived back in England determined to do another trip in our own Vega Gull. We set off for Austria with a full load of suitcases and golf clubs to stay with Count and Countess Munster at their beautiful lakeside castle near Klagenfurt. The flight went smoothly, the Gull performing as it should, and we even kept enough petrol in the tank. Our hostess, formerly Peggy Ward, had been a good friend in London. She made us very welcome and arranged a five-day schedule of golf, dinner parties and sightseeing trips in the scenic, wild countryside.

I remember we were lunching on the terrace the day before we left. 'We'll fly the direct route home,' said Drogo, casually. I blinked. There was a massive mountain range between us and southern Germany; a range we'd flown *round* on our way south.

'The famous Glockner Pass is nearly twelve and a half thousand feet!' said Count Munster.

'We'll make it,' said Drogo.

The next day was bright and clear. With full tanks and a payload of almost nine hundred pounds, we circled upwards, struggling to gain altitude to take us over the tremendous mountain range that spread before us in a continuous wall of massive, snow-covered peaks. Beneath us, the valley of scree and pine, up which we had flown, was broken by foam-white torrents of icy water. 'She's not going to make it,' I said. Thank God the weather, at least, was on our side.

'Chuck the golf clubs out, Jan. Yours too. Then the suitcases.' I did, gritting my teeth against the icy blast of wind from the open door.

'All gone,' I said, as several hundred pounds worth of pigskin, Paris fashions, scent, expensive tweed, metal, leather, wood and rubber went plummeting into the unknown. Drogo then gained height and flew at that mountain. He pulled back the stick and with full throttle took us up and over the shoulder of the Gross Glockner, so close I could have scooped up a handful of snow.

We landed at Frankfurt for lunch; an excellent meal that took three hours longer than necessary. In the meantime, the Germans dismantled the engine and put it back together again. 'Technical fault,' they said. I know now why they had good reason to be curious. In some respects the Vega Gull was a test-bed for the Spitfire. We flew home without incident; both a bit subdued, I thought, remembering, perhaps, that solid wall of glistening mountain in front of us. Our lost belongings were cheap at the price. We were alive. But I have often wondered who, if anyone, ever found our things. Did an Austrian peasant girl once wear the latest fashions from Lanvin's autumn collection? Did a struggling Russian infantryman return home from the war carrying a matched set of Dunlops? I like to think so.

When the German army spewed into Austria in March 1938, a lot of people professed to welcome them. Lily Ernst, a Jewish ballet dancer, was someone who did not, and Father liked her well enough to fly her out of Vienna under the noses of the Gestapo. He installed her at The Vineyard as his long-term guest. Jean, who enjoyed one of the cottages on the Cherkley estate, didn't appear to mind too much under the circumstances, but didn't delude herself that this arrangement was solely one of political and ethnic expediency. I remember going to London, at Father's request, to meet Lily, and I think it was on this occasion that Drogo finally went too far. He had already sold the house in Chelsea Square, so we took a room at the Hotel Maurice for the two nights we were to be in town. 'Just going round to White's for a nightcap.' As usual, I gave him the benefit of the doubt and prepared for an early night.

Then the inevitable happened; the thing I dreaded most. The phone rang. 'Drogo's in the Café de Paris with Peggy,' said a female voice. 'Thought you'd like to know.' She hung up. I tried to ignore it but couldn't. When he came back in the early hours of the morning, I instinctively knew. And he knew I knew.

'We can still be friends, can't we?' He was already reaching for his suitcase.

'Give it time,' I said, 'lots of time.'

I was at a pretty low ebb. My first husband had been obsessed with gambling, my second with pretty women. Two marriages on the rocks in just over ten years – an unenviable record. I needed to clear my mind of it, to stop thinking and wondering how much of the blame was mine and how much was somebody else's. I honestly didn't consider myself the sort of woman who drove men to seek refuge in either the casino or the extra-marital bed. But I thought about it. I was fed up with being the victim. I needed someone I could talk to, someone who could make me believe that, at thirty, life wasn't over and that there were better things to do with it than be a 'wronged' wife.

Father was my best friend, but I couldn't talk to him. Anyway, he was too busy working. Hitler had smothered the whole of Czechoslovakia now, and Sir Samuel Hoare, Father's spy in the cabinet, was keeping him informed on just how far Chamberlain was likely to go in his policy of appeasement. I suspect that the erroneous 'no war' policy of the *Express* at the time owed much to this hot line to No. 10. They were all wrong except Winston.

I didn't go to Jean either. With the advent of Lily Ernst, she was beginning to have problems of her own. Max was too busy. When he wasn't flying, his attentions centred round Cynthia Monteith, an outstandingly beautiful debutante whom he was soon to marry. Peter lived for his motor-racing and Janet MacNeill, in that order, and had just won third place in a BRDC road race in his privately entered ERA. He was seldom around. Two delightful newcomers had arrived at Cherkley, and I could have talked to them, had I known it. Both would have understood how I felt. Michael Foot was to become one of Father's closest and best-loved friends. Both he and his wife, Jill, were to be very special in my life too, but at the time, I hardly knew them.

There was one other person, however, to whom I knew I could take my troubles. She, at least, would know how real they were. Caroline Condon was an American of about my own age who had separated from her husband and was living in Paris. We had already spent much time together, both there and in the south of France. She had met Drogo with me on several occasions and always succeeded in making me feel as if I, not him, was the one liable to kick over the traces. As she knew very well the reverse was true, this was no small achievement and a great boost to the ego. So I called her: 'Let's go somewhere.' A pause.

'Come and talk about it,' said Caroline. So I went to Paris. I just ran away without telling anyone. Jeanne and Bill would be fine. Jeanne had so many interests of her own, and Bill was too small, at two, to know if I was there or not. Or so I told myself. They already had the best care money could buy. From Paris, Caroline and I went to Marseilles and took the first boat we could find that looked comfortable and clean. It was going to Alexandria.

King Farouk's Egypt was a pretty exotic place if one averted one's eyes from the poverty and squalor. The beggars who roamed the streets of Cairo were seldom seen in the British sector, which housed the famous Shepherds Hotel and the homes of the high-born and affluent. A limited number were tolerated, however. They added to the general atmosphere of mystery and promise expected by all tourists arriving at the gateway to the East.

Caroline and I arrived at Shepherds Hotel with the intention of having a good time, beggars or no beggars. And a very good time we had. For three weeks, we stepped outside ourselves and plunged into a wild and fantastic world of glamour and excitement that absorbed us to the exclusion of all else. Soon we would have to step back again, pick up where we had left off and revert to being people with pasts, futures and responsibilities. But for that one glorious stretch, we were just two young women, intent on living life in the present without a backward glance.

We were lucky. The first person I saw in the hotel was a journalist I had known in London. Through him we met the officers of the Camel Corps, a group of terrific young men who, like us, were only too aware that their present life-style would soon come to an end. Their picturesque and romantic way of soldiering would be changed for ever and they would be rudely pitchforked from the past into the present by the grim facts of modern warfare.

Riding a white camel across a moonlit desert within sight of the Great Pyramid is an experience I shall never forget. No one spoke much on these occasions. The phantom shapes of other riders, spread out on either side, seemed to swim forward as if suspended over the white sand. When a cloud passed over the moon and all images disappeared, only the sound of creaking saddles and the dull thud of the animals' feet broke the magical silence. I had ridden camels before, and I soon got used to their curious gait, but I never ceased to be amazed by their speed or, indeed, their height, which seemed to raise me far above the desert floor.

On other occasions we would ride out on Arab ponies; swift and responsive creatures, fine-boned and intelligent. They flew along over the sun-baked sand, their small hooves scarcely seeming to touch it. We raced cars, too, joining a rally which led us far out into the desert, up escarpments and across endless blistering plains to rendezvous at some half-forgotten oasis, where, centuries before, caravans of merchants from the south had camped and watered their stock.

We spent a lot of time in the desert with our friends in the Camel Corps. Neither Caroline nor I had a particular beau, although we probably would have had if we'd stayed longer. For some reason, these young men just welcomed us into their world and seemed to enjoy our company. Perhaps the fact that we accepted anything they suggested by way of adventure and excitement endeared us to them. I don't know. Maybe it was just because there was safety in numbers, not that Caroline or I were particularly concerned with being 'safe'. There was one occasion, however, when we had to run for it, or rather dive for it; straight into the Nile. We had been invited on a boat-picnic by two of King Farouk's one thousand cousins, who, perhaps overcome by the beauty of the sunset, started to breathe rather heavily through their noses. Doubtless either Cleopatra or Nefertiti would have frozen these princes with a single withering look, but Caroline and I had to resort to less subtle means:

'Get away, Marmoud! Be your age!'

'Damn it! Who said you could . . .?'

Scuffles and more unseemly lunges, then two splashes and we were swimming hard for the bank, hoping we hadn't already caught one of the dreaded plagues reserved by the Nile for those imprudent enough to duck their heads in her. We were laughing helplessly as we hauled each other, dripping, up the bank. We hitched a cart ride to the Mena House Hotel which, thankfully, wasn't far off. From there we took a taxi the five or six miles to

Cairo and the luxury of a bath at Shepherds.

By now we were running out of money, so we scraped together every penny we could lay hands on and spent it all on one last picnic for our friends in the Camel Corps. This time it was on us. We invited them all, and they all came. It was wonderful. But when at last it was over, and the stars were at their brightest, we found ourselves on the edge of a loneliness such as we had never known before. For as their familiar faces receded into darkness, it was as if they took with them the illusion of freedom and happiness, leaving us to face our own futures in the stark reality of another day. When I cabled Father, guessing something of the wrath to come, he sent money by return, together with a suspiciously polite reply asking if perhaps I wouldn't mind coming home now. For Caroline and I it was the last of our happy times together. I saw her once more when she was in a hospital in Switzerland being treated for consumption. After that she returned to America and went out of my life for thirty-six years.

In 1975, she called me, out of the blue – to say goodbye. She was dying. The damn thing had got to her other lung.

'Where are you? I'll come there.'

'No, Janie. I look too awful. Let's remember us the way we were – and those wonderful days in the desert.' I didn't know what to say. So she said it for me: 'They were the best, weren't they?'

'Yes,' I said, weakly. Silence. She was gone again.

*   *   *

I phoned Father as soon as I got home to Tracadie. When we talked about Egypt, I realized he already knew a good deal about what had happened there. 'Feel better now?' he asked. I remembered the journalist we'd met that first day in Shepherds Hotel. 'Yes,' I said, 'and thanks for sending the money.' I was both relieved and gratified that he seemed to understand. I asked him what had been going on in my absence. 'Valentine's ill,' he said, 'and your cousin Bill Aitken has married a beautiful girl called Penelope Maffey.'

I was to find out more about this. Father nursed Valentine back

166

to health, taking a room for him at Claridges and footing all the bills. And Penelope Maffey was as nice as she was indeed beautiful. She and Bill, who was terribly wounded in the RAF at the start of the war, were later to have two children, Jonathan and Maria, who were both to be successful in their different careers; Jonathan in journalism and politics, and Maria on stage, screen and television, where her patrician good looks and undoubted talent brought her considerable acclaim.

Not long afterwards, Neville Chamberlain returned from Munich, waving his bit of paper. Those of us who had husbands, relatives and friends in the armed forces felt a sense of relief. We knew it was self-induced to some extent, because none of us really believed that the Hitler peace pact would last. But it was a relief just the same. The first person to call me was Sibell Lygon, and she suggested a party for the pilots of 601 Squadron, one of whom, Michael Rowley, was of particular importance to her. They married in the following year. Sibell insisted we use her father's home in Belgrave Square. Her father, Lord Beauchamp, was abroad and she had the place to herself. It was a great success. We managed to find a band that wasn't already booked, and raided the cellar for vast quantities of champagne, claret and Burgundy. All our friends from the Squadron came, and many others besides. Max arrived with Paddy Green and two barristers, Michael Peacock and Roger Bushell. Both were weekend pilots. Then, when Willie Rhodes Morehouse and Jimmy Little turned up, I could at last begin to put faces to names I already knew.

Peter, whose marriage to Janet MacNeill had already ended despite the birth of their daughter Caroline, came with a new friend, Barbara, whom I instantly liked. He poured himself half a pint of champagne and sat down next to Noel Coward.

'Father's got it wrong,' he said. 'There'll be war with Germany.'

'Nonsense,' said Noel.

I remember Peter fixing him with a baleful stare. 'Look, Noel,' he said, 'Adolf doesn't like your type. If he gets here, you could end up on a lamp-post.' Noel moved away.

The laughter, drinking and dancing continued far into the night. It was the party to end all parties, and in a way that's exactly what it turned out to be. Within months, 601 Squadron was moved from its peacetime base at Hendon to Biggin Hill and put on a war footing. I went there with others to help pack parachutes and found myself working beside Primula Rollo, who later married David Niven but died so tragically in 1946 when it was all over.

Father was in Canada when I got the call from Duncan Davies, my old instructor from Brooklands. It was August 1939 and Hitler's armies were massing on the Polish border.

'How'd you like to fly a Hurricane?' he asked.

'Very much,' I replied, waiting for the tag-line. It was no joke. They desperately needed women pilots to fly this new aircraft to the fighter bases. I knew that 601 Squadron still had Blenheims, most of them without guns or ammunition. This was my chance to help them. 'Where do I go to train?' I asked. Two weeks later, on 3 September, we were at war.

10

I flew a Hurricane for the first and only time from a Midlands Maintenance Unit to Biggin Hill and landed half an hour ahead of the first air-raid siren of the war. After only two hours instruction at the MU, I was thankful for every moment I had spent flying the Vega Gull. There were similarities, but the Hurricane was much faster and heavier, although unarmed. By the time I made my rather bumpy landing, I could remember little about the flight itself other than how hard I had concentrated on getting there in one piece. I doubt if that particular Hurricane went to 601 Squadron after all. They were worth their weight in gold and regular squadrons of the RAF also had to be equipped. 601 continued to fly Blenheims in the opening months of the 'phoney war'. As a fighter, it was a disaster.

Duncan Davies was delighted with this first successful delivery. The Air Ministry was already involved in setting up the Air Transport Auxiliary, an outfit comprising many women pilots which did such great service later on. I looked forward to flying regularly with the ATA, with such fine pilots as Diana Barnato, who was the daughter of the well-known millionaire racing-driver, 'Babe' Barnato. She went on to make a great name for herself, delivering aircraft to the fighter bases throughout the war. Later she became the first woman to fly faster than sound.

I was excited and pleased that I had now found a way to be of real help. But it was not to be. Father had returned from Canada and summoned me to Cherkley. 'No,' he said, 'and that's final. Max will do the flying in this family. Your responsibilities are with your children. I'm asking you – for their sake – stop it.' So that was that. I was grounded. I knew there was no point in arguing. When father made up his mind about something, it was impossible to make him change it.

So I went home to Tracadie and called Duncan Davies. 'I know,' he said, 'your father just told me. What you are going to do now?'

'Farm, I suppose. What else is there?'

'Nothing more important than that,' he said. 'Good luck.'

From that moment, my frustration gave way to feverish activity. I decided to keep pigs, buying three hundred 'large whites' and converting barns, stables and outhouses to accommodate them. I also built a row of new piggeries and enlisted the help of Sibell Lygon, who came to Tracadie as often as she could. Jeanne helped too, either on the farm or taking care of Bill, not yet four. I was also lucky to have a wonderfully reliable neighbour, Betty Lamb, who loved them both and took care of them, inviting them to her own house whenever I was away.

Peter, now in the Royal Fusiliers, came to Tracadie on leave, bringing Barbara with him. He hated going to Cherkley, complaining that Father's attitude towards him was like that of a disinterested martinet. By now, I'm afraid, the breach between them was too wide for any attempt at reconciliation. Neither would give way, and that was how it would remain to the end. But I enjoyed having him with me and liked Barbara more and more as I watched her affection for him grow deeper. I also welcomed their help on the farm.

I don't remember exactly what I was doing or who I was with when the news reached me that Drogo had been killed. My first reaction was to talk to our son, Bill, then walk with him in the garden, saying nothing to anybody until the sense of numbness and shock began to wear off. Later in the war, I somehow came to terms with the idea of death. Friends came and went, killed in action, never to return. But this was the first. The war, and the 'phoney' war at that, had touched me personally. Drogo was dead and Bill would never know him.

The funeral at Hinchinbrook was a harrowing experience. I went there with Father who sat in the back of the car with his secretary while I perched on one of the occasional seats facing him. Lunch was an ordeal. Drogo's mother made one of her rare appearances, surrounded by her family; her husband, her remaining son and her two daughters, Betty and Faith. The atmosphere was sombre, as one might expect, but I couldn't help thinking how Drogo himself would have laughed at our grim-faced, black-clothed figures sitting round the table. Two senior RAF officers came to the church, and by the time the service was over, I had reached such a depth of depression that all I wanted to do was to go away and be by myself. Drogo had died on a training flight, an accident that had also killed the young man he was teaching to fly. It was all so unfair, and such a terrible waste.

On the journey home, the secretary saw my obvious misery and suggested I sit in his more comfortable seat. I was grateful, but Father objected. When he saw I was close to tears, he followed up by demanding that I should be present at dinner as there were to be several guests. 'When we get home,' he said, 'go and have a good cry. Get it over with.' I found it wasn't that easy. I read a telegram of sympathy from Tanis and went up to my room. In spite of everything, Drogo had wanted to remain my friend. I couldn't forget my last words to him: 'Give it time.'

The 'phoney war' spluttered and smoked like a freshly lit fire. During the first three months of 1940, I built up my herd of large whites and, like everyone else, hoped for the best. Paddy Green came over from nearby Tangmere and told me that 601 Squadron was at last being equipped with Hurricanes. Father, who had been to Washington and had established a warm relationship with President Roosevelt, told me he believed that if Hitler attacked at all, he would do so through Sweden and not the Low Countries. He was wrong about that, of course, but he did predict correctly that, contrary to the opinion of the entire Air Ministry (except Sir Hugh Dowding), the daylight bomber would be no match for the fighter.

Throughout the war, Father wanted me to go to Cherkley whenever possible. He liked me to help entertain his guests and we enjoyed our rare evenings together when he would ask my opinion, no matter how ill-informed, on widely differing issues. His private life was beginning to centre round Lily Ernst who was soon to move into Jean Norton's cottage on the estate. Jean simply went away, and became deeply involved in war work. It all seemed a bit too convenient to me but I didn't ask questions. Lily Ernst, however, proved to be of great help to Father, translating Hitler's speeches and other Nazi broadcasts heard on an enormous radio receiver he had installed at Cherkley. Their relationship was deeper than I had thought and was to last several years.

When Hitler invaded Norway on 8 April, I thought Father had been right. Then, a month later almost to the day, the German army swept into Holland and Belgium, removing all opposition from its path. The 'phoney war' was over.

* * *

I was at Stornoway House on 11 May, the day after Winston became Prime Minister. An urgent message had reached me via Tracadie that I was wanted at Shoreham air base. I went looking for Father to say goodbye. We met in the hall. 'Is my asthma very bad?' he asked. It was an unusual question. Asthma was something we had both learned to live with. We seldom spoke about it. 'No,' I said, hesitatingly, 'I don't think so. No worse than usual. Why?' He didn't answer me. A quick kiss goodbye and he was gone again, back into his study.

When I arrived at Shoreham, I was met by a harrassed station commander who ushered me into his office and pointed at a cardboard box with holes in it. 'For you,' he said. 'Probably against the law, but I promised.'

'Who? What is it?'

'Don't know,' he replied, 'but it squeaks. A Hurricane pilot flew it in last night. He's gone again now.'

We never established the name of that pilot. He was probably killed during those first terrible days of the Battle of France. But his story survived. He had been waylaid by an elderly Dutchman in the streets of Amsterdam shortly before the city fell to the Germans. The Dutchman had pleaded with him to take the box to England, to a farm somewhere, and to preserve the culmination of his life's work. The box contained six uniquely bred chicks. They were North Holland Blues; marvellous, dual-purpose birds, with a high yield of eggs and meat. I contacted Vere Harvey who, apart from being a member of 601 Squadron, was also a director of Phillips, the giant Dutch company. It was he who somehow provided me with one hundred hatching eggs. So started a twenty-year project, throughout which I always clung to the hope that either the pilot or the Dutchman from Amsterdam would hear about its success and come forward to share in it.

The Battle of France opened to such a crescendo of horror and confusion I can remember little of it in detail, except the names of some of the pilots who were killed at the very start; names like Jackie Munro-Hindes, Guy Branch, Americans Billy Clyde and Billy Fisk, and a Pole whose name was Oscar Ostowicz. Over half our aircraft were lost within a few days as the allied armies reeled and then buckled under the sudden, devastating onslaught of the *Wehrmacht* and their new *Blitzkrieg*. On 14 May, Father told me he had accepted the job of Minister of Aircraft Production. I knew then why he had asked about his asthma three days earlier. He didn't want to let anybody down. He knew the job was vital at the time, scarcely less important than that of the Prime Minister himself, because, as we all now realized, the fate of the army and indeed the nation depended on our ability to defend ourselves, to fight and eventually to win the war in the air.

Winston had often referred to Father as his 'foul weather friend'. During all the years of their close personal friendship, Father had been able to advise and encourage him, cheer him up, even make him laugh in times of trouble and adversity. 'Lord Beaverbrook was at his very best when things were at their very worst,' Churchill later wrote. Things could not have been much worse in May 1940. In the month before Father took the job, 256 new fighter planes had been produced. Aircraft production, under the aegis of the Air Ministry, was geared to bring the RAF to its peak in 1942. Now, squadron commanders, with both the BEF in France and the home bases, were crying out for replacement aircraft to combat the vastly superior numbers of the *Luftwaffe*.

Father used Stornoway House as his headquarters. He brought George Malcolm Thompson and David Farrer from the *Express* to be his personal assistants. They both worked themselves into the ground to make a success of it. He then asked Patrick Hennessy,

173

chairman of the Ford Motor Company, and Trevor Westbrook, from the City, to be his principal lieutenants. All his life, Father had the knack of choosing the right men for the job. Never before had this gift been so amply rewarded. Between them, Patrick and Trevor worked miracles. Father drove himself to the limit during those early days of the MAP. Under his inspiring leadership he encouraged, bullied and cajoled as the situation demanded. But he made enemies among those in the Air Ministry whom he ignored or bypassed at will – it mattered not: Churchill backed him, as did Air Marshall Sir Hugh Dowding, head of Fighter Command.

When I was finally able to reach him on the telephone, his questions were about Max, who, with his wife, Cynthia, was living close to Tangmere. 'How is he? Tell him to keep calling me.' Then he was off again, working round the clock to boost production, open new factories and workshops, not only to make the desperately needed fighters but also to repair them. Defying established Air Ministry policy, he and Trevor worked out a system of cannibalization – turning two or more damaged planes into one perfect, serviceable machine. Beg, borrow, buy or steal – he didn't care. The country needed fighters and he would supply them.

The battle on the Continent raged on, each day bringing new reverses, new anxieties. 601 had given birth to 92 Squadron the previous autumn. Now both were flying four or five sorties every day in support of the hardpressed army. Max was in the thick of it, shooting down seven Germans and earning himself the DFC.

One day I was at Tracadie when I saw a parachute descending over the nearby fields. The pilot dropped safely and walked in through the garden gate dragging his chute and demanding a double Scotch. It was Paddy. His Spitfire had been hit over the French coast on his way home. This was as far as he had got before the machine caught fire and he was forced to bale out. I drove him back to Tangmere and decided to stay on, sharing a house with Sibell Rowley on the edge of the airfield itself.

It was the most exciting, and the most heartbreaking time of my life. In the days that followed, I shared Cynthia's anxiety for Max and Sibell's for Michael Rowley. Time and again the squadrons set out for the skies above the beleaguered army now falling back towards Dunkirk. I offered Tracadie as a place for rest and relaxation, telling every pilot I met that my home, just sixteen miles away, was theirs as often as they needed it, whether I was there or not.

Apart from my brother Max, my special concern was now for Paddy. He was flying with 92 Squadron and had become very close to me. Often I would listen for their return, counting the number of planes coming in to land, and dreading the inevitable. They came in ones and twos, some with no more than a cupful of petrol left in their tanks, others with their wings and fuselages riddled with bullet holes, their engines coughing and streaming black smoke. In the late evenings, many of them would come to the house and I would see the exhaustion on their faces, an aching tiredness hidden behind their indomitable courage and forced gaiety. I was to get to know and recognize that look, through this battle and the next, until they had beaten the enemy fair and square.

As the nights drew on and vast quantities of drink were consumed, friends would fail to appear. Some were asleep in their own quarters, some late, having baled out over the south coast, others were never to return. We waited in vain for Willie Rhodes Morehouse, Jimmy Little and the neat and tidy barrister, Michael Peacock, but all were killed in the skies over France. Paddy's fellow South African, Roger Bushell (known as 'the Führer'), had taken command of 92 Squadron, flying Spitfires. Both he and Paddy survived those first weeks, but the Americans were not so lucky. Several fought with the RAF, before their own Eagle Squadron was born. One of them was Whitney Straight, a friend of Diana Barnato. He was later shot down and taken prisoner. Another was Billy Fisk. He came in to land at Tangmere, his plane so badly shot up I could see smoke in the cockpit and flames creeping along the fuselage. I watched in horror as his spluttering engine seemed to cut out on landing, then burst into flames. He was pulled out by firemen and taken to hospital, where his wife Rosie and I sat with him for two days and nights before he died in agony.

They were all 'aces' in their way. Living or dying, they would tell you, was largely a matter of luck. Some lengthened the odds very slightly by being superb flyers, although they would never admit to it. Brian Kingcome was one of these, together with Humphrey Gilbert and Roy Dutton. They counted their victories and were proud of them, but they would all say the same thing: 'It's the last battle that counts.'

As the British army fell back on Dunkirk, yet more desperate efforts were made to support them. Remnants of the fighter squadrons that had been based in France were now without airfields from which to operate. They flew back to England with their few remaining serviceable aircraft. 601 and 92 Squadrons flew round the clock as the days grew longer and the situation became more desperate. On 23 May, Roger Bushell was shot down over France and captured. Some years later, after two previous attempts, he organized the famous 'Great Escape'. Unlike Whitney Straight, who reached freedom through France and Spain, Roger himself was recaptured, then shot by the SS. That same day, Paddy, his friend and second-in-command, landed at Hawkinge, his cockpit swilling in blood from a terrible wound in his thigh.

Then the miracle of Dunkirk was upon us. For nine days the navy and the armada of valiant little ships struggled back and forth across the channel to rescue 340,000 British and allied soldiers. High above them, often unseen by the men on the beaches, the airmen fought on. I went to Folkestone to see if I could help. They gave me an ambulance to drive and told me to bring soldiers to the hospital from every ship that docked. The hastily written notice erected over the entrance lives in my memory to this day:

Dead to the Right – Wounded to the Left

There were men from many different countries and regiments among the rescued, but most were British or French. I saw one soldier from a Scottish regiment and wondered about Ian, fighting with the Argyll and Sutherland Highlanders. Later I was to know he had been captured at St Valery, badly shell-shocked, and spent the rest of the war as a prisoner. I was told how hard he had tried to keep the hopes and spirits of his men alive. He was helped in this by a regular supply of parcels sent by his wife, Louise, who became head of the Red Cross in Portugal.

Farming at Tracadie in 1940, where I kept three hundred 'large white' pigs.

ABOVE: 'You mustn't overdo it,' I used to say to Father.

LEFT: My brother Peter, who was killed in a yachting accident just after the war.

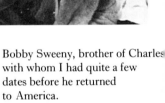

Bobby Sweeny, brother of Charles with whom I had quite a few dates before he returned to America.

ABOVE LEFT: Valentine Castleross who was responsible for the *Sunday Express* Londoner's Log, smoking his pipe amidst friends of mine at Cherkley Court

LEFT: The German Heinkel which was shot down by Peter Dunning-White after it had fired bullets and dropped incendiaries over my farm, killing four pigs and destroying a large piggery.

ABOVE RIGHT: My brother Max, waiting to take off in a Mosquito.

RIGHT: Paddy Green and Bolshie Bartley, two of my greatest friends in fighter command.

Captain Edward Daltry Kidd and I were married on 11 July 1942.

Cappy, as he was always called, relaxing on forty-eight hours' leave.

RIGHT: Cappy and Max.

Our first child, Margaret Jane, playing with her father.

My four children at Tracadie: Bill, Jeanne,
Jane and Johnny.

Grown up: (left to right) Bill, Jeanne, Jane and
Johnny, with me in the middle.

Chatting with Father in the garden at Cherkley
Court on his 84th birthday.

My good friends Lord and Lady Avon with me
in Barbados.

An important win in combined
driving at the Hickstead
Driving Derby.

Painting in my studio at Slythehurst.

LEFT: Captain Bob Baff handing Johnny and me our
helicopter licences on 9 July 1968, my 60th birthday.

When the last defeated but defiant soldier had been disembarked, I went to see Paddy in hospital and from there drove to London. I owned a Railton in those days; a car with a prodigious thirst but the ability to get me quickly from one place to the next. Three hectic weeks had passed since I had last seen Father. During that time, he had revolutionized the system of aircraft production. In the first month, he had increased the supply of fighters to 325 and quadrupled the number repaired. He had also instigated the transatlantic ferry run (which the Air Ministry had said was impossible), putting a colourful Canadian, Jack Bickell, in charge. In the summer of 1940, they flew 160 American war planes to the UK. Only one was lost. Air Chief Marshal Sir Hugh Dowding wrote in his official report: 'I saw my resources slipping away like sand in an hour glass. . . . The effect of Lord Beaverbrook's appointment can only be described as magical. . . .'

At Cherkley, the first thing I noticed was its transformation from being a meeting place for top politicians and international newspaper owners, to one for engineers, designers of fighter planes and armament specialists of all kinds. They doubled up in bedrooms and ate in shifts. The housekeeper, who had been with us for fifty years, began to think her world had been turned irrevocably upside down. When I saw Father, I noticed the strain already showing in his eyes. But he seemed to have his asthma under control. 'I'm treading on a lot of people's corns,' he said cheerfully, 'but it can't be helped. We'll win in the end.'

Trevor Westbrook took me to supper. 'The first thing your father did was to call a few of the senior pilots,' he told me. 'They came to Cherkley. All of them were young and on active service. He asked *them* whether they preferred canons or guns. The answer was canons.' This was typical of Father. To him, the men that mattered most were the ones that did the fighting. He would back them to the limit. Increased manoeuvrability, more speed, canon over machine gun (Air Ministry sacrilege!), the ten-ton bomb, the Whittle jet – all were things Father fought for, some of them in the teeth of resentment and opposition from the air marshals. He was responsible to only one man, Churchill, who had given him draconian powers and supported his efforts to the end.

I was with him on two of his lightning trips at that time; to Bristol and Southampton, where I watched him win the hearts of men and women on the production lines by his enthusiasm and the power of his personality. Some loved him, but even those who did not were inspired by his words and his obvious sincerity. It was a race against time. As the *Wehrmacht* turned south towards Paris and beyond, the *Luftwaffe* began to mass planes at newly captured airfields on the French north coast. On 13 June, Father interrupted his efforts and went with Winston to Tours in a last despairing effort to stiffen French resistance. But three weeks later, with her armies in total disarray, France surrendered.

*　　*　　*

At Tracadie, my main concern was pigswill. With various helpers, including two girls from the Land Army, to take care of the animals themselves, I hitched a trailer to the Railton and foraged far and wide in search of edible garbage. The Savoy Grill in London was one of my main suppliers. I knew some of the older staff from pre-war days and visited them once a week, carrying off drums of the precious stuff. Then I found the wonderful Bartholomew family who owned the Norfolk Hotel in Brighton. Apart from providing me with plenty of swill, they donated a swimming pool for the pilots at Biggin Hill in memory of their son, killed with the RAF. That pool didn't last long, I'm afraid. Biggin Hill was bombed incessantly during the Battle of Britain. 92 Squadron, now without Roger Bushell and Paddy, their founder members from 601, flew continuously from this historic airfield until the battle was won.

My brother Max didn't fly in the Battle of Britain. With over forty missions to his credit, and 601 Squadron posted for regrouping and re-equipment, he was summoned to the Air Ministry in London and from there sent to a northern base to train night-fighters. New faces appeared at Tracadie now, many of them introduced by Paddy, who, although grounded by his terrible wound, would later be flying again on high-altitude reconnaissance missions. I was determined that my home should continue to provide as much of a sanctuary as possible to any fighter pilot who had twenty-four hours leave; more or even less. I wish I could mention the names of all who came there. Some were no more than fleeting visitors, their faces forgotten but their names forever recorded on the RAF memorial at Runnymede. I remember Peter Dunning-White; Henry Cavendish, a fine, careful and much-liked pilot; Brian Thynn and Johnny Peel. Then there was Billy Drake, full of fun and practical jokes; and Bob Holland, who played a great jazz piano when he wasn't shooting down Germans.

Old friends continued to come to Tracadie too; Brian Kingcome, soon to be in command of 92 Squadron; and Harry Edwards, the Canadian, soon to die. Humphrey Gilbert also came. He was a natural pilot, a man who lived as hard as he fought. He finally died flying tandem with a friend in a Spitfire; a feat few have attempted and lived to talk about. They had girlfriends naturally enough; friends of mine who, apart from their own personal relationships, were deeply involved in every life-or-death struggle being fought out in the skies above us. Our stories, sometimes frivolous, often tragic, illustrate something of the feverish pace at which we lived; one minute with laughter, the next with sadness and compassion, but always with the desire to take and give happiness while there was still time. Tomorrow might be too late.

Naomi Bourne has been my friend ever since those days. In 1940, she was waiting for a divorce from her prewar husband and had fallen in love with two pilots; Brian Thynn, kinsman to the Marquess of Bath, and Johnny Peel. Johnny was renowned as a swimmer, having been shot down three times in the English Channel and survived. 'I'll marry one of them,' Naomi said, 'on the day the divorce comes through.'

'Which one?' I asked.

'Don't know yet.' And she still didn't know at noon on the appointed day. Brian and Johnny waited. They had no idea which one it would be. At 1 p.m. she chose Brian. I never knew why particularly, but the afternoon was one long celebration. Both pilots were on 'ops' the next day and never ceased to be friends.

Then there were the twins, Sheila and Moira MacNeal. Everybody loved them. Sheila, whose husband had already been killed in action, had a young daughter, Leslie. When Brian Kingcome was badly wounded, I visited him in hospital. His thoughts were for Moira that day, little knowing that when the war was over, he would marry Sheila's daughter. Sibell, by then Lady Sibell Rowley, lived from day to day, wondering if or when her husband, Michael, would return to her. Michael survived the war but died soon afterwards from a brain tumour, the accumulated result of the unbearable strain of continuous air combat. Sibell nursed him till the day he died.

My own experiences were less heart-breaking and often hilarious, although some of them were frightening. We were bombed at Tracadie. 'Straffed' might be more accurate, because, apart from dropping incendiary bombs, the Heinkel that attacked us opened up with machine guns too. I was in the big field with my young daughter Jeanne and Sibell, rounding up a selection of large whites from the main herd, when I looked up and saw a strange, twin-engine aircraft circling overhead. To start with, I thought it might be one of the boys from Biggin Hill or Tangmere. They sometimes buzzed the farm just to say hello. But this was no Blenheim, the silhouette looked wrong. Then I saw the markings. I yelled at Jeanne, who was some way off, to run for the ditch, then Sibell and I threw ourselves flat as the first bullets started snapping into the grass around us. The Heinkel banked and circled again, keeping up a continuous fire, before levelling out to fly down the line of pig pens, dropping incendiaries as he went. Then he departed, only to do the same thing to the village of Henfield, straffing the main street and shopping area. But luckily it was a Sunday and nobody was killed. Our own casualties at Tracadie were four pigs dead, one wounded and a fire in one of the pens.

That evening the phone rang. It was Peter Dunning-White. 'We got that Heinkel that straffed you,' he said. 'Thought you might like to know.' By 'we', I knew he meant 'I'. It was typical of them somehow. 'Thank you,' was all I could find to say.

'Was anyone hurt?' asked Peter.

'No,' I said. 'Do you like roast pork?' He did. At our celebration feast he told me where the Heinkel had crashed. The next day I went and took a photograph of it.

Paddy was a very jealous man. Perhaps it was his wound, and

the frustration it was causing him, that made him so jealous. He went through a stage of firing warning shots from his service revolver at anyone in air force blue who came up the drive. He did this from his bedroom window, alternately shouting with laughter and feigned outrage, but he was careful not to hit anybody. The only person to take genuine umbrage at being shot at was Roy Dutton. He was a regular RAF pilot who lived for the Service and retired, highly decorated, as an Air Commodore. Roy and Paddy developed a healthy dislike for one another, made more acute by the fact that Roy liked me, and loved farming. He was good at it and helped a great deal, as did many of them. Paddy's wound, however, confined him to light work, if any at all. Things came to a head one night when Roy complained to the assembled company that Paddy's last shot had passed inches over his head. 'We get shot at all day by Germans,' he said, 'now the bloody Boer's doing it!' Hoots of laughter from the pilots. I hoped Pady hadn't heard, but he had.

'Stay out of her bedroom,' he growled. 'You've been warned!' My own embarrassment was swamped in more laughter, but when I looked at Roy, I saw a new glint in his eye.

The next morning, a lone Spitfire flew low over Tracadie while Paddy and I were drinking coffee in the garden. Two pants and a bra floated earthwards to land on the lawn and surrounding flowerbeds. They were mine. Paddy's fury was an unforgettable sight.

We went to Biggin Hill quite often during the Battle of Britain. Paddy spent hours with the fighter pilots, sharing their experiences, encouraging them, and wishing with all his heart that he could be one of them again. I saw the havoc caused by enemy bombs, the pitted runway and the wrecked and burnt-out aircraft dotted round the perimeter. More than once we had to dive for the shelters, as another wave of German aircraft appeared overhead and the deadly bombs dropped once more, sucking and blasting at the air, sending up huge gouts of flaming earth and debris. The noise was ear-splitting, punctuated by harsh shouts, anti-aircraft fire, explosions and the sound of furiously revving engines as those Spitfires still on the ground, rearming and refuelling, struggled to get airborne through the crash of bombs and their still-smoking craters.

At the end of each day they would count the cost, as battle-weary pilots converged on their mess, eager for a drink to celebrate the victory and deaden the sadness. Aircraft could be replaced. Father would see to that, or die in the attempt. But for the men themselves, the pilots, it was a different story. They were so valuable, so desperately needed, so few. Each death was a blow at the heart of the nation.

One evening early in 1940, while 92 Squadron was forming in Gatwick, a young man smiled at me over the top of his beer mug. 'Who's that?' I asked.

Paddy recognized him instantly. He seemed surprised we hadn't already met. 'Meet Tony Bartley,' he said.

'Can we take him back with us for dinner?'

'To Tracadie? No, he's been too bolshie today.' On the drive home, I remarked how young he had looked. 'Don't let that one fool you,' said Paddy. 'He's fought in almost every air battle since before Dunkirk.'

'Why was he being bolshie?' I asked.

'He gets that way sometimes,' said Paddy vaguely. Pilots knew each other very well in those days. So 'Bolshie' it was, and 'Bolshie' it has remained to this day. For Tony Bartley has been one of my dearest friends ever since.

The bar at Tracadie assumed an even greater importance with the arrival of Bolshie. We all tried to keep it well stocked and developed an alarm system for the occasions when Father paid us a visit. Father disapproved of my bar and offered me £1000 to close it down.

I think it was Bolshie who devised the 'Bar Alert' and honed it to perfection. One minute the place was hopping with up to twenty hard-drinking pilots and their girlfriends, and within moments it resembled a library reading-room, with young men and women sitting about in twos and threes looking studious and innocent. Every bottle and glass had its own hiding place. Father never discovered the truth, and I never collected the £1000.

On 16 August we organized a fête at Tracadie in aid of Father's

Spitfire Fund. Most of the pilots at Biggin Hill were on 'ops' that day, but they must have spread the word because other flyers turned up from different squadrons, many of them wounded, others on overdue leave. All came to help. One young officer dressed himself as an old woman and told fortunes, peering knowledgeably into an upturned glass bowl and voicing his predictions at a pound a time, between slurps from a gin bottle hidden under the table. I was returning to the house to fetch more lemonade for the soft drinks booth, when I saw a flight lieutenant with his back towards me, gazing away across the open fields. 'Hello,' I said. 'Do you want to help?' The man turned. He had no face; just two lidless eyes above nostrils and an oval gap where his mouth had once been. His skin was paper thin, livid and scarred, his hands no more than claws.

'I'd like to.' His voice seemed no part of him. I had seen men like this before; pilots who had struggled out of their blazing cockpits, hands and face seared by the sudden, blinding flames.

'We'll think of something for you,' I said. 'In the meantime, relax and help yourself from the bar.' He did his own thinking. He made his friends erect a small tent and set himself up as an exhibit. They painted a notice on a board and hung it outside. It read:

FREAK SHOW
Come and see the man with no face!
Admittance £1
Adults only

And they queued, those English people, because they knew. They went inside and talked to him; ordinary civilians, men and women, with a sprinkling from the army and navy as well. When it was all over, they counted up the money. He had collected over £100 for the fund, yet fewer than fifty people had entered his tent. There had been no time for more. I am not sure who that burned pilot was. Some say Richard Hilary, others Geoffrey Page. But of one thing I am certain. Either John Gillies or Archibald McIndoe would have given him a new face once the scars had had time to heal. Their brilliance as plastic surgeons in those early days, when burned pilots were referred to as 'guinea pigs', became legendary.

The fête was a huge success. Everyone contributed something. Ambrose and his famous orchestra performed for nothing, and the Dewar family contributed no less than half of our total take of £10,000, which I handed to Father.

Father was in the War Cabinet and he had produced no less than 942 fighter aircraft. He received a letter from Winston Churchill saying, 'The figures you gave me of the improvement of operational planes between 10 May and 30 August are magnificent. The country is your debtor, and of your Ministry.' By October 1940, the Battle of Britain had been won. Almost a quarter of our front-line pilots were either dead, wounded or prisoners-of-war. We had lost 915 aircraft, as against 1733 of the enemy's which had been destroyed. Hitler had been forced to think again before attempting an invasion. Then came the Blitz. For nine months the *Luftwaffe* concentrated on London and the industrial cities in a series of massive night-time bombing raids, aimed at the destruction of Britain's war material – particularly aircraft – and the morale of her people.

In early September I went to Cherkley to be with Father. During the previous four months I had seen him whenever possible, particularly on my forays to London in search of pigswill. On each occasion I had noticed his deteriorating health; his weakness caused by overwork and the increasingly frequent attacks of asthma which resulted in his inability to sleep. His old friend R. B. Bennett, no longer Prime Minister of Canada, had arrived in England and bought a house near Cherkley. He immediately offered his services to Father's Ministry and was accepted with gratitude. They saw each other frequently, all differences on Empire Free Trade now forgotten. Father never asked me to go with him on his visits to the factories. It was not his way. But when he climbed into the back of the car and saw me already waiting for him, I'd get a grunt and a half smile. I knew he was pleased.

'Winston won't let me go,' he said on one occasion. 'I told him I was too old and sick. Don't want to let him down.' We would drive on in silence after that, Father studying the sheaf of papers in his lap. No detail escaped him. 'Vickers were bombed. They're down a bit – not much. That's where we're going.' I remember the occasion well. It was 1 September 1940. Trevor Westbrook was with us. We arrived at Brooklands and within minutes thousands of workers were assembled to hear him. He spoke through a portable loud-hailer which he always carried with him. 'You're in the front line,' he told them. 'You and you alone can win this war.' They cheered him, and cheered again when he asked them to keep working when the sirens sounded and not go to the shelters. Then, in answer to some dissenting voices, the majority sang 'Run, Rabbit, Run'. We left soon afterwards, but not before Father had walked about among them, shaking hands, encouraging them, asking for problems, details, anything that hindered the urgency of their work.

Then on to Southampton and the Supermarine works where many of the workforce seemed to know him and welcome him as an old friend. Then on to Bristol and back to Cherkley, wheezing and coughing, still poring over his papers, glad to be back in his study where he could use the telephone. Sometimes he worked all night. Three days later, Vickers received a direct hit. One hundred and seventy workers who had stuck to their posts were killed. Five hundred and fifty more were injured. I was still at Cherkley when the news reached Father and I saw tears in his eyes.

On 20 September, the Supermarine works at Southampton was also hit. Fifteen people died and forty were injured. Father was up all night, prowling through the house, knowing that something drastic and immediate had to be done if the successes of the past months were not to be wiped out in a heap of smoking rubble. By morning he looked haggard and exhausted, but an idea was already beginning to take shape. Soon, Trevor Westbrook and Patrick Hennessy arrived and together they hammered out the answer: Dispersal.

Father now embarked on a period of feverish and continuous activity as an entire industry was dismantled and relocated. Time and again he drove with Patrick or Trevor to the major centres of production – Brooklands, Southampton, Bristol, Coventry – and from there to the hundreds of small locations dotted throughout England. Here, aircraft components could be made, safe from the massive city bombing. They found workshops, garages, small rural factories, film studios, farm buildings, warehouses and even laundries; commandeering, emptying and refitting them for the vital task ahead. On some occasions I went too, and once saw him wheel a barrow-load of scrap iron out through the door of an ancient factory, then turn to the astonished manager: 'See, didn't take long. You can do it.' An overly dramatic gesture, perhaps, but it made them all laugh, and the work got done.

They continued with no halt, no let-up, spiriting away the vital machinery from the devastated cities until production was once again running at full tilt. Only Father's dynamic personality could have achieved this goal. Often he had to demand, even hijack, the materials or manpower he needed, later confronting the Air Ministry and officialdom, and when necessary riding rough-shod over their objections. 'Nobody knows the trouble I've seen,' he wrote to Churchill. 'I do,' Winston replied.

The Blitz raged on and shortly afterwards Stornoway House was razed by a direct hit. Father bought himself an armoured car and moved into a flat in the Admiralty air raid shelter for the nights he wanted to be in London. With the new year, his health broke down completely and Winston was at last persuaded to at least consider shifting the burden of aircraft production on to someone else's shoulders. But it was not until May 1941 that he finally did so. He appointed Moore Brabazon to the job and made Father Minister of State with offices at No. 12 Downing Street. I think he wanted to keep his 'foul weather friend' close to him.

Britain now had all the fighter aircraft she needed, and many more were on the way. Bomber production was fast increasing, along with aircraft for army support and the Royal Navy. It had been a close-run thing. Much later, the two people most concerned with the nation's fortunes during the Battle of Britain and the Blitz were to write the following:

From Air Marshal Lord Dowding, Head of Fighter Command:

We had the organization, we had the men, we had the spirit which could bring us victory in the air but we had not the supply of machines necessary to withstand the drain of continuous battle. Lord Beaverbrook gave us those machines, and I do not believe that I exaggerate when I say that no other man in England could have done so.

And from Winston Churchill, Prime Minister:
'He did not fail. This was his hour.'

11

At Tracadie the quest for pigswill and petrol still kept me occupied. I needed the latter to get the former, on which my entire project depended. I still kept open house for all fighter pilots. They drank, ate, played, slept, rode horses, worked on the farm and, when possible, contributed petrol coupons. Unknown to anybody, Peter's unit of the Royal Fusiliers had been serving in London's dockland, and at the height of the Blitz my younger brother had been very badly wounded in the leg. He now came to Tracadie to recuperate. His relationship with Barbara had sadly come to an abrupt end when, furious with her for some reason, he had thrown her wedding ring out of the window. He never found it, so she never got it. But his good fortune with the girls didn't desert him. Shortly afterwards he met Patricia Maguire, a charming and delightful Australian, who selflessly nursed him as his horribly mangled leg slowly began to mend.

Paddy, still furiously jealous, was now sufficiently recovered to begin to fly reconnaissance missions from Hawkinge. Bolshie, like most veteran pilots after the Battle of Britain, had been posted to a training squadron and then tested new Spitfires, straight from the factory. He came to Tracadie on leave, frustrated at not being in the thick of a battle somewhere. The truth was that he had been in continuous action for one year, had been shot down, landed in a haystack, and burst both eardrums in a vertical dive on a Messerschmidt 109. He didn't seem to care much for counting his 'kills', but the final records show that there were between fifteen and twenty-two.

The Blitz highlighted the RAF's desperate need for nightfighters. Max, in his northern training base, was now deeply involved in this new, difficult and largely untried technique using the new Beaufighter. His lovely wife, Cynthia, crashed her car into a fallen tree and lost for ever the use of her left arm which had been almost severed in the accident. Feeling sad and depressed by this tragedy, I could do no more than ask her to Tracadie to recuperate as soon as she came out of hospital.

On 22 June 1941, Hitler attacked Russia and in doing so made the greatest mistake in German military history. In the same month, Father had been made Minister of Supply, and soon afterwards flew out to join Churchill and Roosevelt aboard the battleship *Prince of Wales* in Placentia Bay, Newfoundland. Father's view that no war against Germany could be won without Russia's help was now becoming widely held. The *Wehrmacht*, revealed in all its awesome strength, had rolled back the massive Russian armies and now stood poised at the gates of Moscow. Britain's communist ally needed help, fast.

Father returned to London with Averell Harriman, one of the most thoughtful and courageous friends England has ever had. Together they were to visit Moscow, meet Stalin, and find out what the Russians needed most. I went to London to see them off. Father looked cheerful and optimistic. His asthma seemed under control. He had just returned from interviewing Rudolf Hess who had parachuted into England with an outrageous suggestion from Hitler to the effect that Russia was our mutual enemy. Father took a transcript of that interview to Moscow and showed it to Stalin, an action which served to instil added trust and confidence. When they left to join the cruiser HMS *London* at Scapa Flow for the voyage to Archangel, I asked Averell to take care of him. 'Sure,' he said, 'if I can keep up.'

From Moscow, Father sent a report vividly describing the desperate situation he found there. The Germans were only a few miles outside the city, and most foreign embassies were making plans to evacuate. When he returned to London, he was more than ever convinced that Russia should be given all possible aid, even to the extent of diverting much-needed American arms and equipment destined for the UK and the Middle East.

In early December 1941 I was in London with Father. He was already thinking of a second front, or at least some diversionary move to draw off German military strength and ease the pressure on Russia. He advocated this in spite of the fact that the United States was still not directly involved. He did not have long to wait. On 7 December, the Japanese attacked Pearl Harbor, and in doing so made *their* greatest mistake. I was dining with Father, Averell and others in a room deep beneath the fortified building adjoining the Admiralty Arch. The news of Pearl Harbor had already prompted Roosevelt to tell Winston: 'We are all in the same boat now.' But when, on the following night, after America had officially declared war, I heard Averell say, 'There is a future for us now,' I felt a deep conviction, perhaps for the first time, that, in spite of the sacrifices, the tragedies and the enormous loss of life yet to come, we could and would now win the war.

A week later, Father went to Washington with Churchill. Father, more than anyone else, underlined the urgency of Britain and Russia's need for military aid. He had long enjoyed a close relationship with the American President and the results were impressive. 'Max has been magnificent . . .' Winston cabled back to London.

In February 1942, Father resigned from the Government and in the following month flew again to see President Roosevelt, who himself favoured a second front that year. He spoke on American radio and when he returned he addressed a crowd of fifty thousand people in Birmingham, echoing his newspapers' call for a 'Second Front Now' which was spread by graffiti all over the kingdom. Churchill was against it, and events were to prove him right. The military reverses of Tobruk, Singapore and Dieppe delayed the longed-for European invasion for two years.

*   *   *

American and Canadian troops were arriving in ever-increasing numbers by March 1942. One morning at Tracadie I opened the door to find a young Canadian army officer standing there with a letter in his hand. 'I'm Chip Drury,' he said, 'your cousin.' He was as charming and as much fun to be with as his father, my mother's brother, with whom I had spent those happy months on the Canadian ski-slopes in the company of Jacques Hubert, my first boyfriend, seventeen years earlier. Having discussed the family, the war and the weather, we got around to the ever-pressing subject of pigswill. I knew that the Canadians, like the Americans, got plenty to eat. Did they have much left over? 'Tons of it,' replied Chip. 'You'd better meet the Captain.' I couldn't wait.

Captain Edward Daltry Kidd, of Kingston, Ontario, had been one of the first Canadians to arrive in England. He and his artillary unit had fought in the Battle of France and had been evacuated, without their guns, from Bordeaux at the time of Dunkirk. This had happened before Chip had joined them, and now the unit was stationed about five miles away, in the requisitioned house and grounds of Sir Benjamin Brodie, where they were being reorganized and re-equipped. 'Sure we've got garbage,' said the Captain. 'Take all you want.' I took the lot. It was manna from heaven. I filled up my containers and asked when they were next going to eat. 'Tonight,' he said. 'Tomorrow you get the leftovers.'

And that's the way it happened. 'Cappy', for we all called him that, was one of those fortunate people whom strangers liked on sight. I was no exception. He was very tall and lean, with a strong face and a glint of humour always in his eyes. 'I wooed her with the swill,' he would say for years after. But it was not quite true. Admittedly, the swill played an important part in it to start with, but more than anything else I liked the quiet, confident way he did things, and his unruffled good nature when they went wrong, as they often did. He was a solitary person at times, retiring with a book for long periods, after which he would emerge like a recharged battery to brighten the lives of all who came near him.

As the weeks passed, and the large whites munched happily on the regimental leftovers, I discovered that Cappy was filling a gap in my life I never knew existed. I could depend on him as a person; not so much on what he did, but because, success or failure, I knew he would still be there afterwards – and still be the same person. The other men in my life had been like stars flashing in a sky filled with excitement and uncertainty. Ian, Drogo, even Paddy; all were wonderful in their way, but unstable. Cappy was different.

'But he's a coolie,' said Max on the phone, 'you can't be serious.'

191

All fighter pilots referred to soldiers as 'coolies' in those days. God knows what they called the sailors. When they met, however, Max liked him immediately, as I knew he would. So did Peter. Paddy, on the other hand, indulged in a fit of such jealousy I thought he'd gone mad. 'I'll blow us up!' he raved. 'Crash my bloody plane on your house and we'll all go together.' But he didn't. He flew his sky blue, unarmed Spitfire high into the atmosphere and took photos of German installations for the bombers who came later. Paddy returned to South Africa when the war was over, and married a different Canadian girl.

So that left Father, because by now Cappy and I were serious. Our feelings for each other had grown rapidly throughout the spring and early summer months. Unlike Peter, who was soon to marry Patricia Maguire in a registry office, little caring if Father was there or not (which he wasn't), I wanted my brilliant, if unpredictable, parent to like, or at least meet, the man I now loved. We drove to Cherkley and parked in the yew forest. We hid the car because Father took a very dim view of anyone using petrol for pleasure trips – except RAF pilots on leave, for whom he had already organized a small ration. We were going to tell him we came by bus.

I showed Cappy the tree house, which looked small and forlorn, its timbers rotten after so many years of neglect. He listened to my childhood memories of Bonar Law, Kipling, Lloyd George and Winston; all seen from up there. And I told him about Tim Healy, my best friend, who had hammered in some of these nails which now hung, rusted, from the blackened, broken wood. We were standing in the bridle path when we saw two horsemen approaching through the trees. Father and Michael Foot rode up.

'Is that your car parked back there?'

'Father, I'd like you to meet . . .'

'Why are you hiding it? How did you get the petrol?'

'How do you do?' said Michael Foot. Father glared at the uniformed figure of Cappy standing beside me. He was studying the insignia. Slowly a broad grin spread over his face.

'We're thinking of getting married,' I said quickly, taking advantage of his sudden change of mood.

He wasn't a bit shaken. 'Then we'd all better go to the house,' he said, 'to celebrate.' Cappy thanked him. Canadians have a way of backing each other up at awkward moments. We were drinking champagne when we heard the sound of a light aircraft circling very low. It was some sort of communications plane, probably a Proctor. After one more circuit, it executed a perfect landing and taxied up to the garden gate. Max and Bolshie got out and walked towards us. 'Why are *you* here?' Father asked Max angrily. 'Where have you been?'

I already knew the answer, and felt again the sudden, familiar sadness. They had been to a funeral. 'Humphrey Gilbert was killed,' said Max shortly. Father was silent. He turned away.

'I'm sorry,' said Cappy. 'Was he a great friend of yours?' Max and Bolshie merely nodded.

'Well, you must leave,' Father said gruffly. 'I can't have private aircraft landing here in wartime.'

Max took off again soon afterwards. But first he asked me to walk with him to the plane. 'Take care of Bolshie,' he said quietly. 'Take him to Tracadie if you can. He's got a bit of leave. Make him rest. You'll see why.' One close look was enough. Behind the friendly grin, Bolshie's eyes looked haunted. We kept him for twenty-four hours, then he was off again, this time to command a Spitfire squadron at Debden. Later, he was sent to do the same thing in North Africa where he won his second DFC. Bolshie typified so many veteran pilots. Sooner or later, the unrelenting pressure of air combat and the continuous shock and sadness of seeing their friends die, caught up with them.

Cappy and I were married on 11 July 1942 in the old Norman church at Henfield. Father was in London, deep in consultation with Churchill about his forthcoming trip to Russia, so Max gave me away. Peter, his leg still in plaster, arrived with Patricia. It was quite an occasion. The church was full of Canadian officers; a solid phalanx of khaki, headed by General Anderson who acted as Cappy's best man. But here and there, dotted about the church, were figures in RAF blue. Some of their faces I didn't recognize, but I gave them all a big smile of welcome. At the altar rail, Cappy whispered something I couldn't hear.

'What?' I whispered back.

'He insists on doing it,' Cappy whispered louder.

'Who? What?'

'You'll see.' Cappy's batman advanced to the centre of the church as the congregation sat and the organ ground out the opening bars. He then embarked on the most remarkable rendering of 'I'll Walk Beside You' that I have ever heard. His voice, pitched in that nether region between tenor and baritone, rose and fell as if in torment, heedless of the postmistress's efforts to keep up. His final notes, executed with a most theatrical gesture, and well ahead of the organ, ranged from high alto to basso profundo. It brought tears to the eyes.

When the festivities were over, Cappy and I returned to Tracadie which was to be our home for the next three years. Jeanne and Bill both liked my new husband, and he spent much time with them, riding and working on the farm. His headquarters were near enough for him to come home whenever he was free, even for an hour or two. But he often reminded me that everything the army did was now a rehearsal for the invasion of France, and that one day soon we would be parted. They were happy times, but I never allowed myself to forget that beyond the tranquillity of our own home, the war was continuing in all its brutal savagery.

In August 1942, the Duke of Kent was killed in an air crash and mourned by his lovely young wife and the whole nation. I remembered him best as Prince George, that happy midshipman of long ago, with his enormous dog and his ability to make me feel feminine and attractive when, after the car accident, I was in need of that most. Then, in December, Doris Castlerosse died. She was Valentine's first wife and, for better or for worse, his greatest love. Valentine married again shortly afterwards but himself died in September of the following year. I know Father felt deeply the loss of his old friend. I felt it a bit too. I'd never really liked Valentine very much, but he was part of the family in a way.

In May 1943, Father went again to see President Roosevelt, this time with Winston, and a few months later rejoined the Government as Lord Privy Seal. He came to Tracadie soon after that, because on 3 June, my second daughter, Jane, was born. Father was impressed with my new baby but spent most of his time, as I knew he would, with Jeanne, whom he consistently adored. As he walked round the farm, he told us that he had bought a farm at Cricket Malherbie in Somerset and invited Jeanne to stay with him whenever she wished. Jeanne was fifteen now, and I could see that even at that unpredictable age, she always loved being with him. Father also told me that his sister, my Aunt Gyp, now Mrs Stickney, had arrived from Canada and was living at The Vineyard. She had established it as a home and rendezvous point for Canadian servicemen on leave. Aunt Gyp worked twenty-four hours a day at her job and became something of a legend; a sort of universal aunt, of whom many Canadians still cherish very warm memories. Later, I found out that Father was also doing something similar; keeping in touch with relations of friends and sending fruit and flowers to the wounded.

In December, Father flew to Marrakesh to be with Winston Churchill during his convalescence. Winston had caught pneumonia shortly after his meeting with Roosevelt and Stalin at Teheran. Again his 'foul weather friend' was near him. Peter must have made some sort of temporary peace with Father at this time, because when he married Patricia they moved into a cottage at the end of the Cherkley drive. They were to have two sons, Tim and Peter, who grew up to be charming and very, very bright, earning reputations for themselves as shrewd, sharp businessmen on both sides of the Atlantic. Peter's wound never recovered sufficiently for him to resume active service. Later on, he was invalided out of the army before the war ended.

Max, whose DFC had been pinned to his tunic by the Commander-in-Chief himself, now received the Czech War Cross from the hands of President Benes, head of their government in exile. Having completed one tour in night-fighters and another in the Middle East, he commanded a wing of Mosquitos operating over the Norwegian coastline. Later he was promoted to Group Captain and awarded the DSO. He and Cynthia were divorced in 1944. Cynthia came to stay with me, her place in Max's affections now taken by the remarkably attractive Lady Isobel Mills Lade. Cynthia, as beautiful as ever despite the terrible injury to her arm, was obviously deeply depressed. But when, in May, the irrepressible Bolshie arrived after a long absence, she began to regain something of her old vitality and sparkle. 'She's beautiful, Janie. And she's nice. Some other lucky man will come along one day.' The lucky man turned out to be Ben, son of Sumner Wells, and that proved to be a very happy marriage.

The first I knew about the buzz bombs was a terrible racket going on in one of the fields. Silver, the pony I had brought back from California, was tearing round his paddock, wild-eyed and half out of his mind with fear. He had remained indifferent to the straffing and to the crump of bomb explosions, but the sound of that jet engine caused him to sweat and shake in abject terror. As more flying bombs continued to pass overhead, we tried everything, but to no avail. In the end, he had to be put out of his misery. On 6 June, the greatest military invasion of all time was launched on the Normandy beaches. With Cappy gone, and the young men all now playing their part in the great battle, I was left alone to work the farm with my two land-girls, and to take care of my three children.

The long summer months turned to autumn as I became increasingly large from what was to be my last pregnancy. In early December, I put the children into the loving care of our neighbour, Betty Lamb, and Bolshie took me off to hospital. Johnny, my youngest son, was born on 10 December. It was not an easy birth. Repeated asthma attacks, made more acute by the atrocious weather, added to my general debility caused by overwork on the farm and the strain of almost continuous V-1 bombing. Cappy's letters had ceased to arrive. Until now, he had written almost every day, and the awful thought that he might have been killed plagued me through many sleepless nights. Later, it transpired that he had been in action with a regiment helping to stem the great German offensive in the Ardennes, their last, desperate bid for victory. There was no way I could reach him.

The baby was fine, but the doctors were seriously worried about me. They became even more worried when Betty Lamb phoned to tell me that Father had taken Jeanne to Cherkley, saying that she could use it as her home. The winter gales lashed at the windows

196

as I periodically fought for breath and wondered if I had a true friend in the world. But my best friends were, in fact, already on their way to me. Peter carried the fruit, Bolshie the flowers; two of the best friends anyone could have. While one gave me reassuring news about Jeanne at Cherkley, the other told me to buck up and get well enough to go home to Tracadie before the pigs died from overeating. We talked about everything else then, the war and the longed-for peace that would follow, between gulps from Bolshie's hip flask. By the time it was empty, the world seemed a different place and I was lonely no longer.

A day or two later, I was strong enough to leave. Another dear friend – Jean Norton – came to drive us home. Somehow she had scrounged enough petrol. She didn't speak about Father, although I knew she was utterly miserable at losing him, for at that time Lily Ernst was still much in evidence. She helped me carry the luggage into the house, then held Johnny while I made us both a warm drink. I remember noticing how tired she looked. She left soon afterwards, saying she had to be up early in the morning to get to the munitions factory by seven thirty. 'It's important,' she said.

I never saw her again. A few weeks later she died, struck down, still in her forties, by a massive heart attack, in all probability caused by anxiety and overwork. I was so thankful that her sister, Lady Brownlow, was with her at the end because I think that Jean Norton, one of the most unselfish people I have ever known, knew what real loneliness was all about.

During the four months before the European war ended on 6 May 1945, my time was fully occupied taking care of three children and working the farm. My two land-girls left me as soon as they were free to do so, returning to their peacetime lives in the city. Letters from Cappy started arriving again; welcome news amid so much pressure of work. Then, one day, Mary came back. She was one of those rare and priceless people who are capable of any kind of work, from nannying to mucking out stables and pig-pens. She had been with me before the war, and now, with her factory closed down, she came back, and at a time when I really needed her.

As soon as I could, I went to Cherkley to see Jeanne and have it out with Father. 'You've got three other children to cope with now,' he said, inferring that he was doing me a favour.

'Mary's back so Jeanne can come home now. Anyway, I need her on the farm.'

'She stays here.' The only answer was to ask Jeanne herself. When I did, she seemed so completely happy with her life at Cherkley I hadn't the heart to fight it. I think, in a way, her grandfather had become a substitute for her father. In the last few weeks of the war, I went again to Cherkley. This time I bumped into Winston Churchill who, on the threshold of the great victory that lay ahead, seemed preoccupied and unhappy. I remember him prowling up and down Father's study, the words 'Elbe' and 'Poland' constantly on his lips. To cross that river and to go on to liberate Poland from *all* aggressors was his dearest wish. 'They have suffered enough,' he growled. 'We owe it to them.'

Lloyd George, my 'Loved One', died on 26 March. Of Father's old friends who had come so often to Cherkley, only Winston himself and R. B. Bennett now remained. Bonar Law, Rudyard Kipling, Tim Healy, F. E. Smith and Valentine Castlerosse – all were gone. Herbert Morrison, Brendon Bracken and Michael Foot were now Father's closest friends. R. B. Bennett still lived in a house close by, used by Father on occasions as a sort of annexe to Cherkley for any overspill of guests. 'Send the boring ones,' he would say with his impish grin. R.B. married one of those 'boring ones'. Thank God he never found out.

V-E Day came and went. Cappy returned and we had a party at the Savoy to celebrate. It was good to see old friends again – those who were left – but I could never quite forget that men were still dying in Burma and the Far East. For the General Election in July, a 'victory feast' had been planned. It then turned into what Father described as 'the Last Supper' when the Conservatives were defeated at the polls. Winston was out. Personally, I could never understand why they didn't wait for the *whole* war to be over first. Surely they owed him that much.

Two months later, the Japanese surrendered and the millions of men who had fought in that equally ferocious war returned to their homelands. Except Bolshie's unit, who were the first to liberate

198

Belsen. The nauseating smell came from Dante's Inferno. They encountered men, women and children diseased beyond description, dead, and dying everywhere. All this inhumanity will remain in Bolshie's mind for the rest of his life. He came back to Tracadie worn out before he allowed himself to be persuaded into flying RAF transport aircraft from the Palau Islands in the Pacific. The man who did the persuading was Whitney Straight, then head of Transport Command. Bolshie, who could never resist a challenge, flew about over New Guinea, the Philippines, Borneo and China, before repatriating himself because he wanted to get married. By that time, the war was over. Father and I went to his wedding at St George's, Hanover Square, on 28 November. His bride was Deborah Kerr, a young and talented actress who was also, justifiably, ambitious. As I say, Bolshie could never resist a challenge.

Cappy and I left England soon afterwards for Canada. We talked it over very carefully first, and when we left we had no firm ideas as to when we would return. My asthma, and Cappy's understandable wish to see his parents, were the main reasons for our decision to leave. Jeanne was so obviously happy at Cherkley with Father; and Bill, now nearly ten, liked to spend his holidays from school either at Hinchinbrook or with his other aunt, Drogo's sister, Faith, who had married Sir Michael Culme-Seymour and lived at Rockingham Castle – a paradise for any schoolboy.

So we sold Tracadie and the large whites, delivered the North Holland Blues into Father's safekeeping, kissed everybody goodbye and left with the two children, Jane and Johnny, and Mary. It was hard saying goodbye to Tracadie. It had been my home since that first day I had seen it, nine years earlier, with Father and Nye Bevan. It was full of memories – of the war mostly, and of friends I would never see again. The war was over now, but the memories would last forever. It seemed like a good time to go.

12

We flew to Canada by courtesy of the Royal Canadian Air Force. The plane was a military Constellation and it did the trip at an average altitude of 5000 feet, navigated by sextant. We sat on metal benches in an unheated cabin, well wrapped against the cold, knowing we were lucky to be going at a time when air transport was at a premium and millions of men were restless for demobilization. The soldiers and airmen with us competed with one another to make us comfortable and to entertain Mary who was unusually pretty. Johnny spent most of the trip huddled inside my fur coat for warmth.

Cappy's father was a canon of the Episcopal Church and lived in Kingston, Ontario. He and his wife were two of the nicest people one could hope to meet. We rented a house called Keema Lodge on the St Lawrence river, and spent the next three months ensuring that my mother-in-law could see as much as possible of her new grandchildren. It was good to be in Canada again but the cold, damp climate caused me repeated and alarming attacks of asthma, which were equally as bad as those I had left England to avoid. In the end, we simply had to go.

We moved south to Arizona and settled into a hotel bungalow near Nogales, on the Mexican border. Here, the sunshine and the swimming pool soon cured me and turned us all a healthy, russet brown. In the mornings, before the blistering sun drove everything human and animal to seek the shade, we would ride out over the desert hills, enjoying the warm, clean air and the glorious scenery. We rode cow ponies; tough, sure-footed creatures that made up for their lack of good looks by being unaffected by the heat and the often rocky ground. It must have been here that Jane and Johnny rode for the first time, clinging to a Western saddle; a cumbersome piece of horse-furniture which rolls like a boat in a breeze until you get used to it. They were wonderful days. We remained in Arizona for four or five months, during which time we often visited Mexico, on some occasions to see a 'quack' doctor who claimed he could cure my asthma for good. The climate itself cured it, but by no means permanently.

I wrote letters to Father who replied to every one. I was starting to miss him very much. One day he told me he had deposited £25,000 in my Canadian account. That's a lot of money even today, but in 1946 it was a fortune, and I hadn't asked him for a penny. Apart from being a sign of his natural generosity, I think it was his way of asking me to come home. Not long afterwards, Cappy and I decided to return to Canada, to his parents at Keema Lodge, and to go on from there to England. Having made up our minds to do so, we couldn't get home fast enough.

On arrival, we went straight to Cherkley, then moved into East-field Lodge, at the end of our drive, which Max had recently vacated. Now an MP, Max had married Jane Lindsay and moved to Cavendish Square. In due course they had two daughters, Kirstie and Linda. It was wonderful to be with Jeanne and Bill again, and to talk to Father about our plans for buying another farm. Europe had seemed a long way from Arizona, and many things, some important, others not, had happened in the past nine months. Among the latter, Father told me that my ex-husband Ian was now engaged to Margaret Sweeny, that Bend Or and Loelia had obtained an amicable divorce, and Joachim von Ribbentrop had been sentenced to death at Nuremberg. He also suggested we throw a 'coming out' party for Jeanne. She was now eighteen. The party was at Claridge's. Jeanne looked lovely in a dress of sky-blue chiffon. Her father thought so too. 'She does you credit, Janet. How about the next dance?' I studied Ian carefully. He was as good looking as ever, but the same restlessness was still there, if anything more pronounced. On release from the prisoner-of-war camp, he had wandered round Europe, seeing people and places with no apparent plan. He had simply disappeared.

I introduced Ian to Cappy, and I said hello to Margaret who was looking beautiful and composed. The party was well into its stride when Ian again appeared at my side. 'Let's show 'em how we did it in the twenties,' he said, leading me on to the dance floor. Without a charleston it was difficult, but one dance led to the next, and then another, as the lights were dimmed, more champagne flowed and the band played on.

'How have you been, Efelant?' He could call me that, now we were alone.

'Fine,' I said. 'I'm happy. How about you?' I caught a glimpse of Margaret. She was smiling. 'She's very beautiful,' I added. But he didn't seem to hear me.

'Remember the time . . .?' Yes, I remembered that time, and a lot of others as well; some happy, others hilarious, a few too intimate to mention above a whisper, close to the ear, half lost in the sound of music.

When I 'opened my eyes, I saw that Margaret's composure was beginning to wear thin. 'We *must* stop now,' I said, trying to break the spell. But I didn't really try hard enough.

'One more. Margaret will understand,' he said. Years later she told me she did understand, and we became friends again. But at the time, she obviously didn't. One moment she was standing in the doorway, glaring furiously, and then she was gone.

'You'd better go after her,' I told Ian. The music was starting again as I felt a tap on my shoulder. It was Cappy.

'This one's mine,' he said cheerfully. Ian smiled and walked away, lost in the crowd moving out on to the floor for the last dance.

'Sorry Cappy.'

He laughed. 'Enjoy yourself?'

'Yes,' I said, 'we were remembering the *good* times.' Cappy understood.

*　　　*　　　*

Shortly afterwards we went to Devon and rented a furnished house. From there we searched the West Country for a farm and a new home. Cappy decided to take an agricultural course at Cirencester and having found nothing in Devon that suited us, we moved to Gloucestershire to be nearer the college. We found a house at

Mitchinhampton and moved in at the start of 1947. It was a disastrous year. First of all, I broke my back while hunting. My horse failed to clear what looked like an innocent enough hedge, caught a foot in a tangle of low branches and somersaulted on top of me. Once home, they put me on a board and there I remained, flat on my back, for six months.

The visible world is a very limited place with a broken back. Apart from a detailed knowledge of the ceiling, I became keenly aware of every small sound that penetrated the room. Each morning, for instance, a girl would ride past the cottage, leading two or more other horses, and start the descent down a steep hill. I could hear their hooves slipping and sliding on the smooth and often wet surface of the road. 'Pick 'em up!' she would say, 'you old fool. *And* you, Blackie, you're half asleep by the looks of it.' Every day I would listen for that West Country voice as the weeks turned to months and my inspection of the ceiling became increasingly unbearable. When at last I was on my feet again, thankful that no vertebrae had been crushed or any nerve ends severed, I waited and watched from the window. The owner of the voice was young and blond, the horses hard and obviously well worked. They were jumpers by the look of them; probably from the nearby riding school. Eight years later I was to hear her voice again.

When I phoned Father, he told me how pleased and relieved he was by the news of my recovery. But, even as I listened, I sensed that something in his own life had gone very wrong and that he was deeply unhappy. The next day I surrounded myself with cushions and got Cappy to drive me to Cherkley. I know of four occasions when Father wept. I was with him when Mother died, and again when those brave men and women at Vickers were bombed and killed after he had asked them not to stop work while the air-raid warning sounded. The third and fourth times now followed each other closely, and a few weeks later still, I was myself plunged into such abject misery that I cried for days.

On 26 June R. B. Bennett died. He and Father had been friends all their lives, and, in spite of their political differences, their deep personal affection for each other had remained unshaken. I remembered him best, not as the Canadian Prime Minister, but as that friendly, humorous man who had visited us so often in our playroom at Cherkley, with his Bible and his box of chocolates. He was buried at Mickleham. Father and I visited his grave on more than one occasion.

Then, not long afterwards, Lily Ernst left him. I know nothing of her reasons for doing this. Perhaps she just no longer loved him. Anyhow, she married Sir Anthony Hornby instead. But it was the fourth and last occasion when I saw tears in my father's eyes. He didn't *ask* me to stay with him through all this, but I did anyway. I think it helped. We cannot measure another person's sadness nor fully comprehend the extent of the cause. Grief is a very personal thing.

Father was in France when Peter died. The first thing I knew was a call from the Swedish police to tell me he had been killed – nothing more. At first I was numb with shock, then the terrible sadness at losing my much-loved younger brother almost over-whelmed me. Peter – thoughtful and kind, like Mother, erratic yet loyal, and always determined to go his own way, taking happiness where he found it, clear of the overriding dominance of his father. I think it was his rebellion against parental influence that had brought us so close. In a way, I was his family; a substitute for our mother and the father he had never really known. After he married Patricia, and his two sons were born, I was so happy that he had found a family of his own at last. Now it was ended, so soon, so tragically. I finally reached Father by phone, as I had done once before when Mother died. This time his response was different: 'Who?'

'Peter. He's dead.' I was choking on the words.

'Who?'

'*Peter.*'

'My dog?'

'No. Your son.' Silence. I thought perhaps he hadn't heard me, or that the line was bad. So I repeated it, then: 'Come back,' I said quietly. 'Come and help me.' More silence. I hung up.

Father came back. He asked Cappy to go to Sweden and bring Peter home. Cappy was in Stockholm for a long while. When he finally returned, he brought with him my brother's body and a

tragic story of his untimely death. Peter, whose main interest outside his family had switched from racing cars to yachts, had
borrowed a boat in Stockholm and sailed it to Copenhagen, prom-
ising the owner he would return it in two weeks. In Copenhagen
his crew left him, evidently discouraged by a bad storm they had
encountered on the way. Peter then sailed back alone, to keep his
promise. His auxiliary engine had failed and he had drifted in
calm waters close to one of the many small islands of the Stockholm
archipelago. He had then gone over the side to keep the boat off the
rocks by trying to push clear. Although there was no wind, the still
violent swell caused the boat's stem to strike him repeatedly in the
chest. Then more damage was done when he was forced to struggle
back aboard single-handed.

He finally reached Stockholm, secured the boat and checked
himself into hospital complaining of severe pains in his chest. A
KLM pilot, who met him in the hospital reception room, listened
to his story and promised to return later to visit him. Before he
left, the pilot warned the doctors that in his opinion, his new friend
was badly hurt. When he returned, Peter was dead. He had broken
four ribs, one of which had pierced his lung.

Perhaps Father's grief was silent. I don't know. He never spoke
about Peter's death, either then or later. In contrast, I was determined to make the funeral as bright and cheerful as I could, filling
the church with flowers and choosing the right hymns. Peter would
have wanted it that way. We buried him at Mickleham, close to
Mother. Max and three of his best friends carried him to the grave
side. Tears and silence. Yes, grief can be a very personal thing.

*   *   *

It had been an unhappy year, but before it was over we had found
ourselves a new home. Pengelly was a farm at a little place called
Two Waters Foot, on the edge of Bodmin Moor in Cornwall. The
house itself was named Pengelly Barton. It was eighty years old,
with a minstrels gallery, fine views over the green and lush (perhaps
too lush) pastures. We redecorated it throughout and moved in
with the new year. Pengelly was really the central one of three

separate dairy farms, each as rundown as the next. But we took a chance, and decided to combine all three. Shortly after our arrival, Mary married the bailiff, Hugh Murray, and left for Australia. Their places were taken by Mr and Mrs Smith, two West Country people from Plymouth. Charlie, who served with the RASC during the war, and his wife, Phyllis, an ex-Wren, whom I always call Mitzi, have been my good and loyal friends ever since.

Jeanne came to Pengelly whenever she felt like it, as did Bill for part of his holidays. Cappy and I had a hunter each, and I brought ponies from Cherkley for the children. Bill rode occasionally, but it was Jane and Johnny who, even at the young ages of four and three, showed signs of real interest. Sadly, my own riding days came to an abrupt and painful end when one wet day my horse's legs slid from under him. I landed on my damaged spine and, after moments of supreme agony, was once again confined to the dreaded board. I remained there for four weeks, my immobility made more bearable this time by visits to the sea at Looe, on a stretcher, in the capable hands of Mr and Mrs Smith. The doctors eventually decided that nothing had been rebroken. But from then on, the risks were too great. They, and Cappy, made me promise never to ride again. It was quite the most painful promise I have ever tried to keep.

Other promises were being made in 1951. Max, having been divorced by his wife Jane, married Violet de Trafford, one of four daughters of the celebrated racehorse owner and President of the Jockey Club. Their son, Maxwell, was born in December and their daugher, Laura, two years later. Ian was also divorced in 1951 and, having already inherited his title, made Margaret Sweeny the new Duchess of Argyll.

Cappy and I farmed Pengelly for three and a half years, during which time I built up the North Holland Blues, with the help of Professor Hutt of Cornell University, who visited us from the United States and taught me a great deal about genetics. But the dairy farm itself was a failure. Persistent rain and cold turned the shale land into a sea of mud, incapable of providing sufficient ʻgrazing for the herd although heavily supplemented by our quota of hay, grain and edible concentrates which were still severely rationed. We just survived the winter of 1951, with the help of Father and his brilliant manager, Sandy Copeland from New Zealand. Then, seeing that no lasting improvement of the land was possible without a massive injection of fresh capital, we decided to sell.

I think Father must have been waiting for us to tell him we were leaving Cornwall. Almost immediately, he offered us Stowey Court, a lovely eighteenth-century house with a hundred acres of land. I started work on the house, until Father decided he wanted it back. There was nothing I could do but return the deeds to him. Then he gave me Auton Dolwells in Somerset – an estate farm with limited arable acreage but extensive paddocks, barns, stables and other farm buildings. The house itself was rambling but full of charm, with plenty of well-shaped rooms. It suited us perfectly.

The North Holland Blues were now my main concern, and before another year was over hatching had peaked at 24,000 a week. I became the largest exporter in the UK and won First Prize at the Olympia Poultry Show of 1953, as well as at main trials throughout the country. The success of this enterprise, started so tenuously in an Amsterdam street and the cockpit of a Hurricane, did much to offset any feelings of failure we may have had after our Cornish experience. These wonderful birds proved to be worth every pound we had spent on incubators, and every minute of the 4 a.m. hatchings we had been forced to endure over the years. My new manager, a Pole of very aristocratic lineage who, with his son-in-law, had fought with the Polish army in the war, had decided to remain in England rather than return to his now communist homeland. They were nice, hard-working and efficient, and stayed with me for the next five years.

Cappy, on the other hand, now decided to give himself a break from farming; a decision not made lightly but influenced to some extent by the fact that Auton Dolwells was from now on going to concentrate on chickens and horses. Before the war, Cappy had worked for Sir Keith Murdoch as a reporter on his Melbourne newspaper, and I had always been aware of his continuing interest in journalism. Having visited Canada to see his parents, and to recover from the Cornish debacle, he returned to become Industrial

Correspondent with the *Sunday Times*, specializing on profiles of important and interesting people in the world of commerce. He managed to do a good part of his work at home and took a lively interest in what was going on.

It was at this point in my life that I became deeply involved in the breeding and schooling of show-jumpers. In this I was aided and abetted by my two youngest children. The first thing I did was to use some of the money from the sale of the Cornish farm to build a covered riding school. This done, I started to look around for good horses. By 1954 I was beginning to have some success. There had been failures, of course, and I always had to hide my activities from Father who seemed intent on 'protecting' me from such a risky enterprise. Hiding the horses reminded me of the 'Bar Alert' devised by Bolshie at Biggin Hill. Sandy Copland would telephone when he knew Father was going to visit us: 'The Lord is coming!' he would say, and promptly hang up, whereupon the precious animals would be secreted to the most unlikely places until he had gone again.

One day, however, Father arrived, after the usual warning, and met Jane and Johnny in the empty stable yard. 'How many horses has your mother got?'

'Two,' said Johnny.

'Oh, about twelve,' said Jane who, aged ten, either couldn't tell a lie or hadn't got the message.

Father and I had an argument about it, but it probably ended with a kiss and a hug when he left. Arguments with Father usually ended that way, depending on his mood. More than once I thought we had gone too far. But we survived.

I never pushed Jane or Johnny into the world of competitive horsemanship. I think they must have inherited their basic interest and simply gone on from there. They had already won at gymkhanas in Cornwall and Somerset, enjoying the fun of such junior events as egg-and-spoon races, and at the same time accepting the hard work involved in keeping a pony. By 1955, we decided to hold a jumping festival, and invited riders to compete. I charged an entrance fee, put up cash prizes for the winners and gave the profits to charity. The £100 top prize was the highest available at that

time and attracted competitors from neighbouring counties and
further afield. Our jumping festival was to become an annual event
at Auton Dolwells for the next four years. 1955 also marked the
beginning of international showjumping as a major television
spectacle. People and horses, hitherto unknown to the general
public (except for Harry Llewelyn and Foxhunter, and Pat Smythe)
suddenly became household names, competing for prizes which
have since increased to many thousands of pounds. But in 1955,
£100 was well worth going for. We built the fences, loose-boxes
and collecting rings, provided car parks, refreshments and even a
tent for lost children and property.

It was in the collecting ring that I heard that familiar voice:
'Shake him up a bit! You're next. He's half asleep by the looks of
it.' The blond girl I had seen from my bedroom window was
addressing a young rider on a bay gelding. She had herself completed a very competent round and obviously knew what she was
doing. That's how I met Rachel Carpenter. Her natural way with
animals and people has endeared her to me, my family and friends
from that day to this. Even when I first met her, she had probably
forgotten more about horses than most people learn in a lifetime,
having worked with them from an early age in studs, farms, riding
schools and on the competition circuit. It is a hard school. Before
long, Rachel came to work with me permanently. Together we had
the experience to give Jane and Johnny the sort of back-up they
needed to graduate into adult competition. And, although I
seemed to have an instinct for choosing good horses, Rachel's own
opinions were often invaluable.

In the fifties and sixties, showjumping took first place, and both
my younger children managed to arrange time off from their studies
to compete; Jane from Bristol University and Johnny, with the
help of an enthusiastic and understanding housemaster, from
Harrow. They were gaining experience all the time. In winter, they
hunted with the Taunton Vale, often joined by Cappy on his horse,
Mohawk. Green with envy, I would watch them go, remembering
my own happy times with Mary Holmden and the Surrey Union.
Then summer would come round again and more silver cups and
rosettes would be added to the collection.

We were all learning. At one of our earlier jumping festivals, a tousle-headed youth from Bingley, Yorkshire, arrived with an un-shod horse called Farmer's Boy. He borrowed a saddle and the entrance fee, then entered himself for the main event and beat everybody – stars and strangers alike. He collected the £100 prize and walked away with more money than he'd ever had in his life. His name was Harvey Smith.

By 1960, my stud was beginning to attract attention. I was always trying to improve the strain, looking to Europe and Ireland for fresh bloodlines which would compete better in this fast-growing sport. In my search for bone and courage, I studied the Lusitanos of Portugal and the Andalusians of southern Spain. I then went again to Germany and looked carefully at the Hanoverians. In 1956, I was probably the first to introduce this remarkable breed to English showjumping, by importing a three-year-old Hanoverian stallion. Their success has since become legendary, but at the time I knew I was taking a chance. I was also amazed by the number of letters I received from prejudiced and outraged people accusing me of some dark and unpatriotic plot.

Jane and Johnny, separately and together, went on to compete at the Horse of the Year Show, Ascot, Hickstead and many other top events. They were selected to ride for Britain in the junior champ-ionships, and did so in most European capitals. Jane helped to win the British Team Event in Venice and came home with many cups and rosettes. Johnny, riding one of my own horses, won in Berlin, and as a result the National Anthem was played in the same stadium where, twenty-six years earlier at the Olympic Games, I had met Hitler and listened to the Horst Wessel anthem and the thunderous baying of crazed spectators.

I know that Father was impressed by his grandchildren's success, although he was seldom around to see it. His life had settled into a routine governed by the seasons of each year. In the mid-forties, he had bought a house in Nassau in the Bahamas, and later he bought one in Jamaica at Montego Bay. He would visit the Carib-bean each winter, then reappear in the spring, either at Cherkley or in his new London flat in Arlington House. His summers would be spent at La Capponcina, his house on Cap d'Ail, and his autumns in Canada and New York. But, wherever he went, he continued to make two or three calls each day to the editors and managers of his newspapers. In the forty years of Father's ownership, the circulation of the *Daily Express* rose from 735,000 to over four million.

In 1947, he had been installed as Chancellor of the University of New Brunswick which he endowed with new buildings in memory of my mother. Two years later he was at La Capponcina with Churchill. Later, when Winston had his second stroke, he lent him the house during his convalescence. They were together in 1958 when the sad news reached them that Brendan Bracken had died. After that, Winston, who must have loved that house, was there as Father's guest on many occasions. Apart from wanting to protect Winston towards the end of his political career, Father was determined to give him as much comfort and pleasure as he could in his retirement, in spite of his old friend's increasing senility.

In 1954, Father set up the Beaverbrook Foundation, and a year later made Max President of the Board of Beaverbrook Newspapers. Apart from working ceaselessly to augment and improve his art gallery at Fredericton, New Brunswick, which was opened in September 1959, Father found the time to write five books in the last ten years of his life. *Men and Power* and *My Early Life* were followed by *Friends* and *Courage*, featuring the lives of Lord Bennett and Sir James Dunn respectively. Then, in 1963, *The Decline and Fall of Lloyd George* was published. It was probably the best book he wrote, and it sold 14,000 copies in its first year. But even then Father hadn't finished. 'I'm working on a book about Winston,' he told me, 'but I will not publish during his lifetime.' He never finished it, and wasn't to know that Winston would outlive him by seven months.

When Sir James Dunn died in Canada on the first day of 1956, Father lost a warm and loyal friend whom he had known since his schooldays. Who knew what pacts and promises had been made between them in the intervening sixty-five years? They had helped each other become rich and successful, and had never once failed to respond in time of need. In 1957, Father went to Canada where he met Senator John F. Kennedy on the campus of the University of New Brunswick at the annual convocation. He then visited Sir James's widow, Christofor, at her house in Dayspring, Saint Andrews. He found her in a very bad way; weak to the point of immobility, with 'unkept hair' and talk of entering a convent. Father set about trying to pull her out of her depression, and did so with remarkable success. He invited her to Cherkley and La Capponcina, and more or less demanded her presence at numerous other places in between. I suppose it is fair to say he gave her a new reason for living.

It was not all one-sided, however. Father was seventy-nine when he went to find her, and suffering from gout as well as asthma. A few years later, another illness overtook him and he underwent an operation. Cancer was diagnosed, although they wisely didn't tell him. Christofor, who had nursed her husband throughout his final illness, now cared for Father at Cherkley; devoting her entire life, night and day, to the task. Apart from being a trained nurse, she was already extremely rich, James Dunn having left her $9,000,000. This fact caused Father much amusement and no small satisfaction, for here was one of those rare people who apparently needed nothing from him, other than himself. She was therefore something of a novelty.

Father was Father, and Cherkley had been our home; each as familiar and seemingly indestructible as the other. But now everything appeared to be on the point of being swept away, threatening all semblance of the old life at Cherkley, including those small family traditions we had come to expect and look forward to over the years. Everything was changing, as if Cherkley was no longer ours, and we, including Father, were just guests.

*   *   *

Looking back over the events that occurred during the last years of Father's life, I keep reminding myself of the one thing that, perhaps more than any other, determined what he did, and why. Father was becoming increasingly lonely. My eldest daughter Jeanne, with whom he had shared not only his life at Cherkley but also a deep and lasting love, had, naturally enough, gone away to make a life of her own. She left behind her a void that needed to be filled.

I first met Norman Mailer, to whom Jeanne was then engaged, at Jane's coming-out party in September 1961. We held this memorable event in the covered riding school at Auton Dolwells, lighting the entire area with candles and decorating it with flowers, trelliswork, and arches draped with red and white silk. Duke Ellington's nephew, whose famous uncle had played at my own party, provided the music for the hundreds of guests, among whom were many old friends, including Evelyn Waugh, Sibell Rowley and Bolshie. There were also a number of top show-jumpers at that party, which continued well into the morning and finished with some of them, in dinner jackets or long dresses, clearing the candle-lit trestle-tables on horses which performed perfectly, despite the inebriated condition of their bareback riders. It was quite a party.

I don't know what Father thought of Norman Mailer, any more than I knew myself. He was a dynamic personality with a huge zest for life, a monstrous ego, and the ability to charm anyone at any time, provided he saw a valid reason for doing so. Jeanne obviously adored him. Soon afterwards, they got married. In 1962, I went to New York to be with her for the birth of their daughter, Kate. When I wasn't actually in the clinic, I found myself being whirled round the nightspots by my son-in-law, who was already famous for his novels and infamous, to some, for his behaviour. Norman was a mercurial character, loaded with talent, and someone you either loved or loathed. I loved him.

In 1963, I was at Cherkley, staying with Max in one of the cottages. It was June, and I was already desperately looking for a house nearby so that I could see more of Father whom we now knew to be very ill. The previous evening I had dined with Father alone. Christofor had taken to hiding in her room and refused to come downstairs when she knew I was in the house. Max left early the following morning, so I was alone when I met Father in the driveway. He was being driven somewhere, hunched in the back of the car, not looking very happy. He rolled down the window. 'I'm going to keep a promise,' he said. 'It was made a long time ago.' With that he rolled up the window and told the chauffeur to drive on.

At lunch we were together again. However, this time, Christofor

held her ground. Father took my arm. 'I married her this morning,' he whispered. 'Go and give her a kiss and congratulate her.'
I complied, after a sideways look at Max. So that's where he'd
been, and why he'd left early. He alone had been invited to the
Epsom Registry Office. The date was 7 June, Christofor's wedding
anniversary to James Dunn.

Father was in almost constant pain during the last year of his
life. Having sold his houses in Jamaica and the Bahamas, he spent
most of his time at Cherkley, except for a short, last visit to La
Capponcina in February 1964. I went to see him at Cherkley as
often as I could. I was still anxiously trying to find a house nearby.
On each occasion he appeared weaker than before, but when Max
was there, or friends like Michael Foot and Alan Taylor, he would
recover his old puckish humour, his interest in journalism and
political history, and, above all, his concern for other people's
welfare. All his life, I believe Father was a deeply caring man who
disguised his feelings for others because of inner self-doubts and
his desire to be loved for his own sake, and not for his power or
money.

Six months before he died, I spent three weeks alone with him
at Cherkley, Christofor having gone to Canada. It was one of the
happiest times of my life and it will live in my memory always.
Each morning we would look for each other, then ride out over the
downs in his little electric golf-cart, going too fast, laughing, taking
risks. Then he would turn down through the trees of the yew forest
and home again, more slowly now, remembering things; arguments and rows perhaps, the jokes we had played, the fun, the
parties and the people. In the evenings we would sit together, content in each other's company, knowing that boredom and restlessness no longer came between us. Our happiness was obvious, surprising even ourselves and affecting all who came near us, staff and
visitors alike. Each day was better than the last, and the last came
all too soon.

On 25 May 1964, Lord Thompson of Fleet, a fellow Canadian,
arranged a lavish dinner party at the Dorchester to celebrate
Father's eighty-fifth birthday. The guest list was a contemporary
Who's Who of politicians and journalists. Max, who supported him

throughout the evening, told me of the supreme effort of will it cost Father to make that final, farewell speech. Having torn up his notes, he said goodbye to his friends, standing on his feet, speaking to them with humour and with optimism for the future of journalism. It was perhaps the greatest act of courage in a lifetime which had so often demanded it. He knew he was dying. Indeed, that morning, he had taken the precaution of taping a message to his friends in case the doctor's warning that he would never make the banquet was correct. 'It is time for me to become an apprentice once more,' he told them. 'I have not decided in which direction. But somewhere, sometime soon.'

Sadly, it was to be very soon. Ten days later I was with him for what was to be our last evening together. We sat in front of the fire in his bedroom and, after supper, he spoke to me about Mother and the deep love he had felt for her. He spoke of nothing else, during which time he revealed his true feelings, so often suppressed behind an outward veneer of toughness and unpredictability. Although he talked only about Mother, the essence of what he said could be applied, to a lesser extent, to all his relationships with people, both men and women, for whom he felt genuine affection – and there were many. Now at last, when the truth no longer made him feel vulnerable, he could speak from the heart. I think that in those last few hours, we were closer than we had ever been.

He died the next day. I arrived from Somerset at noon, having driven as fast as I could after an urgent call from Allan Everett, the family doctor for twenty years. Father was only semiconscious. In his room were Max, Christofor and George Millar, his righthand man who, with Max, would later burn all Father's private papers. I remember Sir Daniel Davis, the Harley Street specialist, who was himself very ill, coming to say goodbye, and Max being sent away to London by Christofor, presumably to get the will or the papers which were later burnt. My other memories of that day are hazy, obscured by sadness. All I know for certain is that I held his hand until the end, fighting back my tears. He died peacefully that same afternoon.

Five days later he was cremated. There was a memorial service at St Paul's Cathedral on 24 June, then Christofor took his ashes to Canada and placed them in the plinth of the bust by Oscar Nemon, which stands in the town square of Newcastle, New Brunswick. Father had already given Max and me several small things at Cherkley before he died. They were pieces of well-loved furniture which we had set our hearts on for sentimental reasons. He had also, in his earlier will, taken good care of his personal secretaries and the old family retainers. But his new wife had swept it all away. Everything was now left to the Beaverbrook Foundation. Max and I could have disputed this but decided against it. We were just not prepared to argue. We ourselves took care of the old staff (most of whom were dismissed), and walked away from Cherkley forever.

Although Father left me no money when he died, in its place were far more valuable things: touches of his own character, such as determination and the will to work, to accept a challenge and stand up to adversity when it comes. I am grateful to him for this and for much more; for the memories, and the knowledge that he had always loved me as I had loved him – through good times and bad. His death left me feeling empty and alone.

In 1921, Father had written a short book called *Success*. A particular passage in it came to my mind during the drive to the crematorium in Leatherhead, when every car in the procession had gone at breakneck speed and Cappy had hardly been able to keep up. In later years I read it again, and think now that perhaps Father had been ready to die when he did. Work had been his life, death his retirement. There was no point in delaying things. 'The man who holds on beyond his limit is laying up trouble for himself and disappointment for others.' I miss him still.

13

My love affair with Barbados had already begun by the time Father died. Ten years earlier my doctor had banished me from England during the winter months, saying that at forty-five I ran the risk of adding pneumonia to my chronic asthma which was confining me to bed for weeks at a time. We tried Madeira first and thoroughly enjoyed it, until, on our third visit, the weather deteriorated to an unending pattern of cold rain interspersed with long periods of sea fog. It was time to move on. Cappy was content to stay in Madeira, as were the children who had made many friends on the island, so I cabled a friend in England, and suggested a Caribbean cruise.

Grania ffrench-Blake, who liked the sun as much as I did, arrived in Madeira aboard the French liner, *Antilles*. I joined her and together we were carried southwest into the sunshine of the Caribbean. Our first destination was Haiti. I was to visit Haiti again during the time when the Duvaliers, Papa Doc and his son, together with their odious secret police, the Tontons Macoute, cast their evil shadows over that desperately poor but beautiful island. Each time I was amazed by the incredible wealth of artistic talent to be found there, and I spent hours talking to the people and buying as many of their paintings and fabrics as I could carry.

From Haiti we went south to the island of Dominica, which we found shrouded in rain clouds, then on past Martinique to Barbados. The first thing I noticed was the cool breeze flowing in from the Atlantic. This was the steady trade wind, driving armies of small, white clouds before it and cooling everything from the blazing sun. The rocky east coast, pounded by magnificent surf, is in total contrast to the calm, blue waters of the western shore, with its palm-fringed beaches and gently curving lagoons. Inland I found hills and valleys, great sugar plantations and small villages of picturesque wooden houses, clustered round old churches with shingled spires. But it was the people who impressed me most. Everywhere we went, Grania and I were met with warm, welcoming smiles and an abundance of good humour. They seemed to like us, too, and by the end of our first day I knew how much I liked them in return. Those feelings of spontaneous affection have grown steadily as I have come to know them better with each passing year.

In 1960, I returned to Barbados with Cappy and our children, hoping they would love it as much as I did. I was not disappointed, and if the people as a whole attracted us so much, there were two in particular whose friendliness and helpful advice determined Cappy and I to stay there and put down permanent roots. Errol Barrow, soon to be Prime Minister of Barbados, and Wynter Crawford, his First Minister, became our friends and allies throughout. Together we toured the length and breadth of the island and, before we left, bought a cane field in the parish of St James on the west coast. The following year we built a house there and moved in during the winter of 1962. We called it Galena and spent five months there in each of the following three years.

We had many parties getting to know the politicians, sugar-cane planters, and for various friends that lived on the island. Johnny has a lovely voice, and we used to go into the boozy parlour, a pretty annex to the house, where he sang with his guitar. Nearly every evening some steel band would pop in for our singsong. It was a happy house and I was loath to leave it, but I wanted a dairy farm, needed so badly on the island, a new garden, and a show-jumping arena. At last we found the perfect place close to Galena, named Holders Plantation. It stood in two hundred acres of cane fields and wilderness, facing west, on high ground where the cooling breeze rustled in the tall mahogany and tamarind trees which flanked it on three sides. The main building, a typical plantation house, had been built in 1675 by the Holder family, whose bones resided in a big vault sunk beyond the foundations on the eastern side. With mounting excitement, I examined every part of the place; the house itself, the stables, barns and outbuildings, the land and, above all, its situation. Then I went in silence to the government land offices. I offered them £60,000 for the entire two hundred acres, which included two separate houses, and waited in trepidation as the five stern-faced Barbadian officials deliberated my fate. At last they accepted, and the grimness turned to broad smiles of welcome as they shared my happiness.

It was to be two years before we could move into Holders House. Every timber was crumbling with worm and rot. In the end, we pulled them all down and rebuilt it in its original style. We landscaped the garden, cleared the land, planted golden palms, African tulip and frangipani. Then we dug a large swimming pool and transformed the thirteen-acre sugar field into an area of flat, healthy grass, which would later become the finest polo field in the West Indies. To achieve all this, Cappy, Rachel Carpenter and I, with sixty men, worked non-stop through one winter season from 7 a.m. to 4 p.m. We imported precious green heart wood from Guyana, ourselves transporting the timbers from the docks at Bridgetown, to make floors, ceilings, beams and joists. We renovated the adjoining stables, once part of the original house, turning them into guest cottages, re-routed the access road and created a covered courtyard to be used as the main dining area. There were times when I thought it would never be finished. But at long last it was.

I was pleased with what we had done, and rather proud because the essential character of a fine old seventeenth-century planter's house had been preserved. I was grateful, too, for all the help we had received, especially from Oliver Messel, Tony Snowden's uncle, who often dropped in from his house nearby to give advice and encouragement. His unreserved approval of the finished work was our final reward. We celebrated moving into our new home in December 1965, combining it with Christmas and Johnny's twenty-first birthday.

Soon after moving in, we started to develop half of our two hundred acres into a dairy farm. Having cleared the land and planted an abundance of pangola grass, we built a modern dairy parlour. The following year we shipped twenty head of pedigree Friesian cattle from England. They came in two banana boats, and Rachel and Johnny's friend, Tim Fox, took charge of the shipments – ten cows to a boat. Northern Dairies provided milk distribution and artificial insemination, and soon the herd was established.

Farming and developing new land in an unfamiliar climate can be a harrowing experience without local help and expertise. In all our endeavours at Holders, we were lucky to have the advice of Lee Dean, a prominent sugar planter. Before long, the polo ground was beginning to take shape and beside it a showjumping field, which I modelled, as far as possible, on Hickstead.

The gallery at Holders became the meeting place for friends and acquaintances. Lady Churchill had lunch with us, and related some amusing stories about Father and Winston's undying friendship. Her son Randolf was trying to finish his book on his father before he died of cancer. He often came to Holders, a childhood friend never to be forgotten. Greta Garbo came with her host Dru Heinz, and I found the still lovely actress interesting and fun. She had become a great friend of Father in the South of France where their houses were almost adjoining. The rumour was that they were going to get married, and I rather wish they had!

My best and dearest friends in late life were Averell Harriman and his wife Pamela, a friend of long standing, and mother of young Winston Churchill. Averell was also a good friend of Father and travelled to Russia and Washington with him during the war. They had lately bought a beach house designed in and out by Oliver Messel and seemed so happy in it. But not for long. I said goodbye to them one evening at Holders, and very soon afterwards Averell died in America.

Princess Margaret used to drop in for lunch, or a drink and a swim in the pool. She was staying with Oliver Messel, while her house was being built in Mustique.

My children all loved Barbados and came to Holders whenever their own lives and careers permitted it. By 1969, Jeanne, whose marriage to Norman Mailer had foundered, had married John Cram. Later on she brought both her daughters, Kate and Cusi, to visit me. My son Bill also adopted Barbados as his home. In 1966, he had married Bonny McKenzie at St Michael's Cathedral in Bridgetown. They were to have one son, Michael. Jane, who had left Bristol University with honours degrees in politics and economics, was teaching when she wasn't actively engaged in international showjumping. Having won her class at the Royal International Horse Show at White City, she suffered one of those accidents that should never happen to anybody. Someone suddenly opened the door to an indoor riding school when she was schooling a young horse. The resulting bad fall broke her back and put her out of competition for three years, since when she has been forced to concentrate exclusively on dressage.

During her enforced immobility, and afterwards, Jane has written eight books on almost every aspect of horsemanship and has become one of the country's most knowledgeable dressage riders and equestrian writers.

Johnny, whose graduation from junior to senior showjumping was achieved with noticeable ease, competed for Britain in most European capitals and developed into something of a 'puissance' expert. With major wins in Dublin and Milan, he then took to the North American circuit, competing in Madison Square Gardens, and then cleared 7′ 2″ in Toronto on Jane's horse, Grey Owl; an appropriate name for a great Canadian occasion. Johnny jumped with the British team for seven years in all.

Although we had ceased to hold summer jumping festivals at our farm in England, we made up for it in Barbados, holding international events every January for four years on our newly completed show ground. We worked hard to make them a success, and I think we succeeded, for by now Rachel Carpenter, Johnny, Jane and I had gained a lot of experience. Flags, bunting, car parks, refreshment tents, collecting rings and, above all, the jumps themselves were all modelled on the best we had seen on the European circuit. It was also great fun. Prizes were awarded by the Governor General or the Prime Minister, and on one occasion by Anthony Eden, Lord Avon, whom I had first met at Cherkley, and who now, tired and ill, had retired to live with his wife, Clarissa, in a beautiful house up in the hills. English stars such as Ann Townsend and Douglas Bunn took part, as did our Barbadian friends, Lee Dean and Errol Barrow. Errol was by now in his second term as Prime Minister, having won power from Grantly Adams in 1961 and guided his country through Independence five years later. He governed as he rode, with a sure, firm touch, and continued to do so for many years.

Having devoted half of the property to farming, we now decided to develop the land surrounding the polo field and show ground. With planning permission granted, Johnny and I between us built over ten houses, secluded and well spaced out, each with a view of the sea and the broad expanse of grass bordered by trees. Later, we bought what was at first intended to be a beach property on the shore below us, then developed it into the Tamarind Cove Hotel. I was involved in every detail of it, decorating many of the rooms with pictures and designs I had brought from Haiti.

Cappy's quiet enthusiasm and encouragement was behind everything we did. He was well aware of my abundance of energy and need to fill every day to the brim. He also recognized the same characteristics in his son. Often, Johnny and I would find him quietly mulling over plans for a new house, or standing, watching it being built. In 1964, the doctors had told Cappy he had emphysema, and that if he didn't give up smoking he would be dead within three years. He gave up, and lived for fifteen. But the medicines took their toll, increasingly limiting his physical ability and his mental desire for more than minimal activity. But whether in Barbados or in England, he never failed to arrive at my bedside whenever he heard that I was once more laid low with asthma.

In England, the house I had been so desperately seeking in order to be nearer Father at Cherkley now came on the market. Slythehurst, part of which is early seventeenth century and boasts a priest's hole, is an attractive, moderate-sized house with extensive barns and stabling. It stands in two hundred acres of prime grassland near Cranleigh in Surrey. I decided to move there not only because I loved the look of the place but also because it was nearer the centre of things for Jane and Johnny.

I sold Auton Dolwells in the summer of 1967 and left for Barbados in the autumn, entrusting the mammoth task of moving furniture and belongings to Mr and Mrs Smith, whose enterprise and industry I knew to be more than equal to the task. Before I left, however, I bid farewell to the two valiant Poles, who went to Canada, and I sold my much-loved North Holland Blues. The horses were moved to spacious new quarters at Slythehurst which we now named The Maple Stud. Here, with fine pastures and ample room, they would flourish under the watchful care of Fred Willder, our stud-groom. We also constructed an aviary at Slythehurst and filled it with canaries and other exotic birds of many colours; the responsibility and special interest of Charlie Smith. I was sitting watching them one early summer morning, feeling rather frustrated because the Smiths had done such a good job that there was nothing much left to do. Jane was teaching, and Johnny was dashing all over the place getting organized for the new season's showjumping. After all the non-stop work in Barbados, life in England seemed rather tame.

Suddenly, the peace of the aviary was shattered by a mounting roar of sound which sent the little birds darting into a kaleidoscope of colours as a blast of wind swept downwards, rattling the coffee cups and flattening the wildly waving bushes. The helicopter landed and settled, its motor cut. Johnny and the pilot, Bob Baff, climbed out.

'What a way to fly!' said Johnny, grinning.

'Sorry about the coffee,' said Bob Baff, a remarkably attractive New Zealander. 'Any left?' I scarcely heard him. I was too busy staring at the helicopter resting lightly on a corner of the lawn. What a way to fly indeed.

I received my helicopter licence on 9 July 1968, my sixtieth birthday. Johnny got his too. Together we had trained hard, achieving our first solo flights after ten hours of instruction at the hands of Bob Baff at Fairoaks. It had been a challenge, and like all the others, I was eager to meet it. 'If the engine cuts,' said my intrepid instructor, 'you float to earth like a sycamore leaf.'

'And if the rotor breaks off?' I asked.

Bob looked thoughtful for a moment. 'We call it "Jesus",' he said. 'You drop like a bloody brick.' The 'Jesus' predicament was something which, thankfully, I never encountered, but there was to be one moment when I found myself thinking hard about sycamore leaves.

I bought a smart little American machine called a Bell II, which I shared with Johnny, and a deep concrete landing pad was sunk beyond the ha-ha which separated the lawn from the field beyond. From here, Johnny and I could soar away over the woods to set a straight course for anywhere in the south of England. Flying at up to 1500 feet and speeds of 110 m.p.h., we could cut our normal travelling time by two thirds. The required mental and physical coordination, however, was even more exacting than in fixed-wing aircraft, such as the Vega Gull, but, in return, I found the sense of freedom more rewarding. I also admit to a certain satisfaction in the knowledge that I was only the fourth woman pilot to hold a helicopter licence in England.

Flying as a passenger in a helicopter can reveal some unsuspected traits of character. Johnny himself was a far better pilot than me, and an excellent navigator. Cappy liked it, provided we had a specific destination and were not just flying about for fun. Norman Mailer, who continued to visit us despite his break with Jeanne, flew for the first time with me, and showed his relief on landing by untoward expressions of affection involving hugs, kisses and some rather bright-eyed overenthusiasm. I flew to Colonel Sir Mike Ansell's home in Devon and returned with a cockpit full of dachshund puppies who didn't care where they were, and then to the Wiltshire home of Lord Avon, this time with a co-pilot and Mrs Thatcher, then Leader of the Conservative Opposition. Anthony Eden, who had cancer, said he would like to meet her. Margaret Thatcher was a model passenger, showing a probing interest in the machine and its performance. She also seemed to have nerves of steel. On arrival, she talked to Anthony Eden with a deep sensitivity and understanding, then climbed back into the helicopter showing less concern for her safety than I do when catching a bus.

It was on a return trip by helicopter from Hickstead, that greatest of all jumping arenas owned by my old friend, Douglas Bunn, that I thought I might have to imitate a sycamore leaf. My passenger on this occasion was a remarkable beauty from Munich for whom Sir Harry Llewelyn had requested a lift back to London. Her name was Nadine. The trouble started over mid-Surrey when I noticed a sudden reduction in engine power. Having checked and re-checked my instrument panel, I knew the fault lay in the plug, piston or cylinder and it was getting worse by the second. I realized I'd have to put her down, and fast. Stealing a glance at the beautiful Nadine, I saw that her classic profile showed no awareness of impending doom, and I was determined to keep it that way. So I fixed a smile on my face and pointed down. 'The Farquhar place,' I said, 'they're charming. Let's pay them a visit.'

'How nice,' she murmured. 'Do we have the time?' Time was one thing we didn't have. Our descent earthwards was rapid and somewhat erratic as the engine started to develop a curious if discreet cough, accompanied by a good deal of vibration.

We landed tolerably gently in a paddock surrounded by a low fence. I didn't have to switch off. The engine cut. 'Always a bit bumpy coming down,' I lied, stifling a sigh of relief.

My companion merely smiled. 'Is that where they live?' She was pointing at the roof of a corrugated-iron shed. It was the only building in sight.

'The stables, I think. Let's take a walk.' And walk we did, straight to the nearest telephone kiosk where I phoned Fairoaks and demanded a mechanic and a pilot to fly the machine home. Then I sat on a gate with Nadine and told her I wanted an engine check before we took off again. 'Just routine, of course.'

The mechanic, who was also a pilot, arrived and gave the engine a brief turnover. 'Can you fly it home?' I shouted against the noise.

He switched off. 'She wouldn't clear the fence,' he said. 'How on earth did you get down in one piece?'

'Quickly,' I replied, looking away to where Nadine still sat on the gate, well out of earshot. I went and made another call and came back to her. 'The Farquhars are away,' I told her. 'We can go on from here by taxi if you like. It'll be quicker.'

'OK,' she said, climbing down from the gate. She was obviously disappointed. I was pleased about that.

For three years, Johnny and I flew that helicopter all over the south of England, to jumping events, horse shows, sales and trials. Then, for fun, we entered an international competition organized by the Helicopter Club of Great Britain. Johnny was pilot and I was navigator. It was a bit like the treasure hunts of old, following clues written on a sheet of paper. Four miles due east. Alter course to 225 degrees . . . ten minutes. Below you a church . . . identify. The name is the clue. Follow rail track . . . and so on, until you arrive at the rendezvous point, empty of fuel, having flown for exactly ninety minutes at the correct speed and altitude. Then we had to fly between 25-foot poles, pick up buckets of water, land on a sixpence and execute a lot of other intricate manoeuvres. It was great fun. We did our best, but we were up against men and machines from France, Germany and Belgium, not to mention the best from our own country. Then, to our astonishment, the chairman of the Helicopter Club pronounced us the winners. After a celebration drink of lemonade, we flew away home over the Sussex countryside, clutching our trophy of a silver helicopter, happy as two kids returning from their first gymkhana.

*   *   *

When I had promised Cappy and the doctors never to ride again, I did so without being aware of the beauty of an early morning in Barbados. The sun rises with the wind out there, and from the back of a horse, the blazing colours can be seen moving against a backdrop of sea and sky. So I broke my promise. I didn't do anything stupid. Each morning I would canter up the broad fire-breaks, cut into the sugar-cane fields, and ride out on to the open pastures above them. One day I reined in to talk to a dog. We knew each other well and usually exchanged a pat on the head for a lick on the hand. I leaned down as usual to keep my part of the bargain while the dog jumped up to keep his. It was only a gesture of friendship. My horse, however, thought otherwise and stepped smartly sideways.

The Queen Elizabeth Hospital in Bridgetown is a nice place. I emerged after an operation, with a badly bruised lower spine and a tube sticking out of me to drain away the poison. I then made a final promise to Cappy never to ride another horse, though I have not kept it. At Holders I had nothing to do except sit around feeling sore. So I painted a picture. Before we left for England, I showed the finished effort to Hector Whistler, who, to my amazement and intense pleasure, said he thought it was rather good. It was Hector's cousin, Rex, who had done those incredible murals at Philip Sassoon's house. I was flattered and encouraged, and left for England with my ruffled dignity restored and looking forward to a new challenge to suit my immobile state.

Bill's marriage to Bonnie McKenzie had lasted only a few years. In 1971, he met and married his second wife, Edna, with whom he was to have two daughters, Nicola and Monette. I went to Germany, my new daughter-in-law's homeland, for the ceremony, and from there to Copenhagen where Johnny was competing for Britain in an international showjumping event. The city was full of students, handsome young people celebrating something or other, an annual 'rag' perhaps, involving a lot of singing, laughter, fire-crackers, peace slogans and booze. A crowd of them were capering about on a carnival float, piled high with crates of beer, a table and heavy amplifying equipment from which issued a deafening cacophony of music. When the entire contraption began to move, I noticed it was drawn by two horses, perfectly matched, of not more than fourteen hands. They seemed unconcerned by the deafening noise and pulled the float, students and all, effortlessly away down the street.

This was my first viewing of the Norwegian Fjord horse. I call it a horse because, despite the fact that the breed is often slightly below the statutory minimum height, they are far too heavy and powerful to be called ponies. It wasn't just their looks that impressed me, although with their stiff black and white manes, the unusual, almost primitive shape of their heads and well-proportioned bodies, I knew I was looking at something very special. What impressed me most about them was their strength of movement as they dragged that noisy load away.

At the stadium I found Johnny and told him what I'd seen. 'They sound like Norwegian Fjords,' he said. 'Neils Gierston knows about them.' Neils Gierston certainly did. He took me to a stud in Jutland where I promptly bought two and had them shipped to England. So started a hobby, an occupation which changed my way of life for the next seven years. I had already been thinking seriously about carriage driving, having spoken to Mike Ansell some weeks previously. He had suggested it, knowing my love of horses and the frustration I felt at no longer being able to ride. He also told me that he and Prince Philip, who could no longer play polo having badly hurt his wrist, were establishing the Combined Driving Association of Great Britain and predicted a great future for it. As a sport, three-day-event carriage driving was virtually unknown outside Germany, Belgium and Holland.

As soon as I returned to England, we set about getting organized. The Fjords came up to and exceeded my expectations in every way. They are responsive and courageous creatures, bred by the Scandinavians over hundreds of years to drag logs, carry produce, pull sleighs and provide transport over rough mountain tracks in all weather. The only trouble I ever had with them was because of their strength. I couldn't cope with more than two at a time, so I concentrated on pairs and never drove them in competitions as a team.

I bought an iron-tyred dog-cart, the perfect vehicle for cross-country events, and slowly built up my string of horses, including breeding stock, by selective buying. For the show events, I borrowed a one-hundred-year-old phaeton from Alan Bristow. Being himself an avid collector of fine old carriages, he wouldn't sell it to me, and, as it was an original Lawton, the Rolls Royce of makes, I could hardly blame him for not wanting to part with it.

Not having driven a horse-drawn vehicle of any kind since that disastrous day at Richmond sixty years earlier, I had to start from scratch. I schooled myself and my horses for hours, days, weeks on end. Every morning, Rachel and I harnessed up a pair of Fjords and went to work. We practised all three types of event; dressage, obstacles and cross-country until we got it right. Then we practised again to make sure. We switched horses continually until the right pair emerged, then kept them together, to get to know each other and work in unison. It was exhausting work. But the will to win was there – and the challenge.

The great day of our first competition arrived in the summer of 1972. It was at Lincoln, and we were up against nine or ten entries. It was a proud moment for me. I wore boots and a coat, a skirt, topper and veil, all of navy blue, and drove into the ring. The Fjords caused a sensation. They performed beautifully – supple, strong and responsive, their distinctive manes dancing as they entered the dressage ring and faultlessly executed each manoeuvre like veterans. 'If they had stripes, they'd be zebras!' I heard someone shout. But they weren't zebras. They were a pair of very highly trained, intelligent horses that took us to an outright win in all three events, enabling us to carry off the trophy at our first attempt.

From Lincoln, we went on over the years to compete annually at Goodwood, Lowther, Hickstead and Cirencester. In Scotland, we drove at Edinburgh and Mellerstain. We competed in events at many of the beautiful parks of great houses and castles, such as Tatton in Cheshire and, of course, Windsor. For several years, we entered the International Horse Show at Wembley and, on one occasion, completed the only clear round. Abroad, we were invited to compete in the indoor stadiums of Paris and Brussels, and returned having collected more rosettes to add to our collection.

Having reluctantly given up my helicopter, owing to the enormous cost of maintenance, Cappy and I went by car or commercial airline to the events that were far from home. I bought a good, reliable horse-box, on the back of which we hitched a 16-foot trailer to carry the dog-cart and phaeton. Rachel and Keith, our Barbadian groom, drove this equipment, which measured 38 feet overall, for many thousands of miles. During those seven years, we averaged twenty competitions a year. They were never once late.

We made a lot of good friends on the circuit, and always looked forward to meeting them again as event followed event throughout the long summer months. Prince Philip would often attend, and I remember him best for his friendliness and willingness to give advice, and to share his enthusiasm with all who asked him, particularly beginners. His advice was much sought after as one of the world's most experienced team drivers, working with big horses that required not only strength but a high degree of professionalism.

It is not an easy sport, and there have been some bad accidents in the cross-country events. Dressage is a question of schooling and control with a smart turnout. The obstacle section requires judgement to a hair's breadth as you race against the clock, turning and weaving through the painted bollards, knowing that the slightest touch will dislodge the ball balanced on top and incur penalty points. The cross-country event, also carefully timed, can be very exhausting for both humans and animals. The marathons, run over distances of up to twenty-two kilometres, include hazards of alarming intricacy – steep banks, tight corners, ditches, woods and rivers, the latter often strewn with boulders.

I remember tackling one of these after heavy rain. The Fjords disappeared altogether beneath the cold, muddy water but kept going, totally submerged until their heads again broke surface at the far bank. I was swept out of the driving seat and only saved by Rachel, my time-keeper, grabbing me by the leg and hauling me aboard. Luckily, we never had an accident during our seven years of competition. Severe or fatal damage to horses is unexpectedly rare although not unknown. But I have seen a few human limbs broken when carriages hit walls or turn over; things that can happen after the slightest error of judgement.

Cappy's enthusiasm for the sport was unflagging. Throughout the 1970s, his health continued to deteriorate but he never failed to come with me to the various competitions. During the marathons, he would always be ready with a welcome drink at the two or three official stopping places along the route. He was intensely interested in all that was going on in our family, particularly his children. He was happy for Jane when she got married, and unhappy for her when, shortly afterwards, she decided she had picked the wrong man and separated from him. Then, when she had recovered from that terrible riding accident and started to compete again, her father followed her career in dressage closely and was always pleased and proud at her success.

In 1973, Johnny married Wendy Hodge and in the following year decided to retire from showjumping which, at international level, was demanding all his attention. To give himself more time for the all-important business of earning money to meet his new responsibilities, he switched to polo, a sport he loves and in which he had excelled, but which, despite many invitations to play abroad, makes fewer demands on his time for work and family. Cappy was overjoyed when his first grandson, Jack, was born, followed by his first granddaughter, Jemma, a year and a day later.

Jodi, their sister, followed after six years but sadly he was never to know her.

I wanted to be with Cappy as much as possible during the last two years of his life. He knew he was dying but even towards the end when he was confined to a wheelchair, he urged me to continue. His unselfishness and enthusiasm for all the family's success in their chosen fields never diminished. In 1979, his brother Herbert, known affectionately to all as 'Bub', came to England from Canada to see him. A month later, Cappy died. The end came quietly, as he would have wished it, for Cappy was a quiet man. I held him in my arms, knowing that I was losing one of the finest people I had ever known – or loved.

Jane and Johnny took me to Barbados soon afterwards, sharing my sadness and deep sense of loss. We filled each day with activity and tried not to let Cappy's death dwell in our thoughts. It was not easy. Cappy and I had been happily married for thirty-seven years. I returned to England three months later and plunged once more into the world of carriage driving. But it was never the same again. I had had my first and last driving accident when the bridle of one of a pair of young horses I was schooling broke. They bolted, blind with fright and totally out of control. I was thrown out of the dog-cart and I landed on concrete in a sprawling heap twenty feet beyond. Amazingly, despite the fact that, aged seventy-one, my bones were supposed to be brittle, nothing was broken. I was taken to hospital with a bad gash on my leg which needed stitching and a strained neck tendon.

A month later, Fred Willder, our head groom, died in a car crash on his way to Olympia. He had been one of the family and loved by everybody, particularly Cappy. It was the final blow. Feeling sad and discouraged, I decided to retire from competitive driving. It had been a wonderful seven years. Over ninety first-prize rosettes hung in the hallway of the house, while outside, sixty Norwegian Fjords, probably the finest stud in the world, grazed in the paddocks. To be honest, we had won everything there was to win – again and again. Now it was time to go. A younger generation would take over.

14

The great thing about painting is that you can take it with you and do it wherever you happen to be. For the traveller, I suppose writing is even better, requiring only a pencil and some paper. On the other hand, the writer cannot evaluate his entire work at a single glance, either during or afterwards. Nor can his critics. Writing a book takes a long time, so I think in future I'll stick to painting.

In Barbados I found plenty of time to take up this new challenge. I had sold the dairy farm, as I was away from the island for such long periods of time. My flying had also stopped with the sale of the helicopter, although for one glorious season I flew a light air-craft, a Cessna, round the island in the early mornings, following the beautiful coastline and waving my wings to friends having breakfast on their terraces. By now I had a lot of friends in Barbados. Some were there before me; others, like Sibell, Bolshie, Naomi Bourne and Johnnie Johnson, have since come to live or visit. Paddy, also, once arrived from Canada for a brief stay. Together we remember the old days and talk about who is doing what and where, and who has died. Ian Campbell died at the Travellers Club in Paris in 1973. I was in Barbados so did not go to the funeral, but good and bad memories flowed back, mostly of the many happy times we had together.

Wherever I am, in Barbados, England or that other beautiful island, Mallorca, where I go each year to stay with Betty Alexander, a friend for fifty years and a cousin of Drogo's, I continue to paint. We talk about those hectic days in the thirties and laugh together about the things we said and did; so important at the time, so trivial in retrospect. On one occasion she introduced me to a charming and courteous Frenchman, Michel Trippier, who became very dear to me and from whom I received news of Jacques Hubert which took me back even further, to the twenties, and my first, innocent love affair.

It was Rachel who bought me my first box of paints, and Johnny who pushed me into my first exhibition. It was held at Cranleigh, our local town in Surrey, where my embarrassment ended when I was told that all my pictures had been sold. The next exhibition was in a London bank, and the third at Simpson's in Piccadilly, where Dr Simpson, himself an artist, enthusiastically hung my work in the Gents Outfitting. From here my exotic tropical blooms and birds peered out between the overcoats, bowler hats and umbrellas. Again, much to my surprise and pleasure, many pictures were sold.

The fourth exhibition was a splendid affair at the Chelsea Town Hall, in a beautiful room which we decorated for the occasion. Hundreds of people arrived for the opening night viewing for which we had provided food and drink and a steel band. My grandchildren acted as waiters. I was watching the growing number of red dots with excitement when two royal gentlemen from the Sultanate of Oman came up to me. They had bought the two most expensive pictures in the exhibition. They had also recently purchased eighteen large, black horses from my Maple Stud for use by their ceremonial police. The result of the conversation that followed was that I found myself on a plane to Oman, together with Jane and Rachel, transporting forty new pictures. My Arab friends had offered to exhibit them at the Intercontinental Hotel in Muscat, and at the same time had enlisted Jane to help train their mounted police for dressage and jumping.

The trip was full of delightful surprises. The country itself was beautiful – where I had expected endless vistas of desert, I found mountains and green pastures sloping to the sea. The hotel and the palaces, with their Aladdin's caves of exotic plants, fabulous pools of multicoloured fish and glittering fountains, were enchanting. Olympic-sized swimming pools were to be seen everywhere, and from the gardens of the hotel itself, ablaze with colour, a glass lift gave a bird's-eye view of the sparkling grandeur.

When I was not required at the exhibition, I was whisked away to the police barracks in a gleaming Rolls Royce. Here, from the edge of a vast parade ground, I watched the diminutive, blond figure of Jane coaching the Sultan's police forces, each magnificently mounted, wheeling in formation, their white helmets and lance pennants weaving patterns in the bright sunlight.

It was a great experience that came to an end all too soon. We had been in Oman for two weeks, and I had sold a large number of pictures. I have no illusions about my talent as an artist, but I love colour, and if that gives pleasure through my paintings, I am pleased in return – and gratified.

After all this, England was something of an anticlimax, made more so for me by a sudden attack of hepatitis. Hepatitis lingers, to the point when you wonder if it will ever go away. Some months later, I was back in Barbados, sitting on the terrace at Holders House feeling rather old and ill, when the bushes below me parted to reveal Prince Andrew, on leave from *Invincible* after the Falklands War. Within minutes, this delightful and irrepressible young man, who had walked over from a house nearby, did for me what his great-uncle, Prince George, had done sixty years earlier. He cheered me up and made me feel human again. Having filled the place with laughter and good spirits, he left, 'buzzing' the house as the great carrier swept once more out to sea. Then I received an enormous bunch of flowers. Young or old, the navy always seems to appear in my life at exactly the right time.

In that same year, 1983, I saw my brother Max for the last time. We had grown apart during the years immediately before and after the rundown and sale of the *Express* empire when he was in no fit state to handle the final negotiations. In my opinion few of those involved on either side emerged with much credit. Soon it would be too late to do more than just be with him as he sat in his wheelchair, struck down by the massive series of strokes which ended his life two years later. Poor, dear Max. I wanted him to die peacefully, without pain, and hoped with all my heart that he felt no awareness or frustration at living on the edge of consciousness, unable to move or speak. We had been such good friends once, especially when things were bad and we needed each other. He died, mercifully, in 1985, and was buried at Mickleham Church, near Mother and my brother Peter. *The Times* carried a warm obituary, dwelling on his gaiety and bravery.

So that leaves me. In a year or two I'll be eighty, but there's no point in dreading old age. Illness is probably the thing we fear most, but facing that can be a challenge too, no matter how young or old we are. To the asthma, tuberculosis, hepatitis, broken back, gashed face and damaged kidneys, I can now add cancer and a stroke. These last two have left me in a fairly fragile condition, but each day I swim a bit, and paint, and think about how lucky I am.

Not long ago I saw a young Barbadian girl walking down the lane carrying a basket on her head. She walked with the grace of youth and gave me a big smile as she passed. When she'd gone I went looking for a fresh canvas, happy for her and for me too, because a moment earlier the lane had been empty. I am lucky that life and colour is still all around me. I just have to open my eyes to see beautiful things that I once took for granted.

It would be wrong to say that life had been full. It still is.

Index

236